The History of Christian Doctrines

L. Berkhof

*This volume is a
companion volume
to the author's
Systematic Theology
and contains the
historical material
to be used
with that work*

The Banner of Truth Trust

THE BANNER OF TRUTH TRUST
3 Murrayfield Road, Edinburgh EH12 6EL
P.O. Box 621, Carlisle, Pennsylvania, 17013 U.S.A

Copyright 1937 Louis Berkhof

This edition published by
The Banner of Truth Trust
November 1969
Reprinted 1975
Reprinted 1978

ISBN 0 85151 005 1

This book is set in
11 on 13 pt Plantin 110

Printed in Great Britain by
Billing & Sons Ltd
Guildford and London

PREFACE

The Historical Volume of what was originally called *Reformed Dogmatics* now appears with a new title, namely, *History of Christian Doctrines*. Works on the gradual development of theological truth in the Church of Jesus Christ usually appear alongside of those which deal with the systematic reproduction of it, and thus stand out as separate works. It was thought best to follow this practice, since this will stress the fact that, after all, the history of the development of Christian thought in the Church is a separate study.

But while it is a separate study, it is not one which students of theology can afford to neglect. The study of doctrinal truth, apart from its historical background, leads to a truncated theology. There has been too much of this in the past, and there is a great deal of it even in the present day. The result has been the lack of a sound understanding and a proper evaluation of the truth. There was no appreciation of the fact that the Holy Spirit guided the Church in the interpretation and development of the truth as it is revealed in the Word of God. The checks and the roadsigns of the past were not taken into consideration, and ancient heresies, long since condemned by the Church, are constantly repeated and represented as new discoveries. The lessons of the past are greatly neglected, and many seem to feel that they should strike out entirely on their own, as if very little had been accomplished in the past. Surely, a theologian must take account of the present situation in the religious world, and ever study the truth anew, but he cannot neglect the lessons of the past with impunity. May this brief study of the history of doctrines serve to create a greater interest in such historical study, and lead to a better understanding of the truth.

L. BERKHOF

Grand Rapids, Michigan
1 *August* 1949

CONTENTS

The doctrine of the Trinity

The doctrine of Christ

The doctrine of sin and grace and related doctrines

The doctrine of the atonement or of the work of Christ

The doctrine of the last things

PROLEGOMENA

I: THE SUBJECT-MATTER
OF THE HISTORY OF DOGMA

The History of Dogma is not concerned with theology in general. It deals primarily with dogmas in the strict sense of the word, and only secondarily with the doctrines that have not yet received ecclesiastical sanction.

I. THE MEANING OF THE WORD 'DOGMA'

The word 'dogma' is derived from the Greek *dokein*, which in the expression *dokein moi* meant not only 'it seems to me', or 'it pleases me', but also 'I have definitely determined something so that it is for me an established fact'. The last word 'dogma' became the designation of a firm, and especially a public, resolution or decree. It was applied to the self-evident truths of science, to well-established and admittedly valid philosophical convictions, to government decrees, and to officially formulated religious tenets.

Derivation of 'dogma'

The Bible uses the word as a designation of government decrees in the Septuagint, Esth 3:9; Dan 2:13; 6:8; Luke 2:1; Acts 17:7; of the ordinances of the Old Testament, Eph 2:15; Col 2:14, and of the decisions of the Assembly of Jerusalem, Acts 16:4. While it was the philosophical and not the biblical usage of the term that gave rise to its later meaning in theology, yet its use in Acts 16:4 has points of resemblance with its later usage in theology. The Jerusalem Assembly, it is true, did not formulate a doctrine but a regulation for the ethical life of the Church; yet its decision was occasioned by a doctrinal controversy, had doctrinal bearings, and was not merely a piece of advice but a positive injunction with ecclesiastical sanction.

'Dogma' in Scripture

While the word 'dogma' is sometimes used in religion and

theology with a great deal of latitude, as practically synonymous
with 'doctrine,' it generally has a more restricted meaning. A
doctrine is the direct, often naive, expression of a religious
'Dogma' in truth. It is not necessarily formulated with scientific precision,
theology and when it is, may be merely the formulation of a single person.
A religious dogma, on the other hand, is a religious truth based
on authority and officially formulated by some ecclesiastical
assembly. This meaning of the word is not determined by its
scriptural usage, in which it always denotes a decree, a com-
mandment, or a rule of practical life, but is more in harmony
with the philosophical use of the word to denote a proposition or
principle. Some of the early Church Fathers used it to describe
the substance of doctrine. Cf Hagenbach, *History of Doctrines*
I, p 2 f; Hauck, *Realencyclopaedie,* Art *Dogmatik.*

2. THE ORIGIN AND CHARACTER OF DOGMAS

Religious doctrines are found in Scripture, though not in fin-
ished form, but dogmas in the current sense of the word are not
found there. They are the fruit of human reflection, the reflection of the Church, often occasioned or intensified by theological
controversies. Roman Catholics and Protestants differ some-
Catholic what in their description of the origin of dogmas. The former
conception of minimize, if they do not exclude, the reflection of the Church *as*
dogma *the body of believers,* and substitute for it the study of the teaching Church or the hierarchy. Whenever a new form of error
arises, the teaching Church, that is the clerus, which now has
its infallible spokesman in the Pope, after careful examination,
formulates the doctrine taught in Scripture or by tradition, declares it to be a revealed truth, and imposes its acceptance on all
the faithful. Says Wilmers in his *Handbook of the Christian
Religion,* p 151: 'A dogma, therefore, is a truth revealed by
God, and at the same time proposed by the Church for our belief.' Similarly Spirago-Clarke in *The Catechism Explained:* 'A
truth which the Church puts before us as revealed by God is
called a truth of faith, or a *dogma.*' p 84. And since the Church is
infallible in matters of doctrine, a truth so proposed is not only

authoritative but also irrevocable and unchangeable. 'If any one shall assert it to be possible that sometimes, according to the progress of science, a sense is to be given to doctrines propounded by the Church different from that which the Church has understood and understands: let him be anathema.' *Dogmatic Decrees of the First Vatican Council, Canons* IV 3.

The Reformers substituted for this Roman Catholic view another which, in spite of its similarity, yet differs from it in important points. According to them all truly religious dogmas derive their material contents from Scripture and from Scripture only. They do not recognize the unwritten word or tradition as a source of dogmas. At the same time they do not regard dogmas as statements taken directly from the Bible, but represent them as the fruit of the reflection of the Church, as the body of believers, on the truths of revelation, and as the official formulations of competent representative bodies. Since the reflection of the Church is often determined and deepened by doctrinal controversies, the formulations to which Church Councils or Synods are finally led under the guidance of the Holy Spirit often bear the earmarks of past struggles. They are not infallible but yet have a high degree of stability. And they are authoritative, not merely because they are proposed by the Church, but *formally* as defined by the Church and *materially* as based on the Word of God. *Protestant conception of dogma*

Under the influence of Schleiermacher, Ritschl, Vinet, and others, a radically different conception of the origin of dogmas was developed, which found ready acceptance in many Protestant circles. It represents the Christian consciousness, Christian experience, the Christian faith, or the Christian life as the source of the material contents of dogmas, and regards this as more in harmony with the principles of the Reformation. The dogmas of the Church are simply the intellectual formulations of its experiences, sentiments, and beliefs, which, according to some, are awakened by an objective factor, in which piety recognizes a divine revelation. Schleiermacher contends for the immediacy of these religious experiences, while Ritschl and his School maintain that they are mediated by some objective fac- *Modern conception of dogma* tor, which faith honours as a revelation of God. The religious community reflects on these experiences and finally by some competent body gives them formal intellectual expression and thus transforms them into dogmas. On this view, as well as on the other, the formulation of dogmas is not the work of an individual theologian, but of a community, either the Church (Schleiermacher), or the State going hand in hand with the Church (Lobstein). This view of the origin of dogmas is held by Schleiermacher, Ritschl, Kaftan, Lobstein, Vinet, Sabatier, Is. Van Dijk, and others. It should be noted, however, that it does not describe the way in which the existing dogmas actually originated in the Protestant Churches, but only the way in which, according to these writers, dogmas should come into existence. They regard the old dogmas as antiquated, because they are too intellectual and do not give adequate expression to the life of the Church, and call for a new dogma vibrant with the life of the religious community.

Harnack's view of dogma

Harnack's view deserves special mention here. In his monumental work on *The History of Dogma* he seeks to discredit the whole dogma (i.e. the whole complex of dogmas) of the early Church by representing it as an unnatural mixture of Greek Philosophy and Christian truth, in which the foreign philosophical ingredient is the preponderating element. Says he: 'Dogma in its conception and development is a work of the Greek spirit on the soil of the Gospel.' The Church yielded to the temptation to represent its message in a form that would make it appear as wisdom rather than foolishness and thus to gain for it the proper respect of the educated people. The practical faith of the Church was transformed into an intellectual concept, a dogma, and this became the real pivot of the history of the Church. This was a great mistake, and a mistake that was continued in the later formation of dogmas, so that the whole history of dogma is really the history of a colossal error. It is the great ambition of the Ritschlian School, to which Harnack belongs, to eliminate all metaphysics from theology.

A dogma may be defined as a doctrine, derived from Scripture, officially defined by the Church, and declared to rest upon

divine authority. This definition partly names and partly sug- *Definition of dogma*
gests its characteristics. Its subject-matter is derived from the
Word of God and is therefore authoritative. It is not a mere
repetition of what is found in Scripture, but the fruit of dogmatic reflection. And it is officially defined by a competent
ecclesiastical body and declared to rest upon divine authority.
It has social significance, because it is the expression, not of a
single individual, but of a community. And it has traditional
value, since it passes the precious possessions of the Church on
to future generations. In the History of Dogma we see the
Church becoming ever increasingly conscious of the riches of
divine truth under the guidance of the Holy Spirit, mindful of
her high prerogative as the pillar and ground of the truth, and
engaged in the defence of the faith once delivered to the saints.

II: THE TASK OF THE HISTORY OF DOGMA

Task of history of dogma

The task of the History of Dogma is, briefly stated, to describe the historical origin of the dogma of the Church and to trace its subsequent changes and developments; or, in the words of Seeberg, 'to show how the Dogma as a whole and the separate dogmas have arisen and through what course of development they have been brought to the form and interpretation prevailing in the churches of any given period'. The following general remarks may be made respecting its presuppositions, its general contents, and the point of view from which it is written.

I. ITS PRESUPPOSITIONS

Dogma changeable

The one great presupposition of the History of Dogma would seem to be that the dogma of the Church is changeable and has, as a matter of fact, undergone many changes in the course of its historical development. That which is unchangeable is not subject to development and has no history. Protestant theology has always maintained the position that the dogma of the Church, while characterized by a high degree of stability, is yet subject to change and has in the course of history been enriched with new elements, received more careful formulation, and even undergone certain transformations. It has no difficulty, therefore, with the idea of a history of dogma. The situation is somewhat different, however, in Roman Catholic theology. Roman Catholics

Catholic dogma unchangeable

glory in the fact that they have an unchangeable dogma and feel far superior to the Protestant who, in the words of Cardinal Gibbons, 'appeals to the unchanging Bible in support of his ever-changing doctrines'. He says that the creed of the Church 'is now identical with what it was in past ages'. *Faith of our Fathers,* pp 11, 87. Wilmers speaks in a similar vein when he says, 'The Christian religion is unchangeable in all its *revealed doctrines* – in all those *precepts* and *institutions* which are intended for all men. No article of faith (for of doctrine there is mainly question) can be added or subtracted; nor can any dogma receive a different meaning from that given it by Christ.' *Handbook of the Christian Religion,* p 67. We are told repeatedly by Roman Catholic authors that the Church cannot make new dogmas, but can only hand down the sacred deposit that was entrusted to her.

But if the repeated assertions that the Church cannot make new dogmas is true, then it follows that the dogmas were already given in the original deposit, in the faith once delivered to the saints and contained in Scripture and in the apostolic tradition. No dogma was ever added to the sacred deposit, and no dogma contained in it was ever changed. The Church only has power to declare a truth to be revealed by God and to give it an infallible interpretation, thus dispelling uncertainty and increasing the positive knowledge of the faithful. It did this in the past and will continue to do it whenever historical occasions call for it. The dogma itself then does not develop and therefore has no history; there is development only in the subjective apprehension of it, and this determines the Roman Catholic conception of the History of Dogma. Says B. J. Otten, the Roman Catholic author of *A Manual of the History of Dogmas* (third edition): 'It [the History of Dogmas] presupposes that revealed truths are objectively permanent and immutable, and also that their subjective apprehension and outward expression admits of progress.' Vol I, p 2.

Catholic dogma in Scripture

For a long time Roman Catholics looked askant at the History of Dogma. Neander says that a 'modern theologian, Hermes of Bonn, has asserted that to treat the History of Dogmas as a special branch of Study, on account of the change in development which it presupposes, militates against the Catholic Church, and for that reason he has scrupled to give Lectures upon it'. *The History of Christian Dogmas,* I, p 28. Petavius was the first of the Roman Catholics to suggest something like a doctrine of development, but his work was not well received, and he had to

Catholic view of history of dogma

qualify his statements. Later on Moehler and especially Newman advocated a theory of development which met with considerable, though not universal, favour. The latter's theory is to the effect that many of the doctrines of the Church were only germinally present in the original deposit. They were like seeds implanted in the mind of the Church that were pregnant with unsuspected possibilities and in course of time unfolded into full-blown doctrines. While opposition often arose to the new doctrinal expressions, they gradually gained ground and increased in popularity. Finally the teaching Church, the hierarchy, stepped in to test the results of this new development and to set the stamp of its infallible approval on some of them by declaring them to be divinely revealed truths. This theory found favour with many of the Roman Catholics, but did not commend itself to all and never received official approval.

Development of dogma organic   A second presupposition of the History of Dogma is that the development of the dogma of the Church moved along organic lines and was therefore in the main a continuous growth, in spite of the fact that the leaders of the Church in their endeavours to apprehend the truth often wandered into blind alleys, chasing will-o'-the-wisps and toying with foreign elements; and that even the Church itself, as a whole or in part, sometimes erred in its formulation of the truth. God's special revelation is the progressive unfolding of the ectypal knowledge of God and of the redemptive idea in Christ Jesus. It is an organic whole in which all the parts are interrelated, the comprehensive expression of divine thought. The Church in its endeavours to apprehend the truth is simply seeking to think the thoughts of God after Him. It does this under the guidance of the Holy Spirit, which is the Spirit of truth and as such guarantees that it will ever-increasingly see the truth as an internally connected organism. The History of Dogma may not be a mere chronicle, recording the external history of the various dogmas of the Church. It is the history of an organic growth and of the inner workings of the mind of the Church, and therefore presupposes a rather continuous development of the ecclesiastical dogma.

If the Church in the past had proceeded on the assumption,

[22]

now advocated by many, that the changing conditions of the religious life ever and anon call for a new dogma, and that every age must formulate its own dogma, discarding the old and substituting for it another more in harmony with the spiritual condition of the times, it would have been quite impossible to write a history of dogma in the organic sense of the word. We shall have to proceed on the assumption that the Church, despite the melancholy aberrations that characterized her search for the truth and often led her into ways of error, yet gradually advanced in her apprehension and formulation of the truth. We shall have to assume that even such a tremendous religious upheaval as the Reformation did not constitute a complete break with the doctrinal development of the past. While many errors were exposed and corrected, the Reformers sought support for their views in the early Church Fathers, and did not even hesitate to adopt some of the views that were developed during the Middle Ages. There was continuity of thought even here.

Gradually advancing development

2. ITS SUBJECT-MATTER

The fact that the History of Dogma deals primarily with the dogmas of the Church does not mean that it need not concern itself with those doctrinal developments that were not yet, and perhaps were never to be, incorporated in the official Creeds. It would be a mistake to assume that it can begin with the Council of Nicaea and end with the adoption of the last of the historical Confessions. In order to describe the genesis of the earliest dogmas of the Church, it must take its starting point at the close of the period of special revelation in the study of the Apostolic Fathers. It will have to take account of those preformations of the dogmas of the Church that resulted from the theological discussions of the day and met with rather general approval, though they did not receive the official stamp of the Church; of those peripheral truths that necessarily followed from the central and controlling dogma, and yet did not receive special ecclesiastical sanction; and of those further developments of doctrinal truth that point forward to and prepare the way for additional

Dogma not the only material for history

formulations of theological dogmas. Since the dogma of the Church is not the fruit of a mechanical construction but rather of an organic growth, the study of its history cannot afford to limit its attention to the clearly defined results obtained at various times, but must also consider the intervening stages with their promise of even better and richer fruits.

Consideration of doctrinal controversies

From this it follows that, as far as the external history is concerned, the History of Dogma cannot neglect the study of the great doctrinal controversies of the Church, which were the birth pangs of new dogmas and often had a determining influence on their formulation. Though this study may not always be edifying, it is absolutely essential to a proper understanding of the genesis of ecclesiastical dogmas. In these controversies differences of opinion became apparent and in some cases gave rise to different lines of development, and doctrinal formulations arose which were at variance with the united consciousness of the Church in general or of some particular denomination. Even these departures from the main line of thought are important for the History of Dogma, since they often led to a clearer and sharper formulation of the truth.

Inner development of thought

But while the History of Dogma cannot afford to ignore any of the external facts that bear on the development of dogma, it should never lose sight of the fact that it is primarily concerned with the development of theological thought in the consciousness of the Church and should therefore trace the development of the idea which is inherent in the revealed revelation of God itself. Hegel and Baur rendered good service to the History of Dogma, when they directed attention to the fact that the development of dogma is controlled by an inner law, though their principle of interpretation does not commend itself to Christian thought. We can discern a certain logical necessity in the successive stages of the development of each dogma, and in the order in which the various dogmatical problems presented themselves. In general it may be said that the logical order, usually followed in the study of Dogmatics, is reflected more or less in the History of Dogma.

III: METHOD AND DIVISIONS OF THE HISTORY OF DOGMA

There has been considerable difference in the division of the subject-matter of the History of Dogma and in the method followed in its treatment. We briefly call attention to some of these differences.

I. DIVISIONS OF THE HISTORY OF DOGMA

The common division found in most of the older works on the History of Dogma is that into General and Special History of Dogma. This division is followed in each of the successive periods, the General History sketching the general philosophic background, the main themes of discussion, and the general direction of doctrinal study in each period under discussion; and the Special History tracing the genesis and development of the separate dogmas, especially those which are central and have a controlling influence on the formation of more peripheral dogmas. The special dogmas are usually discussed under the customary rubrics of Dogmatics: theology, anthropology, christology, and so on. This is called the *lokal-methode*, and is followed by Hagenbach, Neander, Sheldon, and others. Ritschl objected to both parts of this method of division on the ground that they represented an anatomic rather than an organic method of treatment; and in later works on the History of Dogma both its division into General and Special History and the *lokal-methode* are abandoned. This is one of the striking differences between the words of Harnack, Loofs, Seeberg, and Fisher on the one hand and most of the previous Histories on the other hand. The great objection to the division of the History of Dogma into General and Special is that it separates what

General and special history

Later divisions

[25]

belongs together; and to the *lokal-methode*, that it is artificial rather than historical and does not do justice to the difference of emphasis in the various periods, or to that which is distinctive in the discussions of each period. The later writers, though not in complete agreement as to the division to be applied in the study of the History of Dogma, all strive to give a more unified view of the genesis and development of the dogma of the Church. The divisions of Harnack and Loofs reveal great similarity, while that of Seeberg runs to a great extent along similar lines. His division is as follows: I. *The Construction of Doctrine in the Ancient Church.* II. *The Preservation, Transformation, and Development of Doctrine in the Church of the Middle Ages.* III. *The Development of the Doctrinal System through the Reformation, and the Opposing Crystallization of Doctrine by Roman Catholicism.*

2. METHOD OF TREATMENT

Under this general head two distinctions call for consideration.

Horizontal and vertical method

[a] *That between the horizontal and vertical method.* Some follow the horizontal and others the vertical method in their study of the History of Dogma. They who adopt the former take up the history of doctrinal development as a whole by periods and trace the genesis of all the various dogmas in each particular period, leaving them at the stage at which the close of the period finds them, and taking them up again at that point, to trace their further development. Thus the unfolding of the doctrine of God is studied up to the beginning of the Middle Ages; then this is dropped and is followed by a study of the development of the doctrine of Christ up to the same point; again, this is discontinued and is succeeded by a consideration of the gradual expansion of the anthropological doctrines of sin and grace within the same period of time; and so on all along the line. They who follow the latter method, however, take up the study of the separate dogmas in the order in which they become the centre of attention in the Church, and trace their development until they

reach their final form. The doctrine of God is taken up first, because it was the first to engage the special attention of the Church, and its development is traced up to the time of its final formulation in the historic Creeds of the post-Reformation period. In a similar way the remaining central doctrines, such as those of Christ, of sin and grace, of the atonement, and so on, are studied in their various stages of growth until they reach their final official form. The former method is followed by Hagenbach, Neander, Sheldon, Harnack, Loofs, and Seeberg; the latter, though with certain differences, by Thomasius, Shedd, and Cunningham. Each one of these has its advantages and disadvantages. In our brief discussion it seems preferable to follow the latter, because it keeps the separate dogmas more prominently before the mind, and enables us to trace their development from start to finish without diverting the attention from the regular flow of thought by a more or less mechanical division. Of course, the danger lies at hand, and ought to be avoided as much as possible, that the doctrines under consideration will appear more or less detached from their historical setting and from their logical connection in the systems of thought of the great theologians of the Church, such as Tertullian, Origen, Augustine, Anselm, Thomas Aquinas, Luther, Calvin, and others. Happily, this danger is obviated to a great extent by the fact that the central doctrines of the Church, with which we are mainly concerned, did not occupy the centre of the stage simultaneously. Moreover, the reading of another work on the History of Dogma, such as that of Seeberg, Sheldon, or Fisher, will help to off-set this handicap. While pursuing this method, we shall not terminate our historical discussion of each one of the dogmas at the point of their incorporation into the last of the great historic Creeds, but shall also consider the changes or developments suggested in later theological literature, since they may in course of time lead to sounder, clearer, or more complete dogmatical formulations.

[b] *That between a purely objective and the confessional method.* Some are of the opinion that the only proper, the only

Objective and confessional method scientific way, to treat the History of Dogma is according to the purely objective method. They regard it as the task of the historian to describe the genesis and development of the dogma of the Church without any prepossessions, without manifesting any sympathy or antipathy, and without in any way judging of the truth and falsity of the various doctrinal formulations. Such judgment, we are told, is not in place in the History of Dogma, but only in Dogmatics proper. And so, whenever the general course of doctrinal development divides itself into various currents, which yield diversified and even antithetical doctrines, as in the Greek, the Roman Catholic, the Lutheran, and the Reformed Churches, the historian should simply describe these, one after another, without testing them and without expressing any preferences. Dr. Kuyper correctly calls attention to the fact, however, that no one could follow this method in describing the history of his country, or in writing the biography of a friend, since one would not be able to write as a disinterested spectator.

Just so the historian, who has definite doctrinal convictions and subscribes to a certain Creed, will find it difficult, if not impossible, to write a history of dogmas without any prepossession and without revealing his ecclesiastical standpoint. He will prefer the confessional method, according to which he will take his starting point in his own Confession and will seek to give a genetic explanation of its contents. In judging of the various doctrinal developments he will employ not only the standard of God's Word, but also the criterion of his own Confession: the former as the absolute standard of religious truth, and the latter as the well-considered and carefully formulated result of previous investigations which, while not infallible, should yet be regarded as a true representation of Scripture truth until the contrary is proved. History so written will not be colourless, but will naturally reflect the standpoint of the author on almost every page. It will not wittingly pervert the facts of history, but will judge them primarily by the standard of Scripture by which all religious truth should be judged, and secondarily by a predetermined ecclesiastical criterion. This is the method we prefer to follow in our study of the History of Dogma.

[28]

IV: HISTORY OF THE HISTORY OF DOGMA

I. FACTORS THAT GAVE RISE TO THE HISTORY OF DOGMA AS A SEPARATE DISCIPLINE

The study of the History of Dogma as a separate discipline is of comparatively recent date. Valuable materials for such a study were gathered in the centuries preceding the Reformation, but, as Harnack says, 'They scarcely prepared the way for, far less produced a historical view of dogmatic tradition.' *History of Dogma* I, p 24. Since the Church of Rome proceeded on the assumption, and still maintains the position, that dogma is unchangeable, it may be said that the Reformation by breaking with that view opened the way for a critical treatment of the history of dogma. Moreover, it was a movement which, in its very nature, was well calculated to furnish a special incentive for such a study. It raised many questions respecting the nature of the Church and her teachings, and sought to answer these not only in the light of Scripture but also with an appeal to the Fathers of the early Church, thus furnishing a direct and powerful motive for a historical study of dogma. Yet the Reformers and the theologians of the era of the Reformation did not initiate such an investigation. Though they appealed to the Fathers of the early centuries to substantiate their views, they did not feel the need of a careful and critical inquiry into the historical genesis of that whole body of doctrine that constituted the content of their faith. They harboured no doubts as to the scriptural character of the doctrines which they believed. Moreover, these doctrines entered into their very life and were verified by experience. And not only did their robust faith have no need

Origin of history of dogma

Influence of the Reformation

of such a historical investigation, but the dogmatical and polemical interests that were uppermost in their mind left little time for historical study.

The fact remains, however, that the Roman Catholic and Protestant Churches accused each other of departing from the historic faith of Christendom, and that only a careful study of history could settle that dispute. While this motive remained inoperative for a long time, due to dogmatical and polemical interests, it was there and was bound to have some influence in course of time. It did not become operative, however, until it was reinforced by other motives, supplied by movements which were

Influence of Pietism and Rationalism

unfriendly to the dogma of the Church. Pietism was born of the conviction that Protestant Scholasticism exercised a petrifying influence and thus threatened the living truths of the Reformation. It reacted against what it regarded as the barren intellectualism of the seventeenth century and saw in this a departure from the faith of the Reformers. And Rationalism was hostile to the dogma of the Church, because it was based on authority rather than on human reason and with its vaunted stability represented a check on the free inquiry of the human mind. It was interested in showing that the dogma of the Church had been changed repeatedly, and therefore could not lay claim to the permanence and stability usually ascribed to it. These two movements, however different and even antagonistic in some respects, joined hands in their opposition to dogma and began the study of its history with the ill-concealed desire of undermining it.

Influence of historical spirit

Another factor that should be taken into consideration, is the awakening of the historical spirit under the influence of Semler and others. Semler initiated the modern historical study of Scripture and wrote a work entitled, *An Experiment of a Freer Method of Teaching*, which was a pioneer work in which the practical value of the historical method was explained. In Church History the fruit of this new spirit was first seen in the great work of Mosheim. While it did not take up the history of dogma, it nevertheless gave great impetus to this study. Important elements for it are found in the works of Lessing and Semler.

[30]

2. EARLIER WORKS ON THE HISTORY OF DOGMA

Earlier works

The real beginnings of the study of the History of Dogma are seen in the works of S. G. Lange and Muenscher. The work of the former was planned on a large scale, but was never completed. The latter wrote a work consisting of four volumes in 1797, and followed this up with a compendium. By an unbiased study he sought to answer the question, How and why did the doctrine of Christianity gradually assume its present form? His work is marred by the influence of Rationalism and left the question unanswered, whether the proper object of the study is doctrine or dogma. He introduced the division of the study into a General and Special History of Dogma, which is found in many of the later works. The manuals that followed the work of Muenscher did not mark any special advance in the study of the subject.

Under the influence of Hegel a better historical method was introduced. The application of it to the study of the History is seen especially in the work of F. C. Baur, the father of the Tuebingen School of New Testament criticism. The Hegelian principle of evolution was introduced in tracing a definite order and progress in the rise of ecclesiastical dogmas. It was regarded as the object of the History of Dogma (a) to ascertain the facts in their actual settings as attested by accredited witnesses, and (b) to interpret them in accordance with an exact law of inner unfolding. For a long time, however, it was a purely speculative idea of development, as embodied in the familiar Hegelian triad, that was superimposed on this study. This appears most clearly in the work of Baur.

The idea of development, however, gradually acquired other than Hegelian applications. It is assumed in the productions of Schleiermacher's school of theology. It is also applied by such mediating writers as Neander and Hagenbach, who surpass the Hegelians in their estimate of Christianity as a religion and of the religious value of doctrine. They fall short, however, in their application of the historic principle where they continued the old division into a General and Special History and in the latter also apply the so-called *lokal-methode*. Other modifications are found in the writings of such confessionalists as Kliefoth and

Thomasius. In the work of the former the idea of dogma in distinction from doctrine emerges and is made the proper object of this study. According to this writer each epoch yields its own cycle of dogmatic truth and leaves this to succeeding generations as a treasure to be preserved rather than as material to be re-shaped or even to be cancelled (Baur). It is to be incorporated as a whole in the following development. Thomasius carefully distinguished between central and peripheral dogmas, the former being the great fundamental doctrines of God, of Christ, and of Sin and Grace, and the latter the more derivative doctrines which are developed on the basis of the central doctrines. His work is written from the confessional standpoint of the Lutheran Church.

Roman Catholic scholarship was slow in taking an interest in the study of the History of Dogma. And when it did, it took its starting-point in the distinct conception of dogma as the authoritative deliverance of the Church on the fundamentals of the Christian religion. The older works proceed on the assumption that the early Church was in possession of the complete dogma of Christianity, and that there is no possibility of material alteration from one generation to another. It is claimed that there has been no addition to the original deposit but only interpretations of it. Newman introduced the theory of development. According to him the original deposit of revealed truth in the Bible is largely implicit and germinal, and only gradually unfolds under the stimulus of external conditions. The process of development is absolutely controlled, however, by the infallible Church. But even this theory, however carefully put, did not meet with general acceptance in Roman Catholic circles.

3. LATER WORKS ON THE HISTORY OF DOGMA

Later works Later works on the History of Dogma reveal a tendency to break with the mechanical arrangement of the earlier works with their division of the subject into a General and a Special History and their application of the *lokal-methode*. This is still found, indeed, in the work of Sheldon, and partly also in that of Shedd, but is conspicuous by its absence in other recent works. There is a growing conviction that the History of Dogma should be treated more organically. Nitzsch adopted a genetic arrangement under the following heads: *The Promulgation of the Old Catholic Church Doctrine*, and *The Development of the Old Catholic Church Doctrine*. A similar division is found in Harnack, who speaks of *The Rise of Ecclesiastical Dogma* and *The Development of Ecclesiastical Dogma*.

Harnack shows affinity with both Thomasius and Nitzsch, but advances far beyond their position. He limits his discussion to the rise and development of dogmas as distinguished from doctrines, and takes into account the constantly changing aspects of Christianity as a whole, particularly in connection with the general cultural development. His work breaks radically with the *lokal-methode*. But he has an erroneous conception of dogma, regarding it in its inception and structure as a work of the Greek spirit on the soil of the Gospel, a mixture of Christian religion and Hellenistic culture, in which the latter predominates. As he sees it, propositions of faith were wrongly turned into intellectual concepts, which were supported by historical and scientific proofs, but by that very process lost their normative value and dogmatic authority. According to him that corruption began, not in the New Testament itself, as later writers assert, but in the second and third centuries with the development of the Logos doctrine, and was continued in the Roman Catholic Church up to the time of the first Vatican Council, while Protestantism at the time of the Reformation in principle set aside the dogmatic conception of Christianity. Its dogmas are constantly subject to revision. Strictly speaking, it has no place for fixed truths, for dogmas, but only for a *Glaubenslehre*. Harnack takes too limited a view of dogma, does not do justice to the aversion of the early Church Fathers to heathen influence, and makes the whole History of Dogma one gigantic error.

Loofs and Seeberg do not follow the division of Harnack, but seem to feel that the second division of his great work really covers practically the whole of the History of Dogma, though the former still has a separate chapter on the genesis of dogma among the Christians. And though he does not entirely agree with Harnack's conception of dogma, he shows greater affinity with him than Seeberg does in his monumental work. This work is somewhat of a source-book, since it contains numerous quotations from the authors whose doctrinal views are discussed. Like Harnack, Seeberg has also written a textbook in two volumes, which was translated into English by Dr. Charles E. Hay and appeared in 1905 under the title, *Textbook of the History of Doctrines*. It is a work of considerable value for the student.

QUESTIONS FOR FURTHER STUDY

How do the Roman Catholic and the Protestant conceptions of dogma differ? How did Newman's theory change the Roman Catholic view of the history of dogma? What objections are there to Harnack's view of dogma? Has his view met with general favour among the Ritschlians? Are Roman Catholics and Protestants agreed as to the task of the history of dogma? Is the changeable element of dogma, presupposed in its history, found in its form or in its content or in both? What can be said for and against the Hegelian method as applied to the History of Dogma? Did Baur in applying it do justice to the external historical facts? Must the history of dogma, in order to be truly scientific, be written in a purely objective way?

LITERATURE

Harnack, *History of Dogma*, I, pp 1–40; Seeberg, *History of Doctrines*, I, pp 19–27; Loofs, *Handboek der Dogmengeschiedenis*, pp 1–9; Neander, *History of Christian Dogmas*, I, pp 1–32; Fisher, *History of Christian Doctrine*, pp 1–22; Hagenbach, *History of Doctrines*, I, pp 1–47; Shedd, *History of Christian Doctrine*, I, pp 1–48; Rainy, *Delivery and Development of Christian Doctrine*; Kuyper, *Encyclopaedie der Heilige Godgeleerdheid*, III, pp 370–386.

PREPARATORY
DOCTRINAL
DEVELOPMENT

I: THE APOSTOLIC FATHERS AND THEIR DOCTRINAL VIEWS

I. THEIR REPUTED WRITINGS

The Apostolic Fathers are the Fathers who are supposed to have lived before the last of the apostles died, of whom some are said to have been disciples of the apostles, and to whom the earliest Christian writings now extant are ascribed. There are especially six names which have come down to us, namely, Barnabas, Hermas, Clement of Rome, Polycarp, Papias, and Ignatius. The first is generally regarded, though with doubtful warrant, as the Barnabas who is known as the companion of Paul in the Acts of the Apostles. He is the reputed author of a strongly anti-Judaic Epistle of doubtful genuineness. Hermas is supposed to have been the person mentioned in Rom. 16:14, though on insufficient grounds. The Shepherd of Hermas ascribed to him contains a series of visions, commands, and similitudes. It is a work of doubtful authenticity, though it was held in high esteem by the early Church. Clement of Rome may have been Paul's fellow-worker named in Phil. 4:3. He is commonly represented as bishop of Rome, though he may have been, and most likely was, merely an influential pastor there. He was the author of an Epistle to the Corinthians, containing general moral injunctions and special exhortations, occasioned by discords in the Corinthian church. The authenticity of this Epistle is also doubted by some, though without good reasons. It is probably the earliest of the genuine remains of early Christian literature. Polycarp is usually designated 'bishop of Smyrna', but Eusebius speaks of him more correctly as 'that blessed and apostolic presbyter'. He was a disciple of John and wrote a short Epistle to the Philippians, consisting chiefly of practical exhortations in Scripture language. Papias, called 'bishop of Hierapolis' was a contemporary of

Writings of Apostolic Fathers

[37]

Polycarp, and perhaps also a disciple of John. He was the author of an *"Exposition of the Oracles of the Lord"*, of which only a few doctrinally insignificant fragments were preserved by Eusebius. Ignatius, commonly known as 'bishop of Antioch', also lived in the days of the last of the apostles. Fifteen letters were ascribed to him, but only seven are now regarded as genuine, and even these are doubted by some. To these writings two of unknown authorship must be added, namely, the Epistle to Diognetes and the Didache. The former is sometimes ascribed to Justin Martyr, since he wrote an Apology to Diognetes. His authorship is very unlikely, however, in view of internal evidence. The writer gives an account of the ground on which many Christians had abandoned Paganism and Judaism, describes the leading features of the character and conduct of Christians, and traces this to the doctrine of Christianity, of which he gives an admirable summary. The Didache, discovered in 1873, was probably written about the year AD 100. The first part contains moral precepts under the scheme of the Two Ways, the way of life and the way of death, while the second part gives directions pertaining to worship and church government, interspersed with statements respecting the last things.

2. FORMAL CHARACTERISTICS OF THEIR TEACHINGS

Want of originality, depth, and clearness It is frequently remarked that in passing from the study of the New Testament to that of the Apostolic Fathers one is conscious of a tremendous change. There is not the same freshness and originality, depth and clearness. And this is no wonder, for it means the transition from truth given by infallible inspiration to truth reproduced by fallible pioneers. Their productions were bound to lean rather heavily on Scripture and to be of a primitive type, concerning itself with the first principles of faith rather than with the deeper truths of religion.

Meagreness Their teachings are characterized by a certain meagreness. They are generally in full agreement with the teachings of Scripture, are often couched in the very words of the Bible, but add very little by way of explication and are not at all systema-

[38]

tized. And this need not surprise anyone, for there had as yet been but a short time for reflection on the truths of Scripture and for assimilation of the great mass of material contained in the Bible. The canon of the New Testament was not yet fixed, and this explains why these early Fathers so often quote oral tradition rather than the written word. Moreover, it should be borne in mind that there were no philosophical minds among them with special training for the pursuit of the truth and outstanding ability for its systematic presentation. In spite of their comparative poverty, however, the writings of the Apostolic Fathers are of considerable importance, since they witness to the canonicity and integrity of the New Testament Books and form a doctrinal link between the New Testament and the more speculative writings of the Apologetes which appeared during the second century.

A second characteristic of the teachings of the Apostolic Fathers is their want of definiteness. The New Testament records various types of the Apostolic *kerugma* (preaching): the Petrine, the Pauline, and the Johannine. The three are in fundamental agreement, but each one of them represents a different emphasis on the truth. Now it may seem surprising that the Apostolic Fathers, while revealing some preference for the Johannine type, with which they may have been best acquainted, yet did not definitely attach themselves to any one of these types. However, several considerations may be offered in explanation. It requires considerable reflection to distinguish these types. These early Fathers stood too near the Apostles to grasp the distinctive features of their teachings. Then, too, for them Christianity was not in the first place a knowledge to be acquired, but the principle of a new obedience to God. While they were conscious of the normative value of the words of Jesus and the Apostolic *kerugma*, they did not attempt to define the truths of revelation, but simply to restate them in the light of their understanding. And, finally, the general conditions of their life, in so far as these were influenced by the popular heathen philosophy of the day, and by heathen and Jewish-Hellenistic piety, were not favourable to the proper understanding of the characteristic differences between the several types of the Apostolic *kerugma*.

Want of definiteness

[39]

3. MATERIAL CONTENTS OF THEIR TEACHINGS

It is a matter of common observation that the writings of the Apostolic Fathers contain very little that is doctrinally important. Their teachings are generally in harmony with the truth revealed in the Word of God, and are often represented in the very words of Scripture, but for that very reason cannot be said to increase or deepen our insight into the truth or to shed light on the inter-relations of the doctrinal teachings of Scripture.

On God, and Jesus Christ They testify to a common faith in God as the Creator and Ruler of the universe and in Jesus Christ, who was active in creation and throughout the old dispensation, and finally appeared in the flesh. While they use the scriptural designation of God as Father, Son, and Holy Spirit, and also speak of Christ as God and man, they do not testify to an awareness of the implications and problems involved.

On work of Christ The work of Christ as the Redeemer is not always represented in the same way. Sometimes His great significance is seen in the fact that He, by His passion and death, freed mankind from sin and death; and sometimes in the related, but not correlated fact that He revealed the Father and taught the new moral law. In some cases the death of Christ is represented as procuring for men the grace of repentance and as opening the way for a new obedience, rather than as the ground of man's justification. This moralistic strain is, perhaps, the weakest point in the teachings of the Apostolic Fathers. It was related to the moralism present in the heathen world of that day and characteristic of the natural man as such, and was bound to serve the interests of legalism.

On the sacraments The sacraments are represented as the means by which the blessings of salvation are communicated to man. Baptism begets the new life and secures the forgiveness of all sins or of past sins only (Hermas and II Clement); and the Lord's Supper is the means of communicating to man a blessed immortality or eternal life.

On faith and good works The individual Christian apprehends God in faith, which consists in true knowledge of God, confidence in Him, and self-committal to Him. Man is said to be justified by faith, but the relation of faith to justification and the new life is not clearly understood. An anti-Pauline strain of legalism becomes manifest at this point. Faith is simply the first step in the way of life, on which the moral development of the individual depends. But after the forgiveness of sins is once granted in baptism and apprehended by faith, man next merits this blessing by his good works, which become a second and independent principle alongside of faith. Christianity is often represented as a *nova lex*, and love, leading on to a new obedience, takes the leading place. Not the grace of God, but the good works of man sometimes appear in the foreground.

The Christian is represented as living in a Christian community, the Church, which still rejoices in the possession of charismatic gifts, but also shows an increasing respect for the ecclesiastical offices mentioned in the New Testament. In some instances the bishop stands out as superior to the presbyters. A vivid sense of the vanity and transitory character of the present world, and of the eternal glory of the future world, is manifest in their writings. The end of all things is thought to be very near, and the representations of the end of the present world are derived from Old Testament prophecy. The Kingdom of God is regarded as the supreme good and as a purely future blessing. According to some (Barnabas, Hermas, Papias) its final form is preceded by a millennial kingdom. But whatever attention is devoted to the millennium, there is far greater emphasis on the coming judgment, when the people of God will receive the rewards of heaven, and the wicked will be condemned to everlasting destruction. *On the Church* *On the future world*

QUESTIONS FOR FURTHER STUDY
How is the indefinite character of the teachings of the Apostolic Fathers to be explained? On which point are these teachings defective? What seeds of the doctrines peculiar to Roman Catholicism are already present in these writings? How can we account for their different representations of the work of Christ? In what particular points does the moralism or legalism of the early Fathers appear? What can be said in explanation of this phenomenon? Could it have been occasioned in any way by Scripture statements? Is Harnack correct when he says that the Christology of the Apostolic Fathers is in part 'Adoption Christology'?

LITERATURE
Lightfoot, *The Apostolic Fathers;* Lechler, *Das apostol. u nachap. Zeitalter;*
Moxom, *From Jerusalem to Nicaea,* pp 99–162; Cunningham, *Historical
Theology,* I, pp 94–120; Scott, *The Nicene Theology,* pp 82–86, 142–160;
Moody, C. N., *The Mind of the Early Converts,* pp 10–101; Harnack, *History
of Dogma,* I, pp 141–221; Seeberg, *History of Doctrines,* I, pp 55–82; Loofs,
Handboek der Dogmengeschiedenis, pp 57–66; Otten, *Manual of the History of
Dogmas,* I, pp 62–98; Fisher, *History of Christian Doctrine,* pp 41–47.

II: PERVERSIONS OF THE GOSPEL

In the second century the Christian religion as a new force in *Outside* the world, revealing itself in the organization of the Church, had *dangers* to engage in a struggle for existence. It had to guard against dangers from without and from within, had to justify its existence, and had to maintain the purity of doctrine in the face of subtle error. The very existence of the Church was threatened by State persecutions. The first persecutions were entirely Jewish, due to the fact that the Church was largely limited to Palestine, and that the Roman Government for some time considered the followers of Christ as a Jewish sect and therefore regarded their religion as a *religio licita*. But when it became apparent that Christianity laid claim to a universal character, thus endangering the State religion, and that the Christians largely disregarded the affairs of the State and refused to join in the idolatrous worship of the Romans, and particularly in their emperor worship, the Roman government inaugurated a series of persecutions which threatened the very existence of the Christian Church. At the same time Christianity had to suffer a great deal from the written attacks of some of the keenest minds of the age, such as Lucian, Porphyry, and Celsus, men of a philosophical bent of mind, who hurled their invectives against the Christian religion. Their arguments are typical of the philosophical opposition to Christianity throughout the centuries and frequently remind one of those employed by rationalistic philosophers and higher critics in the present day. But however great these dangers from without were, there were even greater dangers which threatened the Church from within. These consisted in different types of perversions of the Gospel.

[43]

I. JEWISH PERVERSIONS

There were three groups of Jewish Christians which revealed a Judaistic tendency. Traces of them are found even in the New Testament.

Inside dangers: Nazarenes

[*a*] *The Nazarenes.* These were Jewish Christians who adopted the tenets of the Christian religion. They used only the Hebrew Gospel of Matthew, but at the same time recognized Paul as a true apostle. In distinction from other Jewish sects they believed in the divinity and the virgin birth of Jesus. And while they bound themselves in practice to a strict observance of the law, they did not demand this of Gentile Christians. 'They were', as Seeberg says, 'really Jewish Christians, whereas the two following groups were only Christian Jews.'

Ebionites

[*b*] *The Ebionites.* This sect really constituted the continuation of the Judaistic opponents of the Apostle Paul and was of a Pharisaic type. Its adherents refused to recognize the apostleship of Paul, whom they regarded as an apostate from the law, and demanded that all Christians should submit to the rite of circumcision. They had a Cerinthian view of Christ, which was probably due to their desire to maintain the Old Testament monotheism. Both the divinity of Christ and His virgin birth were denied. In their opinion Jesus distinguished Himself from others only by a strict observance of the law, and was chosen to be the Messiah on account of His legal piety. He became conscious of this at the time of His baptism, when He received the Spirit, which enabled Him to perform His task, the work, of a prophet and teacher. They were reluctant to think of Him as subject to sufferings and death.

Elkesaites

[*c*] *The Elkesaites.* This group represented a type of Jewish Christianity marked by theosophic speculations and strict asceticism. While they rejected the virgin birth of Christ and claimed that He was born as other men, they also spoke of Him as a higher spirit or angel. They regarded Him as an incarnation of the ideal Adam, and also called Him the highest archangel. Circumcision and the sabbath were held in honour; there were repeated washings, to which a magical cleansing and reconciling meaning was ascribed; and magic and astrology were practised

[44]

among them. They had their secret doctrines respecting the observance of the law. Their movement was probably an attempt to gain general recognition for Jewish Christianity by adapting it to the syncretistic tendencies of the age. In all probability the Epistle to the Colossians and First Timothy refer to this heresy.

2. GENTILE PERVERSIONS: GENTILE–CHRISTIAN GNOSIS

In Gnosticism we meet with a second perversion of Christianity. It had this in common with the Judaistic sects, that it conceived of the relationship between the Old Testament and the New, and between their respective religions, as one of opposition. Its original form was rooted in Judaism, but it ultimately developed into a strange mixture of Jewish elements, Christian doctrines, and heathen speculative thought.

[a] *Origin of Gnosticism.* There are indications in the New Testament that an incipient Gnosticism was already making its appearance in the days of the Apostles. There were heretical teachers even then who drew their immediate impulse from Judaism, engaged in speculations respecting angels and spirits, and were characterized by a false dualism, leading on to asceticism on the one hand, and to an immoral libertinism on the other hand, who spiritualized the resurrection and made the Church's hope the object of derisive mockery; Col 2:18 ff; I Tim 1:3–7; 4:1–3; 6:3 f; II Tim 2:14–18; Tit 1:10–16; II Pet 2:1–4; Jude 4,16; Rev 2:6, 15, 20 f. There was also a tendency to religious philosophical speculation, which appeared especially in the heresy of Cerinthus, who distinguished between the human Jesus and Christ as a higher spirit which descended on him at the time of his baptism and left him again before the crucifixion. John indirectly combats this heresy in his writings, John 1:14; 20:31; I John 2:22; 4:2, 15; 5:1, 5, 6; II John 7.

Gnosticism in the New Testament

From the early part of the second century these errors assumed a more developed form, were openly proclaimed, and at once had an amazingly wide circulation. This can be understood only in the light of the general syncretism of the period. There was a widespread religious unrest and a surprising eagerness to absorb

Gnosticism in the second century

[45]

all possible religious ideas, and to generalize and harmonize them. Western religions had ceased to satisfy, and Eastern cults, diligently propagated by itinerant preachers, were eagerly embraced. The great aim was to gratify the thirst for deeper knowledge, the desire for mystic communion with God, and the hope of securing a sure path for the soul in its ascent to the upper world at death. It is no wonder that this tendency attached itself to Christianity, which seemed to address itself to the same task with marked success. Moreover, it found support in the claim of Christianity to be the absolute and universal religion. It may be said that Gnosticism mistakenly sought to elevate Christianity to its rightful position, that of universal religion, by adapting it to the needs of all, and by interpreting it in harmony with the wisdom of the world.

[b] *The essential character of Gnosticism.* Gnosticism was first

Gnosticism as a speculative movement

of all a *speculative movement.* The speculative element was very much in the foreground. The very name *Gnostikoi*, adopted by some of its adherents, indicates that they laid claim to a deeper knowledge of divine things than could be obtained by common believers. The Gnostics grappled with some of the deeper problems of philosophy and religion, but approached them in the wrong manner and suggested solutions totally at variance with the truths of revelation. Their two greatest problems were those of absolute being and of the origin of evil, problems not of Christian but of heathen religious thought. They developed a phantastic cosmogony, in which they borrowed freely from oriental speculation, and with which they sought to combine the truths of the Gospel. Undoubtedly, they were serious in their attempts to make the Gospel acceptable to the educated and cultured classes of their day.

Gnosticism as a popular movement

In spite of its speculative character, Gnosticism was also a *popular movement.* In order to sway the masses, it had to be something more than mere speculation. Therefore attempts were made in special associations to popularize the general cosmical theory by symbolic rites, mystic ceremonies, and the teaching of magic formulas. In the initiation into these associations strange formulas and rites formed an important part. These were

[46]

supposed to form a necessary and effective protection against the power of sin and death, and to be a means of gaining access to the blessedness of the world to come. In reality their introduction was an attempt to transform the Gospel into a religious philosophy and into mystic wisdom. Yet Gnosticism claimed to be Christian in character. Whenever possible, it appealed to the words of Jesus explained in an allegorical way, and to a so-called secret tradition handed down from the times of the Apostles. Many received its teachings as genuine Christian truth.

Gnosticism was also a *syncretistic movement* within the sphere of Christianity. It is still a matter of discussion, whether the Gnostics were Christians in any sense of the term. According to Seeberg Gnosticism was pagan rather than Gentile Christian. It addressed itself to the solution of problems that originated in the religious thought of the heathen world, and merely gave its discussions a somewhat Christian colouring. Apparently it placed a high estimate on Jesus Christ as marking the decisive turning-point in human history, and as a teacher of absolute truth. Harnack speaks of it as 'the acute Hellenizing of Christianity', and calls the Gnostics 'the first Christian theologians'. Prof. Walther is more correct, when he says that Gnosticism is ' . . . a stealing of some Christian rags to cover heathen nakedness'. This corresponds with the description of Seeberg when he speaks of it as 'an ethnicizing of Christianity'.

Gnosticism as a syncretistic movement

[c] *The main teachings of Gnosticism.* We cannot discuss the various Gnostic systems, such as those of Valentinus and Basilides, but can only briefly indicate the teachings of Gnosticism in general. A trait of dualism runs through the whole system and manifests itself in the position that there are two original principles or gods, which are opposed to each other as higher and lower, or even as good and bad. The supreme or good God is an unfathomable abyss. He interposes between Himself and finite creatures a long chain of aeons or middle beings, emanations from the divine, which together constitute the Pleroma or fullness of the divine essence. It is only through these intermediate beings that the highest God can enter into various relations with created beings. The world is not created by the good God, but is

Gnostic teachings

the result of, probably, a fall in the Pleroma, and is the work of a subordinate, possibly a hostile, deity. This subordinate god, is called the Demiurge, is identified with the God of the Old Testament, and is described as an inferior, limited, passionate, and vengeful being. He is contrasted with the supreme God, the source of goodness, virtue, and truth, who revealed Himself in Christ.

The world of matter as the product of a lesser and possibly an evil god, is essentially evil. There is found in it, however, a remnant from the spirit-world, namely, the soul of man, a spark of light from the upper world of purity which in some inexplicable way became entangled in evil matter. Its deliverance can be obtained only through some intervention of the good God. A way of deliverance has been provided by the sending of a special emissary from the kingdom of light into the world of darkness. In Christian Gnosticism this emissary is regularly identified with Christ. He is variously represented, either as a celestial being appearing in a phantasmal body, or as an earthly being, with whom a higher power or spirit temporarily associated himself. Since matter is in itself evil, this higher spirit could not have an ordinary human body.

Participation in redemption, or victory over the world, was gained only through the secret rites of the Gnostic associations. Initiation into the mysteries of marriage to Christ, of peculiar baptism, of magic names, and of special anointing, by which the secret knowledge of Being was secured, formed the path of redemption. At this point Gnosticism became more and more a system of religious mysteries. Men are divided into three classes: the pneumatic who constitute the élite of the Church, the psychic consisting of the ordinary Church members, and the hylic or the Gentiles. Only the first class is really capable of higher knowledge (*epignosis*) and thus obtains the highest blessedness. The second class may be saved through faith and works, but can only attain to an inferior blessedness. Those belonging to the third class are hopelessly lost.

The ethics, or moral philosophy, accompanying these views of redemption, was dominated by a false estimate of sensuousness,

[48]

which resulted either in strict ascetic abstinence or in low carnality, born of the assurance that nothing could really hinder those who were favoured of heaven. There was asceticism on the one hand and libertinism on the other. The ordinary eschatology of the Church had no place in this system. The doctrine of the resurrection of the dead was not recognized. When the soul was finally released from matter, it returned to the Pleroma, and this marked the end.

[d] *Historical significance of Gnosticism.* Even Gnosticism, however formidable an enemy of the truth, was not able to check the onward march of Christianity. Many were indeed swept along for a time by its daring speculations or by its mystic rites, but the great body of believers was not deceived by its phantastic representations nor by its alluring promises of secret bliss. In fact, Gnosticism was short-lived. Like a meteor it lit up the sky for a moment, and then suddenly disappeared. It was overcome by the direct refutations of the Church Fathers, by the preparation and circulation of short statements of the fundamental facts of the Christian religion (Rules of Faith), and by a more rational interpretation of the New Testament and a limitation of its canon, to the exclusion of all the false Gospels, Acts, and Epistles that were in circulation. Yet it did not fail to leave a lasting impression on the Church. Some of its peculiarities were absorbed by the Church and in course of time came to fruition in the Roman Catholic Church with its peculiar conception of the sacraments, its philosophy of a hidden God, who should be approached through intermediaries (saints, angels, Mary), its division of men into higher and lower orders, and its emphasis on asceticism.

Failure of Gnosticism

Its lasting impression on the Church

The Church also derived actual profit from the appearance of Gnosticism, but only in an indirect way. It learned to mark off clearly the limits of divine revelation, and to determine the relation of the Old Testament to the New. Moreover, it became keenly alive to the necessity of drawing up short statements of the truth, based on current baptismal formulas, which could serve as standards of interpretation (Rules of Faith). There was also a very evident doctrinal gain. Christianity was now first

Profit derived from Gnosticism

conceived as a 'doctrine' and as a 'mystery'. The intellectual element in the Christian religion was emphasized, and this marked the real starting-point for doctrinal development. The Christian idea of God was rescued from the mythological speculations of the Gnostics. The Church came into conscious possession of the truth that God is the Supreme Being, the Creator and Upholder of the Universe, the same in the Old and in the New Testament. The doctrine of the Demiurge and his creative activity was set aside, and the dualism of the Gnostics, making matter essentially evil, was overcome. Over against the Gnostic tendency to regard Jesus Christ merely as one of the aeons, His unique character as the Son of God was emphasized, and at the same time His true humanity was defended against all kinds of docetic denials. The great facts of His life, His virgin birth, miracles, sufferings, death, and resurrection, were all maintained and set in clearer light. Moreover, the doctrine of redemption through the atoning work of Christ was put forward in opposition to the speculative vagaries of the Gnostics; and the universal receptivity of men for the Gospel of Jesus Christ was stressed in answer to Gnostic exclusiveness and pride.

QUESTIONS FOR FURTHER STUDY

Are there any traces of the Nazarenes, Ebionites, and Elkesaites in the New Testament? How does the Ebionite denial of the divinity of Christ follow from Judaism? Does the New Testament contain any indications of an incipient Gnosticism? Where are these found? Are there any elements of New Testament teaching to which Gnosticism could rightly or wrongly appeal? On which sources did Gnosticism draw? Wherein does the anti-Judaistic character of the movement in its final form appear? Why is its Christology called docetic? What method of interpretation did the Gnostics adopt in founding their system on Scripture? How did the Gnostics distinguish between *pistis* and *gnostis*? Are the Gnostic distinctions between the world and the kingdom of God, between good and evil, of an ethical nature? Is there anything in other systems corresponding to their doctrine of an unapproachable God and intermediate beings? What lent Gnosticism its temporary popularity, its speculations or its esoteric religion? Why is Harnack hardly justified in speaking of the Gnostics as 'the first Christian theologians'?

LITERATURE

Burton, *Heresies of the Apostolic Age;* Mansel, *The Gnostic Heresies of the First and Second Centuries;* King, *The Gnostics and their Remains;* Lightfoot, *Commentary on Colossians,* pp. 73–113; Moody, *The Mind of the Early Converts,* pp 148–203; Scott, *The Nicene Theology,* pp 87–133; Faulkner, *Crises in the Early Church,* pp 9–51; Cunningham, *Historical Theology,* I, pp 121–133; Neander, *History of Christian Dogmas,* I, pp 33–45; Harnack, *History of Dogma,* I, pp 222–265; Seeberg, *History of Doctrine,* I, pp 87–102; Otten, *Manual of the History of Dogmas,* I, pp 99–105; Shedd, *History of Christian Doctrine,* I, pp 105–117; Fisher, *History of Christian Doctrine,* pp 48–58; Orr, *Progress of Dogma,* pp 54–70.

1. MARCION AND HIS MOVEMENT OF REFORM

Nature of Marcion's work   [a] *His character and purpose.* Marcion was a native of Pontus (Sinope), who was driven from his home, so it seems, on account of adultery, and made his way to Rome about the year AD 139. He is represented as a man of deep earnestness and marked ability, who laboured in the spirit of a reformer. He first made the attempt to bring the Church to his way of thinking, and when he did not succeed in his work of reform, felt constrained to organize his followers into a separate church and to seek universal acceptance of his views by active propaganda. He has often been classed as a Gnostic, but the correctness of this classification is now doubted. Loofs says that the statement of Hahn, '*Marcion perperam gnosticus vocatur*, is to the point, since Marcion had a soteriological rather than a cosmological purpose, faith rather than knowledge occupied the most important place in his system, he did not work out oriental myths nor Greek philosophical problems, and excluded allegorical interpretations'. This is in general agreement with the statement of Harnack, who says that he should not be classed with Gnostics like Basilides and Valentinus and gives the following reasons for his opinion: '(1) He was guided by no metaphysical, also by no apologetical, but only by a purely soteriological interest, (2) he therefore placed the whole emphasis upon the pure Gospel and upon faith (not upon knowledge), (3) he did not employ philosophy – at least not as a main principle – in his conception of Christianity, (4) he did not endeavour to found schools of philosophers, but to reform, in accordance with the true Pauline Gospel, the churches whose Christianity he believed to be legalistic (Judaistic) and who, as he thought, denied free grace.

[52]

When he failed in this, he formed a church of his own.' Seeberg also singles him out for separate treatment.

[b] *His main teachings.* The great question for Marcion was how to relate the Old Testament to the New. He found the key to this problem in the Epistle to the Galatians, which speaks of a Judaistic opposition to Paul, and proceeded on the assumption that the other apostles shared in this. He became convinced that the Gospel was corrupted by commingling it with the law. So he set himself the task of separating the law and the Gospel, and worked out his theory of opposites or antitheses. He accepted the Old Testament as the genuine revelation of the God of the Jews, but declared that He could not be the same as the God of the New Testament. He is the Creator of the world, but a God by no means perfect. He rules with rigour and justice, is full of wrath, and knows nothing of grace. However, He is not opposed to the God of the New Testament as the principle of evil, but only as a lesser God.

Teachings of Marcion

The God of the New Testament, on the other hand, is good and merciful. He was unknown until the fifteenth year of Tiberius, when He revealed Himself in Christ, who is often spoken of as the good God himself. Christ is not to be identified with the Old Testament Messiah, since He does not answer to the prophetic delineations of the coming Redeemer. He came as the manifestation of the good God, and did not defile Himself by taking on a real body, since He would take nothing from the kingdom of the Demiurge, but merely assumed an apparent body, in order to make Himself intelligible. He abrogated the law and all the works of the Demiurge, who for that reason secured His execution on the cross by the princes of the world. But because of the unreality of His body, the crucifixion did not harm Christ. He proclaimed the Gospel of love and of freedom from the law of the Old Testament God, thus opening a way of salvation for all who believe and even for the wicked in the nether world. It was understood, however, that the majority of mankind would perish by being consigned to the fire of the Demiurge. The good God does not punish them; He simply will not have them. That is His judgment on the wicked. Since

Marcion believed that Paul was the only apostle who really understood the Gospel of Jesus Christ, he limited the canon of the New Testament to the Gospel of Luke and ten Epistles of the great Apostle of the Gentiles.

2. THE MONTANIST REFORMATION

Origin of Montanism

[a] *Its origin.* While Montanism may be regarded as a reaction against the innovations of the Gnostics, it was itself also characterized by innovating tendencies. Montanus appeared in Phrygia about the year AD 150, and therefore his teaching is often called the Phrygian heresy. He and two women, Prisca and Maximilla, announced themselves as prophets. On the basis of the Gospel of John they held that the last and highest stage of revelation had been reached. The age of the Paraclete had come, and the Paraclete spoke through Montanus now that the end of the world was at hand. The revelations given through Montanus were mainly concerned with those things in which it seemed that the Scriptures were not sufficiently ascetic. From this it would seem that the most essential element in Montanism was its legalistic asceticism.

Teachings of Montanism

[b] *Its main teachings.* According to Montanism the last period of revelation has opened with the coming of the Paraclete. Hence the present age is one of spiritual gifts and especially of prophecy. Montanus and his co-labourers are regarded as the last of the prophets, bringing new revelations. On the whole the Montanists were orthodox and accepted the rule of faith. They strongly emphasized the nearness of the end of the world, and in view of this insisted on strict moral requirements, such as celibacy (or at most a single marriage), fasting, and rigid moral discipline. They unduly exalted martyrdom and absolutely forbade flight from persecution. Moreover, they revealed a tendency to exalt the special charisms in the Church at the expense of the regular offices and officers. While Marcion appealed especially to the writings of Paul, Montanus sought support more particularly in the Gospel and Epistles of John.

[c] *Its reception in the Church.* The Church was placed in a

[54]

somewhat embarrassing position by Montanism. On the one *Judgment of* hand it represented the orthodox position over against the *the Church* speculations of the Gnostics, and as such deserved appreciation. *Montanism* And in view of the Scriptural emphasis on the nearness of the end of the world, on the great importance of the charismatic gifts, particularly prophecy, and on the necessity of keeping oneself unspotted from the world – it is not difficult to understand that many regarded it with favour. On the other hand the Church followed a true instinct in rejecting it, especially because of the fanaticism it involved and its claim to a higher revelation than that contained in the New Testament.

QUESTIONS FOR FURTHER STUDY

Why is Marcion often ranked as a Gnostic? In what respects does he differ from the Gnostics? What contrasts dominate all his teachings? What objections did he have to most of the New Testament writings? To what New Testament books is Marcion's canon limited? How did the Church indirectly profit by the Marcionite controversy? What factors gave rise to Montanism? How do you account for its asceticism, and for its emphasis on special charisms? How should we judge of its claim to a new outpouring of the Holy Spirit and prophetic gifts? Was its strict discipline justified?

LITERATURE

Consult the books on Gnosticism mentioned in the previous chapter for Marcionism: Faulkner, *Crises in the Early Church*, pp 52–75; McGiffert, *A History of Christian Thought*, I, pp 149–174; Harnack, *History of Dogma*, I, pp 266–286; II, pp 94–104; Seeberg, *History of Doctrines*, I, pp 102–108; Fisher, *History of Doctrine*, pp 59, 60, 81–83.

IV: THE APOLOGISTS AND THE BEGINNINGS OF THE CHURCH'S THEOLOGY

I. THE TASK OF THE APOLOGISTS

Pressure from without and from within called for a clear statement and for defence of the truth, and thus gave birth to theology. The earliest Fathers who took up the defence of the truth are for that very reason called Apologists. The most important of these were Justin, Tatian, Athenagoras, and Theophilus of Antioch. They addressed their apologies partly to the rulers and partly to the intelligent public. Their immediate object was to mollify the temper of the authorities and of the people in general towards Christianity; and they sought to do this by setting forth its true character and by refuting the charges proffered against the Christians. They were particularly solicitous to make the Christian religion acceptable to the educated classes by stressing its rationality. With that in view they represented it as the highest and surest philosophy, gave special emphasis to the great truths of natural religion: God, virtue, and immortality, and spoke of it as the fulfilment of all the truth found in both Judaism and Hellenism.

Threefold task of Apologists

Their task assumed a threefold character, defensive, offensive, and constructive. They defended Christianity by showing that there was no evidence for the charges brought against its adherents, that the offensive conduct ascribed to them was altogether inconsistent with the spirit and precepts of the Gospel, and that the character and lives of those who professed the Christian faith were marked by moral purity.

Not satisfied with a mere defence, they also attacked their opponents. They charged the Jews with a legalism that lost sight of the shadowy and typical character of much that was found in the law and represented its temporal elements as

[56]

permanent, and with a blindness that prevented them from seeing that Jesus was the Messiah, promised by the prophets, and as such the fulfilment of the law. Moreover, in their assault on paganism, they exposed the unworthy, absurd, and immoral character of the heathen religion, and particularly of the doctrine of the gods, as compared with the doctrines of the unity of God, His universal providence, His moral government, and the future life. Tatian saw little or no good in Greek philosophy, while Justin recognized a true element in it, which he ascribed to the Logos. A common feature in their writings is a blending of general and special revelation.

Finally, they also felt it incumbent on them to establish the character of Christianity as a positive revelation of God. In demonstrating the reality of this revelation, they relied mainly on the argument from prophecy, but also, though in a lesser degree, on that from miracles. They appealed repeatedly to the remarkable spread of the Christian religion in spite of all resistance, and to the changed character and lives of its professors.

2. THEIR POSITIVE CONSTRUCTION OF THE TRUTH

In stating the doctrinal contents of the divine revelation the Apologetes did not always clearly distinguish between general and special revelation, and often failed to discriminate carefully between that which is the product of the human mind and that which is supernaturally revealed. This is due to the fact that they conceived of Christianity too much as a philosophy, albeit the only true philosophy, superior to all other philosophies in that it was based on revelation. Says Harnack: 'Christianity is *philosophy* and *revelation*. This is the thesis of every Apologist from Aristides to Minucius Felix.' They regarded it as a philosophy, because it contains a rational element and satisfactorily answers the questions that have engaged all true philosophers; but also as the direct antithesis of philosophy, since it is free from all mere notions and opinions, and originates from a supernatural revelation.

They represented God as the Self-existent, Unchangeable,

Their view of philosophy and revelation

*Their
conception
of God and
the Logos* and Eternal One, who is the primal cause of the world, but because of His uniqueness and perfection can best be described in terms of negation. They hardly got beyond the idea of the divine Being as *ho on* or absolute attributeless existence. In speaking of the Son they preferred the use of the term 'Logos', undoubtedly because it was a common philosophical term and therefore appealed to the cultured classes. At the same time its use shows that the Church's attention was focused on the divine and exalted Christ rather than on the man Jesus. The Apologists did not have the biblical conception of the Logos, but one somewhat resembling that of Philo. To them the Logos, as He existed eternally in God, was simply the divine reason, without personal existence. With a view to the creation of the world, however, God generated the Logos out of His own Being and thus gave Him personal existence. Essentially the Logos remains identical with God, but in view of His origin as a person He may be called a creature. Briefly stated, Christ is the divine reason, immanent in God, to which God gave a separate existence, and through which He revealed Himself. 'As the divine reason,' says Seeberg, 'he was not only operative at the creation of the world and in the Old Testament, but also in the wise men of the heathen world.' It should be noted particularly that the Logos of the Apologists, in distinction from the philosophical Logos, had an independent personality.

*Their view
of Christ
and
salvation* The Logos became man by assuming a real human nature, consisting of body and soul. Yet He was not an ordinary man, but God and man, though His divinity was concealed. Hence it was not a mere man, but the very Son of God that hung on the cross. All emphasis is placed on the fact that He became the teacher of the race, as He had already shown Himself before the incarnation. The main content of His teaching is found in the ideas of the one God, the new law requiring a virtuous life, and immortality, particularly the resurrection, carrying with it rewards and punishments. Because God created man free, the latter has the ability to keep the commandments of God. Grace consists only in the revelation of doctrine and of the law. The sufferings of Christ hardly appear to be necessary, except as a fulfilment of

[58]

Old Testament prophecy. Yet the Apologists do insist on the reality and the great significance of these sufferings as obtaining for men the forgiveness of sins and deliverance from sin and the devil.

The origin of the new life is represented somewhat dualistically by the Apologetes. Sometimes it appears to be wholly dependent on the free choice of man, and then again it seems to be entirely contingent on the free grace of God. Baptism stands in the closest relationship to the new birth, and marks the beginning of the new life. The Church consists of the people of God, the true Israel, and the high-priestly generation of God, and is characterized by strict morality, holy love, and readiness to suffer with rejoicing. The Apologists firmly believed in the resurrection of the dead, but there was some difference of opinion among them about the *essential* immortality of the soul. Tatian and Theophilus regarded immortality as a reward for the righteous and a punishment for the wicked, and Justin seems to have shared this view. In their description of the blessedness of the future the millennial kingdom sometimes plays a part (Justin).

Their view of the new life, the Church, and the future

3. THEIR SIGNIFICANCE FOR THE HISTORY OF DOGMA

Harnack and Loofs are of the opinion that the Apologists completely fell away from the right apprehension of the Christian Gospel. They claim that these early Fathers sought the substance of Christianity solely in its rational contents, valued the objective facts of revelation, such as the incarnation and the resurrection, merely as certifying the truths of natural revelation, and Hellenized the Gospel by turning faith into doctrine and by giving Christianity, especially through their Logos doctrine, an intellectual character. But while there may be some semblance of truth in their representation, it is clearly the result of a one-sided contemplation of some of the teachings of the Apologists and fails to take *all* the facts into consideration.

Harnack on the Apologetes

It must be admitted that these early Fathers gave great prominence to the truths of reason and sought to demonstrate their rationality. But it should be borne in mind, (a) that they

Their significance for the development of theology

[59]

were writing Apologies and not doctrinal treatises, and that the nature of Apologies is always determined more or less by the opposition; (b) that the truths which they stressed also constitute a very essential part of the system of Christian doctrine; and (c) that their writings also contain many positive Christian elements, which do not merely serve as props for the fundamental truths of reason.

Again, it must be admitted that they represented Christianity largely in terms of philosophy, that they did not clearly discriminate between philosophy and theology, and that their representation of the truths of revelation, and particularly of the Logos doctrine, suffered from an admixture of Greek philosophical thought. But they evidently meant to give a correct interpretation of the truths of revelation, though they did not always succeed. The fact that they sought to give a rational interpretation of Christianity cannot be held against them, for this does not consist exclusively in religious experiences, as Ritschlians sometimes seem to think, but also has an intellectual content and is a reasonable religion. It is quite evident from the writings of the Apologists that their conception of Christianity still suffered from the same defects and limitations as that of the Apostolic Fathers. This is seen especially in the doctrine of the Logos and in that of the way of salvation (moralism). At the same time their work marked the beginnings of Christian theology, though this was forced into a philosophical framework.

QUESTIONS FOR FURTHER STUDY

How do you account for it that the early Apologetes placed so much emphasis on natural theology; on Christ as the Logos rather than on Christ as the Redeemer; on His teaching rather than on His death? Did they succeed in harmonizing the work of Christ as Logos with His work as Redeemer? How does their moralism compare with that of the Apostolic Fathers? What do you think of the idea that Christianity is a *nova lex*? What was the prominent element in faith as understood by the Apologists? How did they conceive of the forgiveness of sins after baptism? What do you think of their conviction that such Gentiles as Socrates and Plato were saved? Was their Logos doctrine that of the Greeks and therefore a perversion of Christianity?

LITERATURE

Scott, *The Nicene Theology*, pp 160–178, 208–210, 219–229, 271–275; Moody, *The Mind of the Early Converts*, pp 102–147; McGiffert, *A History of Christian Thought*, I, pp 96–131; Harnack, *History of Dogma*, II, pp 169–229; Cunningham, *Historical Theology*, I, pp 134–139; Seeberg, *History of Doctrine*, I, pp 109–118; Loofs, *Dogmengeschiedenis*, pp 72–81; Otten, *Manual of the History of Dogmas*, I, pp 110–137; Fisher, *History of Christian Doctrine*, pp 61–69.

V: THE ANTI-GNOSTIC FATHERS

From the Apologists we naturally pass on to the anti-gnostic Fathers who succeeded them. Three of these stand out with great prominence.

I. THE ANTI-GNOSTIC FATHERS

Irenaeus The first one that comes into consideration here is Irenaeus. He was born in the East, where he became a disciple of Polycarp, but spent the main part of his life in the West. At first a presbyter, he afterwards became bishop of Lyons. He evinces a practical Christian spirit in his writings, and represents a Johannine type of Christian doctrine, though not without some traces of a more sensuous conception. In his chief work, *Against Heresies*, he takes issue particularly with Gnosticism. It is a work marked by ability, moderation, and purity in its representation of Christianity.

The second of these Fathers is Hippolytus, who is said to have *Hippolytus* been a disciple of Irenaeus and greatly resembled his teacher in mental make-up, being simple, moderate, and practical. Less gifted than Irenaeus, he gives evidence of a greater fondness for philosophical ideas. After labouring in the neighbourhood of Rome, he seems to have suffered martyrdom in that city. His principal work is entitled *The Refutation of All Heresies*. He finds the root of all the perversions of doctrine in the speculations of the philosophers.

The third and greatest of the famous trio was Tertullian, a *Tertullian* man of profound intellect and deep feeling, of a vivid imagination, and distinguished by acuteness and great learning. As presbyter of Carthage he represents the North African type of theology. Due to his violent temper he was naturally passionate in his representation of Christianity and somewhat given to extreme statements. As a lawyer he was familiar with Roman law and introduced legal conceptions and legal phraseology into theological discussions. Like Hippolytus he, too, was inclined to deduce all heresy from the philosophy of the Greeks, and therefore became a zealous opponent of philosophy. His native fervour reacted strongly against the lax spirit of the age, and even induced him to embrace Montanism in later life. Convinced of the futility of arguing with heretics, he said it was best to meet them with a simple demurrer. He influenced Western theology more than any of the others.

2. THEIR DOCTRINES OF GOD, MAN, AND THE HISTORY OF REDEMPTION

They regarded the separation of the true God and the Creator as the fundamental error of the Gnostics, as a blasphemous conception suggested by the devil, and stressed the fact that there is but one God, who is both Creator and Redeemer. He gave the law and also revealed the Gospel. This God is triune, a single essence subsisting in three persons. Tertullian was the first to assert the tri-personality of God and to use the word 'Trinity'. In opposition to the Monarchians he emphasized the fact that the three Persons are of one substance, susceptible of number without division. Yet he did not reach the proper trinitarian statement, since he conceived of one Person as subordinate to the others. *Doctrine of God*

In the doctrine of man they also opposed the Gnostics by stressing the fact that good and evil in man do not find their explanation in different natural endowments. If evil is inherent in matter, and therefore in man as such, he can no more be regarded as a free moral being. Man was created in the image of God, without immortality indeed (ie without perfection), but with the possibility of receiving this in the way of obedience. Sin is disobedience and brings death, just as obedience brings immortality. In Adam the whole race became subject to death. The connection of our sin with that of Adam is not yet clearly appre- *Doctrine of man*

[63]

hended, though Tertullian makes some suggestive statements on the subject. He says that evil became, as it were, a natural element in man, present from birth, and that this condition passes over through generation upon the whole human race. This is the first trace of the doctrine of original sin.

History of redemption Irenaeus has something special on the history of redemption. He says that God expelled man from paradise and suffered him to die, in order that the injury sustained might not remain for ever. From the start God was deeply concerned for the salvation of the race, and sought to win it by three covenants. The law written in the heart of man represented the first covenant. The patriarchs were righteous before God because they met its requirements. When the knowledge of this law faded away, the decalogue was given, representing the second covenant. On account of Israel's sinful disposition the law of ceremonies was added, to prepare the people for following Christ and for friendship with God. The Pharisees made it of none effect by robbing it of its chief content, namely, love. In the third covenant Christ restored the original law, the law of love. This covenant is related to the preceding as freedom to bondage, and requires faith, not only in the Father, but also in the Son, who has now appeared. It is not, like the preceding, limited to Israel, but is universal in its scope. Christians received a stricter law than the Jews and have more to believe, but they also receive a greater measure of grace. To these three periods Tertullian, while an adherent of Montanism, still added the era of the Spirit.

3. THEIR DOCTRINE OF THE PERSON AND WORK OF CHRIST

Irenaeus and Tertullian differ considerably in their doctrine of the Person of Christ, and therefore it may be well to consider them separately.

Irenæus' Christology [a] *Irenaeus.* The Christology of Irenaeus is superior to that of Tertullian and Hippolytus and influenced the latter to a great extent. He is averse to speculations about the Logos, because these lead at most to probable guesses. He merely asserts that the Logos existed from all eternity and was instrumental in revealing the Father; and then takes his real starting-point in the historically revealed Son of God. Through the incarnation the Logos became the historical Jesus, and thereafter was at once true God and true man. He rejects the heresy of the Gnostics that in His suffering and death the passible Jesus was separated from the impassible Christ, and attaches the greatest significance to the union of God with human nature. In Christ as the second Adam the human race is once more united to God. There is in Him a *recapitulation of mankind*, which reaches backward as well as forward, and in which mankind reverses the course on which it entered at the fall. This is the very core of the Christological teaching of Irenaeus. The death of Christ as our substitute is mentioned but not stressed. The central element in the work of Christ is His obedience, whereby the disobedience of Adam is cancelled.

[b] *Tertullian*. Tertullian takes his starting-point in the doctrine of the Logos, but develops it in a way that became *Tertullian's Christology* historically significant. He stresses the fact that the Logos of the Christians is a real subsistence, an independent Person, who was begotten by God and thus proceeded from Him, not by emanation, but by self-projection, just as a root projects a tree. There was a time when He was not. He emphasizes the fact that the Logos is of the same substance with the Father, and yet differs from Him in mode of existence as a distinct Person. He did not come into existence by partitioning but by self-unfolding. The Father is the whole substance, but the Son is only a part of it, because He is derived. Tertullian did not entirely get away from the idea of subordination. His work is of lasting significance in connection with the introduction of the conceptions of substance and person into theology, ideas that were utilized in the construction of the Nicene Creed. It may be said that he enlarged the doctrine of the Logos into a doctrine of the Trinity. In opposition to the Monarchian theory he stressed the fact that the three persons in the Godhead are of one substance, susceptible of number without division. Yet he did not succeed in reaching the full trinitarian statement. He too conceived of the

Logos as originally impersonal reason in God, become personal at the time of creation. And subordination of the one person to the other is presented in the crude form of a greater and lesser participation of the first and second persons in the divine substance.

Relative to the God-man and His two natures Tertullian expressed himself very much as the School of Asia Minor did. He surpasses all the other Fathers, except Melito, in doing justice to the full humanity of Christ, and in his clear distinction of the two natures, each one retaining its own attributes. According to him there is no fusion, but a conjunction of the human and the divine in Christ. He is very emphatic on the importance of the death of Christ, but is not entirely clear on this point, since he does not stress the necessity of penal satisfaction, but only that of penitence on the part of the sinner. While he does recognize a punitive element in justice, he exalts the mercy of God. At the same time a certain legalism pervades his teaching. He speaks of satisfaction made for sins committed after baptism by repentance or confession. By fasting and other forms of mortification the sinner is able to escape eternal punishment.

Irenæus on work of redemption

Of the Anti-gnostic Fathers Irenaeus gives the fullest description of the work of redemption, but his representation is not altogether consistent. While he is regarded as one of the most orthodox of the early Church Fathers, there are two lines of thought present in his writings which are hardly Scriptural, the one moralistic and the other somewhat mystical. According to the former, man regains his destiny when he voluntarily chooses the good which he is still able to do. The real significance of Christ's work lies in the fact that He brought the sure knowledge of God and thus strengthened the freedom of man. According to the second Christ recapitulates the whole human race in Himself, and thus establishes a new relation between God and man and becomes the leaven of a new life in humanity. The Logos identifies Himself with humanity in His sufferings and death, and becomes instrumental in raising it to a higher level by sanctifying and immortalizing it. He recapitulates in Himself the whole human race and reverses the course which derives its impetus

[66]

from the fall of the first Adam. He communicates to it the leaven of a new and immortal life. This may easily be, and has frequently been interpreted as teaching atonement by a mystical process begun in the incarnation and resulting in the deification of man. The emphasis on this idea in the writings of Irenaeus may be due to the fact that he was influenced by the Johannine writings more than by the Pauline Epistles. It is quite evident, however, that Irenaeus did not mean to teach a purely mystical or hyperphysical redemption. While he strongly emphasizes the necessity of a living union of Christ with the subjects of his redemption – something which Anselm failed to do – he associates this with other ideas, such as that He rendered for us the obedience required by God, that He suffered in our stead, paying our debt and propitiating the Father, and that He redeemed us from the power of Satan.

4. THEIR DOCTRINES OF SALVATION, OF THE CHURCH, AND OF THE LAST THINGS

Irenaeus is not altogether clear in his soteriology. He emphasizes the necessity of faith as a prerequisite for baptism. This faith is not only an intellectual acceptance of the truth, but also includes a self-surrender of the soul which issues in a holy life. By baptism man is regenerated; his sins are washed away and a new life is born within him. He evidently has no clear conception of the Pauline doctrine of justification by faith, for his representation of the relation between faith and justification is different. Faith necessarily leads on to the observance of the commandments of Christ, and is therefore sufficient to make a man righteous before God. The Spirit of God endows the Christian with new life, and the fundamental characteristic of the new life is that it brings forth the fruits of righteousness in good works.

Irenæus' doctrine of salvation

The work of Tertullian marks no particular advance in the doctrine of the application of the work of Christ. Moralism again appears in the view that the sinner by repentance earns for himself salvation in baptism. His representation of the doctrine of penance is of special interest, however, since he introduces legal terms here which were in later theology applied to the

Tertullian's doctrine of salvation

redemptive work of Christ. He regards God as a Lawgiver and Judge, who looks upon sin as transgression and guilt, and therefore demands satisfaction, and in lieu of satisfaction inflicts punishment. Sins committed after baptism require satisfaction by penance. If this is rendered, the punishment is warded off. In this representation we find the foundation for the Roman Catholic sacrament of penance. The legal terms employed, such as 'Judge', 'guilt', 'punishment', and 'satisfaction', were transferred to the work of Christ in the theology of the Church.

Doctrine of the Church
In their teachings respecting the Church these Fathers reveal a tendency to yield to Judaism in substituting the idea of an external community for that of a spiritual fellowship. They sowed seeds which bore fruit in the Cyprianic or Roman Catholic conception of the Church. They do indeed still retain the idea that the Church is a spiritual community of believers, but represent this as coinciding with an external fellowship. In fact, they represent the visible organization as the channel of divine grace, and make participation in the blessings of salvation dependent on membership in the visible Church. They who separated themselves from the external communion of the Church, which was of Apostolic origin and had as its head the *sedes apostolicae*, thereby also renounced Christ. Due to the influence of the Old Testament the idea of a special mediating priesthood also came to the foreground.

Doctrine of the future
The Anti-gnostic Fathers in general championed the doctrine of the resurrection of the flesh, and based it on the resurrection of Christ and on the indwelling of the Spirit. The end will come when the devil has succeeded in giving the entire apostate throng a new head in Antichrist. Then Christ will appear, and the six thousand years of the world will be followed by the first resurrection and the sabbatic rest of the millennium. In Palestine believers will enjoy the riches of the land. After the millennium there will be a new heaven and a new earth, and the blessed will live in graded order in the mansions prepared for them.

QUESTIONS FOR FURTHER STUDY
Do the Anti-gnostic Fathers mark any advance in the doctrine of God? How must the recapitulation idea in Irenaeus' Christology be understood?

Does it agree with Schleiermacher's mystical theory of the atonement? What other conceptions of the work of Christ are found in his writings? Does his recapitulation theory reckon with sin as individual guilt, and provide for individual redemption? Did he believe in a deification of man? How are divine grace and human merit related in his soteriology? At what point did he change the current conception of the Church? What was his conception of the last things? In what respect was Tertullian's doctrine of the Trinity defective? What was characteristic of his Logos doctrine? What effect did Montanism have on his views? What legal terms did he introduce into theology? Were they applied to the work of Christ? Does the legal element constitute a deterioration of the pure Gospel?

LITERATURE

Scott, *Nicene Theology*, pp 95–102, 178–184, 210–212, 230–236, 281–286; Moody, *The Mind of the Early Converts*, pp 204–237; Cunningham, *Historical Theology*, I, pp 139–146, 158–163; Morgan, *The Importance of Tertullian in the Development of Christian Dogma*; Harnack, *History of Dogma*, II, pp 230–318; Seeberg, *History of Doctrines*, I, pp 118–140; Loofs, *Dogmengeschiedenis*, pp 87–101; McGiffert, *History of Christian Thought*, I, pp 132–148; Otten, *Manual of the History of Dogmas*, I, pp 138–152, 160–169; Fisher, *History of Christian Doctrine*, pp 84–98.

VI: THE ALEXANDRIAN FATHERS

Just as in a former century Jewish religious learning and Hellenistic philosophy combined to produce the type of thought represented by Philo, so in the second and third centuries Hellenistic learning and the truths of the Gospel were combined in a rather astonishing way to give birth to the Alexandrian type of theology. The attempt was made by some of the leading theologians to utilize the profoundest speculations of the Gnostics in the construction of the Church's faith. In doing this they resorted to the allegorical interpretation of the Bible. The truths of the Christian religion were turned into a science couched in literary form. The most important representatives of this form of Christian learning were Clement of Alexandria and Origen.

I. THE ALEXANDRIAN FATHERS

Clement of Alexandria Clement and Origen represent the theology of the East, which was more speculative than that of the West. Both were influential teachers of the school of the catechetes at Alexandria. Clement was not an orthodox Christian in the same measure as Irenaeus and Tertullian. He did not adhere to the Rule of Faith as much as they did, but followed in the path of the Apologetes in seeking to wed the philosophy of the day, as he understood it, to the Christian tradition, and sometimes practically substituted the former for the latter. In distinction from Tertullian he was friendly to philosophy, and insisted on it that the Christian theologian should build a bridge between the Gospel and Gentile learning. He found the sources of the knowledge of divine things in Scripture and reason, exalted the latter unduly, and by his allegorical interpretation opened wide the door for all kinds of human speculation. His estimate of Greek philosophy is not altogether consistent. Sometimes he ascribes it to a partial revelation, and sometimes he stigmatizes it as plagiarism from the Hebrew prophets.

Origen was born of Christian parents and received a Christian *Origen* education. He was a precocious child, and from early childhood practised a rigorous asceticism. He succeeded his teacher, Clement, as catechist at Alexandria. To fit himself for the work he made a thorough study of Neo-Platonism, which was then coming into favour, and of the leading heretical systems, especially Gnosticism. His fame soon spread and large numbers attended his lectures. He was the most learned and one of the profoundest thinkers of the early Church. His teachings were of a very speculative nature, and in later life he was condemned for heresy. He battled against the Gnostics and also struck a decisive blow against Monarchianism. But this was all incidental to his main purpose, that of constructing a systematic body of Christian doctrine. His principal work, *De Principiis*, is the first example of a positive and well-rounded system of theology. Part of his teachings were afterwards declared heretical, but he had an enormous influence on the development of doctrine. It seems that he desired to be an orthodox Christian: he took his stand squarely on the Word of God and on the Rule of faith as a standard of interpretation; and maintained that nothing should be received that was contrary to Scripture or to a legitimate deduction from Scripture. Yet his theology bore the earmarks of Neo-Platonism, and his allegorical interpretation opened the way for all kinds of speculation and arbitrary interpretation.

2. THEIR DOCTRINES OF GOD AND OF MAN

Like the Apologetes, Origen speaks of God in absolute terms, as *Doctrine of* the incomprehensible, inestimable, and impassible One, who is *God* beyond want of anything; and like the Anti-gnostic Fathers, he rejects the Gnostic distinction between the good God and the Demiurge or Creator of the world. God is One, the same in the Old and in the New Testament. He ascribes absolute causality to

God, and since he can conceive of such attributes as omnipotence and justice only as eternally in action, he teaches the doctrine of eternal creation.

Doctrine of the Logos   Clement of Alexandria is by no means clear in his representation of the Logos. He stresses the personal subsistence of the Logos, His oneness with the Father, and His eternal generation; but also represents Him as the divine reason, and as subordinate to the Father. He distinguishes between the real Logos of God and the Son-Logos who appeared in the flesh. From the beginning the Logos mediates the divine revelation by stamping divine wisdom on the work of creation, by imparting to men the light of reason, by making special disclosures of the truth, and by His incarnation in Jesus Christ. The light of the Logos serves the Gentiles as a stepping-stone to the fuller light of the Gospel. Origen says that the one God is primarily the Father, but He reveals himself and works through the Logos, who is personal and co-eternal with the Father, begotten of Him by one eternal act. In connection with the generation of the Son every idea of emanation and division is rejected. But though he recognizes the full divinity of the Son, he uses some expressions that point to subordination. While he speaks of *eternal* generation, he defines the phrase in such a way as to teach not merely an economic but an essential subordination of the Son to the Father. He sometimes calls the Son *Theos Deuteros*. In the incarnation the Logos united himself with a human soul, which in its pre-existence remained pure. The natures in Christ are kept distinct, but it is held that the Logos by His resurrection and ascension deified His human nature.

Doctrine of the Holy Spirit   Clement does not try to explain the relation of the Holy Spirit to the other Persons of the Trinity, and Origen's view of the third Person is further removed from the Catholic doctrine than his conception of the Second Person. He speaks of the Holy Spirit as the first creature made by the Father through the Son. The Spirit's relation to the Father is not as close as that of the Son. Moreover, the Spirit does not operate in creation as a whole, but only in the saints. He possesses goodness by nature, renews and sanctifies sinners, and is an object of divine worship.

[72]

Origen's teachings respecting man are somewhat out of the ordinary. The pre-existence of man is involved in his theory of eternal creation, since the original creation consisted exclusively of rational spirits, co-equal as well as co-eternal. The present condition of man presupposes a pre-existent fall from holiness into sin, which was the occasion for the creation of the present material world. The fallen spirits now became souls and were clothed with bodies. Matter was called into being for the very purpose of supplying an abode and a means of discipline and purgation for these fallen spirits.

Origen's doctrine of man

3. THEIR DOCTRINE OF THE PERSON AND WORK OF CHRIST

Both of these Fathers teach that in the incarnation the Logos assumed human nature in its entirety, body and soul, and thus became a real man, the God-man, though Clement did not entirely succeed in avoiding Docetism. He says that Christ used food, not because He needed it, but simply to guard against a denial of his humanity, and that he was incapable of emotions of joy and grief. Origen maintains that the soul of Christ pre-existed, like all other souls, and was even in its pre-existence united with the Logos. In fact, even before the incarnation a complete interpenetration had taken place between the Logos and this soul. The Logos-filled soul assumed a body, and then even this body was penetrated and divinized by the Logos. There was such a mingling of the divine and the human in Christ that by his glorification He became virtually ubiquitous. Origen hardly succeeded in maintaining the integrity of the two natures in Christ.

Doctrine of the incarnation

There are different representations of the work of Christ, which are not properly integrated. Clement speaks of the self-surrender of Christ as a ransom, but does not stress the idea that He was a propitiation for the sin of mankind. He places far greater emphasis on Christ as the Lawgiver and Teacher, and as the way to immortality. Redemption does not so much consist in undoing the past as in the elevation of man to a state even

Doctrine of the work of Christ

higher than that of unfallen man. The dominant thought in Origen is that Christ was physician, teacher, lawgiver, and example. He was a physician for sinners, a teacher of those who had been purified, the lawgiver of His people, requiring obedience to God and faith in Christ, and the perfect example of a virtuous life for His followers. In all these capacities He makes sinners, as much as possible, partakers of the divine nature. At the same time Origen recognizes the fact that the salvation of believers is dependent on the sufferings and death of Christ. Christ delivers them from the power of the devil, and does this by practising deceit on Satan. He offers Himself to Satan as a ransom, and Satan accepts the ransom without realizing that he would not be able to retain his hold on Christ, the Sinless One. The death of Christ is represented as vicarious, as an offering for sin, and as a necessary atonement. The redemptive influence of the Logos extends beyond this life. Not only men who have lived on earth and died, but all fallen spirits, not excluding Satan and his evil angels, are brought under redemptive influences. There will be a restitution of all things.

4. THEIR DOCTRINES OF SALVATION, OF THE CHURCH, AND OF THE LAST THINGS

Doctrine of salvation The Alexandrian Fathers recognize the free will of man, which enables him to turn to the good and to accept the salvation that is offered in Jesus Christ. God offers salvation, and man has the power to accept it. But while Origen represents faith as an act of man, he also speaks of it as an effect of divine grace. It is a necessary preliminary step to salvation, and therefore salvation may be said to depend on it. However, it is only an initial acceptance of God's revelation, must be elevated to knowledge and understanding, and must lead on to the performance of good works. Faith saves because it ever has works in view. These are the really important things. Origen speaks of two ways of salvation, one by faith (exoteric), and another by knowledge (esoteric). These Fathers certainly did not have the Pauline conception of faith and justification. Moreover, Origen stresses the fact that faith is not the only condition of salvation. Repentance is even more necessary, which consists in the confession of our sins before God. He ascribes to it a more inward, and less legal, character than the Western Fathers, and particularly Tertullian.

Origen regards the Church as the congregation of believers, outside of which there is no salvation. He discriminates between the Church properly so called and the empirical Church. And while he recognizes all believers as priests, he also speaks of a separate priesthood with special prerogatives. Both he and Clement teach that baptism marks the beginning of the new life in the Church, and includes the forgiveness of sins. Clement distinguishes between a lower and a higher state of the Christian life. In the former man attains to holiness under the influence of fear and hope, while in the latter fear is cast out by perfect love. This is the life of real knowledge that is enjoyed by him to whom the mysteries are revealed. The eucharist bestows participation in immortality, for through it the communicant enters into fellowship with Christ and the divine Spirit. In Origen the sacraments are spiritualized. They are symbols of divine influences, though they also represent gracious operations of the Holy Spirit.

Doctrine of the Church

According to both Clement and Origen the process of purification, begun in the life of the sinner on earth, is continued after death. Chastisement is the great cleansing agency and cure for sin. Origen teaches that at death the good enter paradise or a place where they receive further education, and the wicked experience the fire of judgment which, however, is not to be regarded as a permanent punishment, but as a means of purification. Clement asserts that the heathen have an opportunity to repent in hades and that their probation does not end until the day of judgment, while Origen maintains that God's work of redemption will not cease until all things are restored to their pristine beauty. The restoration of all things will even include Satan and his demons. Only a few people enter upon the full blessedness of the vision of God at once; the great majority of them must pass through a process of purification after death. Both of these Fathers were averse to the doctrine of a millennium, and Origen

Doctrine of the future

has a tendency to spiritualize the resurrection. He seems to have regarded the incorporeal as the ideal state, but did believe in a bodily resurrection. According to him a germ of the body remains and gives rise to a spiritual organism, conformed to the nature of the particular soul to which it belongs, whether it be good or evil.

QUESTIONS FOR FURTHER STUDY

How did the theology of the East in general differ from that of the West? How do you account for the difference? What bearing did the allegorical interpretation of Scripture have on the theology of the Alexandrian Fathers? Did the Logos doctrine of these Fathers differ from that of the Apologists? If so, how? How does their doctrine of the Trinity compare with that of Tertullian? Do they shed any light on the relation of the Holy Spirit to the Father and the Son? How do they represent the main sources of sin and its chief remedy? Does Origen have a self-consistent theory of the origin of sin? In what direction did they develop the doctrine of free will? (cf Scott, *The Nicene Theology*, p 212). How do they conceive of the work of Christ? Do the sufferings of Christ form an essential element in their teachings? In what sense do they teach the deification of human nature? How does Origen's theology offer points of contact for Arianism? How does his eschatology compare with that of the Roman Catholic Church? Is Allen justified in considering Greek rather than Latin theology as expressing the Christian faith? What points of similarity may be noted between Greek theology and present-day Modernism?

LITERATURE

Fairweather, *Origen and Greek Patristic Theology*; Scott, *The Nicene Theology*, pp 188–194, 212–219, 236–251, 286–289; Moody, *The Mind of the Early Converts*, pp 258–301; Cunningham, *Historical Theology*, I, pp 146–158; McGiffert, *A History of Christian Thought*, I, pp 177–231; Harnack, *History of Dogma*, II, pp 319–380; Seeberg, *History of Doctrines*, I, pp 140–161; Loofs, *Dogmengeschiedenis*, pp 106–126; Shedd, *History of Christian Doctrine*, I, pp 274–277, 288–305; II, pp 3–10, 31–36, 225–237, 395, 396; Otten, *Manual of the History of Dogmas*, I, pp 190–209; Neander, *History of Christian Dogmas*, cf Index; Fisher, *History of Christian Doctrine*, pp 94–97, 104–116.

VII: MONARCHIANISM

While the great heresy of the second century was Gnosticism, the outstanding heresy of the third century was Monarchianism. The Logos doctrine of the Apologetes, the Anti-gnostic Fathers, and the Alexandrian Fathers did not give general satisfaction. Apparently many of the common people regarded it with misgivings, since it seemed to impinge on their theological or on their Christological interests. Where the theological interest was uppermost, the doctrine of the Logos as a separate divine Person appeared to endanger the unity of God or monotheism; and where the Christological interest was in the foreground, the idea that the Logos was subordinate to the Father seemed to compromise the deity of Christ. In course of time men of learning took notice of the misgivings of the people and attempted to safeguard, on the one hand the unity of God, and on the other hand the deity of Christ. This gave rise to two types of thought, both of which were called Monarchianism (a name first applied to them by Tertullian), though strictly speaking it could justly be applied only to that type in which the theological interest was uppermost. In spite of its partial impropriety, the name is generally used up to the present time as a designation of both types.

I. DYNAMIC MONARCHIANISM

This is the type of Monarchianism that was mainly interested in maintaining the unity of God, and was entirely in line with the Ebionite heresy of the early Church and with present-day Unitarianism. Some find the earliest manifestation of it in the rather obscure sect of the Alogi, but Seeberg questions the correctness of this. In all probability its earliest representative was Theodotus of Byzantium, who was excommunicated by Victor, the bishop of Rome. After that Artemon, a Syrian by birth, tried to prove the peculiar views of this type of Monarchianism from Scripture and tradition. His arguments were effectively refuted, however, in the publication of an unknown author, entitled the *Little Labyrinth*. The sect gradually dwindled away, but was revived again through the efforts of the man who *Paul of* became its most noted representative, Paul of Samosata, the *Samosata* bishop of Antioch, who is described as a worldly-minded and imperious person. According to him the Logos was indeed *homoousios* or consubstantial with the Father, but was not a distinct Person in the Godhead. He could be identified with God, because He existed in Him just as human reason exists in man. He was merely an impersonal power, present in all men, but particularly operative in the *man* Jesus. By penetrating the humanity of Jesus progressively, as it did that of no other man, this divine power gradually deified it. And because the man Jesus was thus deified, He is worthy of divine honour, though He cannot be regarded as God in the strict sense of the word. By this construction of the doctrine of the Logos Paul of Samosata maintained the unity of God as implying oneness of person as well as oneness of nature, the Logos and the Holy Spirit being merely impersonal attributes of the Godhead; and thus became the forerunner of the later Socinians and Unitarians. Like them he was interested in the defence of the unity of God and of the real humanity of Jesus. McGiffert asserts that the latter was his primary interest.

2. MODALISTIC MONARCHIANISM

Sabellianism There was a second form of Monarchianism which was far more influential. It was also interested in maintaining the unity of God, but its primary interest seems to have been Christological, namely, the maintenance of the full divinity of Christ. It was called Modalistic Monarchianism, because it conceived of the three Persons in the Godhead as so many modes in which God manifested Himself; was known as Patripassianism in the West,

[78]

since it held that the Father Himself had become incarnate in Christ, and therefore also suffered in and with Him; and was designated Sabellianism in the East after the name of its most famous representative. The great difference between it and Dynamic Monarchianism lay in the fact that it maintained the true divinity of Christ.

Tertullian connects the origin of this sect with a certain *Praxeas and* Praxeas of whom little is known, while Hippolytus claims that it *Noëtus* originated in the teachings of Noëtus of Smyrna. However this may be, both were evidently instrumental in propagating it. Praxeas was absolutely inimical to personal distinctions in God. Tertullian says of him: 'He drove out the Paraclete and crucified the Father.' Praxeas, however, seems to have avoided the assertion that the Father suffered, but Noëtus did not hesitate at this point. To quote the words of Hippolytus: 'He said that Christ is Himself the Father, and that the Father Himself was born and suffered and died.' According to the same Church Father he even made the bold assertion that the Father by changing the mode of his being literally became His own Son. The statement of Noëtus referred to runs as follows: 'When the Father had not yet been born, He was rightly called the Father; but when it pleased Him to submit to birth, having been born, He became the Son, He of Himself and not of another.'

The most important representative of this sect was Sabellius. *Sabellius* Since only a few fragments of his writings are extant, it is hard to determine in detail just what he taught. It is perfectly clear, however, that he distinguished between the unity of the divine essence and the plurality of its manifestations, which are represented as following one another like the parts of a drama. Sabellius indeed sometimes spoke of three divine persons, but then used the word 'person' in the original sense of the word, in which it signifies a role of acting or a mode of manifestation. According to him the names Father, Son and Holy Spirit, are simply designations of three different phases under which the one divine essence manifests itself. God reveals Himself as Father in creation and in the giving of the law, as Son in the incarnation, and as Holy Spirit in regeneration and sanctification.

[79]

QUESTIONS FOR FURTHER STUDY

What accounts for the rise of Monarchianism? In what countries did it make its appearance? Is it correct to say with McGiffert that Monarchianism was only moderately, if at all, concerned about the unity of God; and that its main interest was Christological? To what other early heresies was dynamic Monarchianism related? Has it any modern counterpart? What did the two types of Monarchianism have in common? Has Sabellianism any modern counterpart? What Fathers combated this type of heresy? Was the position of the Alogi in any way related to this heresy? Is Harnack's sympathy with Monarchianism justified?

LITERATURE

Scott, *The Nicene Theology*, pp 89, 184–188, 275–280; Faulkner, *Crises in the Early Church*, pp 76–96; McGiffert, *History of Christian Thought*, I, pp 232–245; Harnack, *History of Dogma*, III, pp 14–118; Seeberg, *History of Doctrines*, I, pp 162–168; Loofs, *Dogmengeschiedenis*, pp 112–126; Neander, *History of Christian Dogmas*, I, pp 164–171; Orr, *The Progress of Dogma* pp 91–102; Otten, *Manual of the History of Dogmas*, I, pp 153–156; Fisher, *History of Christian Doctrine*, pp 98–104.

THE DOCTRINE
OF THE TRINITY

I: THE TRINITARIAN CONTROVERSY

I. THE BACKGROUND

The trinitarian controversy, which came to a head in the struggle between Arius and Athanasius, had its roots in the past. The early Church Fathers, as we have seen, had no clear conception of the Trinity. Some of them conceived of the Logos as impersonal reason, become personal at the time of creation, while others regarded Him as personal and co-eternal with the Father, sharing the divine essence, and yet ascribed to Him a certain subordination to the Father. The Holy Spirit occupied no important place in their discussions at all. They spoke of Him primarily in connection with the work of redemption as applied to the hearts and lives of believers. Some considered Him to be subordinate, not only to the Father, but also to the Son. Tertullian was the first to assert clearly the tri-personality of God, and to maintain the substantial unity of the three Persons. But even he did not reach a clear statement of the doctrine of the Trinity.

Meanwhile Monarchianism came along with its emphasis on the unity of God and on the true deity of Christ, involving a denial of the Trinity in the proper sense of the word. Tertullian and Hippolytus combated their views in the West, while Origen struck them a decisive blow in the East. They defended the trinitarian position as it is expressed in the Apostles' Creed. But even Origen's construction of the doctrine of the Trinity was not altogether satisfactory. He firmly held the view that both the Father and the Son are divine hypostases or personal subsistences, but did not entirely succeed in giving a scriptural representation of the relation of the three Persons to the one essence in the Godhead. While he was the first to explain the relation of the Father to the Son by employing the idea of

Rise of trinitarian controversy

eternal generation, he defined this so as to involve the subordination of the Second Person to the First *in respect to essence*. The
Father communicated to the Son only a secondary species of
divinity, which may be called *Theos*, but not *Ho Theos*. He sometimes even speaks of the Son as *Theos Deuteros*. This was the
most radical defect in Origen's doctrine of the Trinity and
afforded a stepping-stone for Arius. Another, less fatal, defect is
found in his contention that the generation of the Son is not a
necessary act of the Father, *but proceeds from His sovereign will*.
He was careful, however, not to bring in the idea of temporal
succession. In his doctrine of the Holy Spirit he departed still
further from the representation of Scripture. He not only made
the Holy Spirit subordinate even to the Son, but also numbered
Him among the things created by the Son. One of his statements
even seems to imply that He was a mere creature.

2. THE NATURE OF THE CONTROVERSY

Views of Arius

[a] *Arius and Arianism*. The great trinitarian strife is usually
called the Arian controversy, because it was occasioned by the
anti-trinitarian views of Arius, a presbyter of Alexandria, a
rather skilful disputant, though not a profound spirit. His dominant idea was the monotheistic principle of the Monarchians,
that there is only one unbegotten God, one unoriginated Being,
without any beginning of existence. He distinguished between
the Logos that is immanent in God, which is simply a divine
energy, and the Son or Logos that finally became incarnate. The
latter had a beginning: He was generated by the Father, which
in the parlance of Arius was simply equivalent to saying that He
was created. He was created out of nothing before the world was
called into being, and for that very reason was not eternal nor of
the divine essence. The greatest and first of all created beings,
He was brought into being that through Him the world might
be created. He is therefore also mutable, but is chosen of God
on account of his foreseen merits, and is called the Son of God
in view of His future glory. And in virtues of His adoption as Son
He is entitled to the veneration of men. Arius sought Scripture

support for his view in those passages which seem to represent the Son as inferior to the Father, such as, Prov 8:22 (Sept); Matt 28:18; Mark 13:32; Luke 18:19; John 5:19; 14:28; I Cor 15:28.

[b] *The opposition to Arianism.* Arius was opposed first of all by his own bishop Alexander who contended for the true and proper deity of the Son and at the same time maintained the doctrine of an eternal sonship by generation. In course of time, however, his real opponent proved to be the archdeacon of Alexandria, the great Athanasius, who stands out on the pages of history as a strong, inflexible, and unwavering champion of the truth. Seeberg ascribes his great strength to three things, namely, (1) the great stability and genuineness of his character; (2) the sure foundation on which he stood in his firm grasp on the conception of the unity of God, which preserved him from the subordinationism that was so common in his day; and (3) the unerring tact with which he taught men to recognize the nature and significance of the Person of Christ. He felt that to regard Christ as a creature was to deny that faith in Him brings man into saving union with God. *Strength of Athanasius*

He strongly emphasized the unity of God, and insisted on a construction of the doctrine of the Trinity that would not endanger this unity. While the Father and the Son are of the same divine essence, there is no division or separation in the essential Being of God, and it is wrong to speak of a *Theos Deuteros*. But while stressing the unity of God, he also recognized three distinct hypostases in God. He refused to believe in the pre-temporally created Son of the Arians, and maintained the independent and eternally personal existence of the Son. At the same time he bore in mind that the three hypostases in God were not to be regarded as separated in any way, since this would lead to polytheism. According to him the unity of God as well as the distinctions in His Being are best expressed in the term 'oneness of essence'. This clearly and unequivocally expresses the idea that the Son is of the same substance as the Father, but also implies that the two may differ in other respects, as, for instance, in personal subsistence. Like Origen he taught that the *Athanasius on the relation of the Son and the Father*

[85]

Son is begotten by generation, but in distinction from the former he described this generation as an internal and therefore necessary and eternal act of God, and not as an act that was simply dependent on His sovereign will.

It was not merely the demand of logical consistency that inspired Athanasius and determined his theological views. The controlling factor in his construction of the truth was of a religious nature. His soteriological convictions naturally gave birth to his theological tenets. His fundamental position was that union with God is necessary unto salvation, and that no creature, but only one who is Himself God can unite us with God. Hence, as Seeberg says, 'Only if Christ is God, in the full sense of the word and without qualification, has God entered humanity, and only then have fellowship with God, the forgiveness of sins, the truth of God, and immortality been certainly brought to man.' *Hist. of Doct.* I, p 211.

3. THE COUNCIL OF NICAEA

The Council of Nicaea was convened in AD 325 to settle the dispute. The issue was clear-cut, as a brief statement will show. The Arians rejected the idea of a timeless or eternal generation, while Athanasius reasserted this. The Arians said that the Son was created from the non-existent, while Athanasius maintained that He was generated from the essence of the Father. The Arians held that the Son was not of the same substance as the Father, whileAthanasius affirmed that he was *homoousios* with the Father.

Besides the contending parties there was a great middle party, which really constituted the majority, under the leadership of the Church historian, Eusebius of Caesarea, and which is also known as the Origenistic party, since it found itsimpetus in the principles of Origen. This party had Arian leanings and was opposed to the doctrine that the Son is of the same substance

Council of Nicaea and its decision with the Father (*homoousios*). It proposed a statement, previously drawn up by Eusebius, which conceded everything to the party of Alexander and Athanasius, with the single exception of the above-named doctrine; and suggested that the word *homoiousios*

[86]

be substituted for *homoousios*, so as to teach that the Son is of similar substance with the Father. After considerable debate the emperor finally threw the weight of his authority into the balance and thus secured the victory for the party of Athanasius. The Council adopted the following statement on the point in question: 'We believe in one God, the Father Almighty, Maker of things visible and invisible. And in one Lord Jesus Christ, begotten not made, being of one substance (*homoousios*) with the Father', *et cetera*. This was an unequivocal statement. The term *homoousios* could not be twisted to mean anything else than that the essence of the Son is identical with that of the Father. It placed Him on a level with the Father as an uncreated Being and recognized Him as *autotheos*.

4. THE AFTERMATH

[a] *Unsatisfactory nature of the decision.* The decision of the Council did not terminate the controversy, but was rather only the beginning of it. A settlement forced upon the Church by the strong hand of the emperor could not satisfy and was also of uncertain duration. It made the determination of the Christian faith dependent on imperial caprice and even on court intrigues. Athanasius himself, though victorious, was dissatisfied with such a method of settling ecclesiastical disputes. He would rather have convinced the opposing party by the strength of his arguments. The sequel clearly proved that, as it was, a change in emperor, an altered mood, or even a bribe, might alter the whole aspect of the controversy. The party in the ascendancy might all at once suffer eclipse. This is exactly what happened repeatedly in subsequent history.

[b] *Temporary ascendancy of Semi-Arianism in the Eastern Church.* The great central figure in the Post-Nicene trinitarian controversy was Athanasius. He was by far the greatest man of the age, an acute scholar, a strong character, and a man who had the courage of his convictions and was ready to suffer for the truth. The Church gradually became partly Arian, but predominantly semi-Arian, and the emperors usually sided with

the majority, so that it was said: 'Unus Athanasius contra orbem' (one Athanasius against the world). Five times this worthy servant of God was driven into exile and succeeded in office by unworthy sycophants, who were a disgrace to the Church.

The opposition to the Nicene Creed was divided into different *Opposition* parties. Says Cunningham: 'The more bold and honest Arians *to decision* said that the Son was *heteroousios*, of a different substance from *of Nicaea* the Father; others said that He was *anomoios*, unlike the Father; and some, who were usually reckoned semi-Arians, admitted that He was *homoiousios*, of a like substance with the Father; but they all unanimously refused to admit the Nicene phraseology, because they were opposed to the Nicene doctrine of the true and proper divinity of the Son and saw and felt that that phraseology accurately and unequivocally expressed it, though they sometimes professed to adduce other objections against the use of it.' *Historical Theology* I, p 290. Semi-Arianism prevailed in the eastern section of the Church. The West, however, took a different view of the matter, and was loyal to the Council of Nicaea. This finds its explanation primarily in the fact that, while the East was dominated by the subordinationism of Origen, the West was largely influenced by Tertullian and developed a type of theology that was more in harmony with the views of Athanasius. In addition to that, however, the rivalry between Rome and Constantinople must also be taken into account. When Athanasius was banished from the East, he was received with open arms in the West; and the Councils of Rome (341) and Sardica (343) unconditionally endorsed his doctrine.

His cause in the West was weakened, however, by the accession *Marcellus of* of Marcellus of Ancyra to the ranks of the champions of the *Ancyra* Nicene theology. He fell back on the old distinction between the eternal and impersonal Logos immanent in God, which revealed itself as divine energy in the work of creation, and the Logos become personal at the incarnation; denied that the term 'generation' could be applied to the pre-existent Logos, and therefore restricted the name 'Son of God' to the incarnate Logos; and held that, at the end of his incarnate life, the Logos

[88]

returned to his premundane relation to the Father. His theory apparently justified the Origenists or Eusebians in bringing the charge of Sabellianism against their opponents, and was thus instrumental in widening the breach between the East and the West.

Various efforts were made to heal the breach. Councils were convened at Antioch which accepted the Nicene definitions, though with two important exceptions. They asserted the *homoiousios*, and the generation of the Son by an act of the Father's will. This, of course, could not satisfy the West. Other Synods and Councils followed, in which the Eusebians vainly sought a western recognition of the deposition of Athanasius, and drew up other Creeds of a mediating type. But it was all in vain until Constantius became sole emperor, and by cunning management and force succeeded in bringing the western bishops into line with the Eusebians at the Synods of Arles and Milan (355). *Reconciling efforts*

[c] *The turning of the tide.* Victory again proved a dangerous thing for a bad cause. It was, in fact, the signal for the disruption of the anti-Nicene party. The heterogeneous elements of which it was composed were united in their opposition to the Nicene party. But as soon as it was relieved of external pressure, its lack of internal unity became ever increasingly evident. The Arians and the semi-Arians did not agree, and the latter themselves did not form a unity. At the Council of Sirmium (357) an attempt was made to unite all parties by setting aside the use of such terms as *ousia*, *homoousios*, and *homoiousios*, as pertaining to matters far beyond human knowledge. But things had gone too far for any such settlement. The real Arians now showed their true colours, and thus drove the most conservative semi-Arians into the Nicene camp. *Disruption of the opposition*

Meanwhile a younger Nicene party arose, composed of men who were disciples of the Origenist School, but were indebted to Athanasius and the Nicene Creed for a more perfect interpretation of the truth. Chief among them were the three Cappadocians, Basil the Great, Gregory of Nyssa, and Gregory of Nazianzus. They saw a source of misunderstanding in the use of the term *The three Cappadocians hypostasis* as synonymous with both *ousia* (essence) and *prosopon* (person), and therefore restricted its use to the designation of the personal subsistence of the Father and the Son. Instead of taking their starting-point in the one divine *ousia* of God, as Athanasius had done, they took their point of departure in the three hypostases (persons) in the divine Being, and attempted to bring these under the conception of the divine *ousia*. The Gregories compared the relation of the Persons in the Godhead to the divine Being with the relation of three men to their common humanity. And it was exactly by their emphasis on the three hypostases in the divine Being that they freed the Nicene doctrine from the taints of Sabellianism in the eyes of the Eusebians, and that the personality of the Logos appeared to be sufficiently safeguarded. At the same time they strenuously maintained the unity of the three Persons in the Godhead and illustrated this in various ways.

Early opinions about the Holy Spirit [d] *The dispute about the Holy Spirit.* Up to this time the Holy Spirit had not come in for a great deal of consideration, though discordant opinions had been expressed on the subject. Arius held that the Holy Spirit was the first created being produced by the Son, an opinion very much in harmony with that of Origen. Athanasius asserted that the Holy Spirit was of the same essence with the Father, but the Nicene Creed contains only the indefinite statement, 'And (I believe) in the Holy Spirit'. The Cappadocians followed in the footsteps of Athanasius and vigorously maintained the *homoousis* of the Holy Spirit. Hilary of Poitiers in the West held that the Holy Spirit, as searching the deep things of God, could not be foreign to the divine essence. An entirely different opinion was voiced by Macedonius, bishop of Constantinople, who declared that the Holy Spirit was a creature subordinate to the Son; but his opinion was generally considered as heretical, and his followers were nicknamed Pneumatomachians (from *pneuma*, spirit, and *machomai*, to speak evil against). When in AD 381 the general Council of Constantinople met, it declared its approval of the Nicene Creed and under the guidance of Gregory of Nazianzus accepted the following formula respecting the Holy Spirit: 'And

[90]

we believe in the Holy Spirit, the Lord, the Life-giving, who proceeds from the Father, who is to be glorified with the Father and the Son, and who speaks through the prophets.'

Procession of the Holy Spirit from the Son

[e] *Completion of the doctrine of the Trinity.* The statement of the Council of Constantinople proved unsatisfactory in two points: (1) the word *homoousios* was not used, so that the consubstantiality of the Spirit with the Father was not directly asserted; and (2) the relation of the Holy Spirit to the other two Persons was not defined. The statement is made that the Holy Spirit proceeds from the Father, while it is neither denied nor affirmed that He also proceeds from the Son. There was no entire unanimity on this point. To say that the Holy Spirit proceeds from the Father only, looked like a denial of the essential oneness of the Son with the Father; and to say that He also proceeds from the Son, seemed to place the Holy Spirit in a more dependent position than the Son and to be an infringement on His deity. Athanasius, Basil, and Gregory of Nyssa, asserted the procession of the Holy Spirit from the Father, without opposing in any way the doctrine that He also proceeds from the Son. But Epiphanius and Marcellus of Ancyra positively asserted this doctrine.

Western theologians generally held to the procession of the Holy Spirit from both the Father and the Son; and at the Synod of Toledo in AD 589 the famous 'filioque' was added to the Constantinopolitan Symbol. In the East the final formulation of the doctrine was given by John of Damascus. According to him there is but one divine essence, but three persons or hypostases. These are to be regarded as realities in the divine Being, but not related to one another as three men are. They are one in every respect, except in their mode of existence. The Father is characterized by 'non-generation', the Son by 'generation', and the Holy Spirit by 'procession'. The relation of the Persons to one another is described as one of 'mutual interpenetration' (circumincession), without commingling. Notwithstanding his absolute rejection of subordinationism, John of Damascus still spoke of the Father as the source of the Godhead, and represents the Spirit as proceeding from the Father through the Logos.

This is still a relic of Greek subordinationism. The East never adopted the 'filioque' of the Synod of Toledo. It was the rock on which the East and the West split.

Augustine on the Trinity The western conception of the Trinity reached its final statement in the great work of Augustine, *De Trinitate*. He too stresses the unity of essence and the Trinity of Persons. Each one of the three Persons possesses the entire essence, and is in so far identical with the essence and with each one of the other Persons. They are not like three human persons, each one of which possesses only a part of generic human nature. Moreover, the one is never and can never be without the other; the relation of dependence between them is a mutual one. The divine essence belongs to each of them under a different point of view, as generating, generated, or existing through inspiration. Between the three hypostases there is a relation of mutual interpenetration and interdwelling. The word 'person' does not satisfy Augustine as a designation of the relationship in which the three stand to one another; still he continues to use it, as he says, 'not in order to express it (the relationship), but in order not to be silent'. In this conception of the Trinity the Holy Spirit is naturally regarded as proceeding, not only from the Father, but also from the Son.

QUESTIONS FOR FURTHER STUDY
What different views of the Logos and of His relation to the Father were prevalent before the Council of Nicaea? How did Origen's doctrine of the Trinity compare with that of Tertullian? In what points was his doctrine defective? What conception did Arius have of God? How did his view of Christ follow from this? To what passages of Scripture did he appeal? What was the real point at issue at the Council of Nicaea? What was Athanasius' real interest in the matter? How did he conceive of man's redemption? Why was it essential that the term *homoousios* rather than *homoiousios* should be used? Why were the semi-Arians so opposed to its use? How could they detect Sabellianism in it? What valuable contribution did the Cappadocians make to the discussion? How must we judge of the anathema at the end of the Nicene Creed? How was the question of the relation of the Holy Spirit to the other Persons settled in the West and how in the East? Why was the East unalterably opposed to the famous 'filioque'? Does the final statement of the doctrine of the Trinity by John of Damascus differ much from that by Augustine?

THE TRINITARIAN CONTROVERSY

LITERATURE
Bull, *Defense of the Nicene Faith*; Scott, *The Nicene Theology*, pp 213–384; Faulkner, *Crises in the Early Church*, pp 113–144; Cunningham, *Historical Theology*, I, pp 267–306; McGiffert, *A History of Christian Thought*, I, pp 246–275; Harnack, *History of Dogma*, III, pp 132–162; Seeberg, *History of Doctrines*, I, pp 201–241; Loofs, *Dogmengeschiedenis*, pp. 140–157; Shedd, *History of Christian Doctrine*, I, pp 306–375; Thomasius, *Dogmengeschichte*, I, pp 198–262; Neander, *History of Christian Dogmas*, I, pp 285–316; Sheldon, *History of Christian Doctrine*, I, pp 194–215; Orr, *Progress of Dogma*, pp 105–131.

II: THE DOCTRINE OF THE TRINITY IN LATER THEOLOGY

I. THE DOCTRINE OF THE TRINITY IN LATIN THEOLOGY

Roscellinus on the Trinity

Later theology did not add materially to the doctrine of the Trinity. There were deviations from, and consequent restatements of, the truth. Roscelinus applied the Nominalist theory that universals are merely subjective conceptions to the Trinity, and thus sought to avoid the difficulty of combining the numerical unity with the distinction of persons in God. He regarded the three Persons in the Godhead as three essentially different individuals, which could be said to be one generically and in name only. Their unity is merely a unity of will and power. Anselm correctly pointed out that this position logically leads to Tritheism, and stressed the fact that universal conceptions present truth and reality.

Gilbert of Poitiers on the Trinity

If Roscellinus gave a Nominalistic interpretation of the doctrine of the Trinity, Gilbert of Poitiers interpreted it from the point of view of a moderate Realism of the Aristotelian type, which holds that the universals have their existence in the particulars. He distinguished between the divine essence and God and compared their relation to that between humanity and concrete men. The divine essence is not God, but the form of God, or that which makes Him to be God. This essence or form (Latin *forma*, ie that which makes a thing what it is) is common to the three Persons and in that respect they are one. As a result of this distinction he was charged with teaching Tetratheism.

Abelard on the Trinity

Abelard spoke of the doctrine of the Trinity in a way that caused him to be charged with Sabellianism. He seemingly identifies the three Persons in the divine Being with the attributes of power, wisdom, and goodness. The name of Father stands for power, that of Son for wisdom, and that of Holy Spirit for

[94]

goodness. While he also uses expressions which seem to imply that the distinctions in the Godhead are real personal distinctions, he employs illustrations that clearly point in the direction of Modalism.

In Thomas Aquinas we find the usual representation of the doctrine of the Trinity, and this was the prevailing view of the Church at the time.

2. THE DOCTRINE OF THE TRINITY IN THE PERIOD OF THE REFORMATION

Calvin discusses the doctrine of the Trinity at length in his *Institutes* I. 13, and defends the doctrine as formulated by the early Church. On the whole he preferred not to go beyond the simple statements of Scripture on the matter, and therefore during his first stay at Geneva even avoided the use of the terms 'person' and 'trinity'. In his *Institutes*, however, he defends the use of these terms and criticizes those who are averse to them. Caroli brought a charge of Arianism against him, which proved to be utterly baseless. Calvin held to the absolute equality of the Persons in the Godhead, and even maintained the self-existence of the Son, thereby implying that it is not the essence of the Son, but His personal subsistence that is generated. He says 'that the essence both of the Son and the Spirit is unbegotten', and 'that the Son, as God, independently of the consideration of person, is self-existent; but as the Son, we say, that He is of the Father. Thus His essence is unoriginated; but the origin of His person is God Himself.' *Institutes* I. 13, 25. It is sometimes said that Calvin denied the *eternal* generation of the Son. This assertion is based on the following passage: 'For what is the profit of disputing whether the Father always generates, seeing that it is foolish to imagine a continuous act of generating when it is evident that three persons have subsisted in one God from eternity.' *Institutes* I. 13, 29. But this statement can hardly be intended as a denial of the eternal generation of the Son, since he teaches this explicitly in other passages. It is more likely that it is simply an expression of disagreement with the Nicene

Calvin on the Trinity

speculation about eternal generation as a perpetual movement, always complete, and yet never completed. Says Warfield: 'Calvin seems to have found this conception difficult, if not meaningless.' *Calvin and Calvinism*, p 247 f. The doctrine of the Trinity, as formulated by the Church, finds expression in all Reformed Confessions, most completely and with the greatest precision in chapter III of the Second Helvetic Confession.

Socinians and Arminians on the Trinity

In the sixteenth century the Socinians declared the doctrine of three Persons possessing a common essence, to be contrary to reason, and attempted to refute it on the basis of the passages quoted by the Arians, cf above, p 89. But they even went beyond the Arians in denying the pre-existence of the Son and holding that Christ, as to His essential nature, was simply a man, though He possessed a peculiar fullness of the Spirit, had special knowledge of God, and at His ascension received dominion over all things. They defined the Holy Spirit as 'a virtue or energy flowing from God to men'. In their conception of God they were the forerunners of the present day Unitarians and Modernists.

In some quarters subordinationism again came to the foreground. Some of the Arminians (Episcopius, Curcellaeus, and Limborch), while believing that all three Persons shared in the divine nature, yet ascribed a certain pre-eminence to the Father over the other Persons in order, dignity, and power of domination. In their estimation belief in the equality of rank was almost sure to lead to Tritheism.

3. THE DOCTRINE OF THE TRINITY AFTER THE PERIOD OF REFORMATION

Clarke on the Trinity

In England Samuel Clarke, court preacher to queen Anne, published a work on the Trinity in 1712, in which he approached the Arian view of subordination. He speaks of the Father as the supreme and only God, the sole origin of all being, power, and authority. Alongside of Him there existed from the beginning a second divine Person called the Son, who derives His being and all His attributes from the Father, *not by a mere necessity of nature, but by an act of the Father's optional will*. He refuses to commit himself on the question, whether the Son was begotten from the essence of the Father, or was made out of nothing; and whether He existed from all eternity or only before all worlds. Alongside of these two there is a third Person, who derives His essence from the Father through the Son. He is subordinate to the Son both by nature and by the will of the Father.

New England theologians on the Trinity

Some of the New England theologians criticized the doctrine of eternal generation. Emmons even called it eternal nonsense, and Moses Stuart declared that the expression was a palpable contradiction of language, and that their most distinguished theologians, for forty years past, had declared against it. He himself disliked it, because he regarded it as contrary to the proper equality of the Father and the Son. The following words seem to express his view: 'Father, Son, and Holy Spirit are words which designate the distinctions of the Godhead as manifested to us in the economy of redemption, and are not intended to mark the eternal relations of the Godhead *as they are in themselves.*'

Modern views of the Trinity

Sabellian interpretations of the Trinity are found in Emanuel Swedenborg, who denied the essential Trinity and said that what we call Father, Son, and Holy Spirit is simply a distinction in the eternal God-man, assuming human flesh in the Son, and operating through the Holy Spirit; in Schleiermacher, who says that God in Himself as the unknown unity underlying all things is the Father, God as coming into conscious personality in man, and especially in Jesus Christ, is the Son, and God as the life of the risen Christ in the Church, is the Holy Spirit; and in Hegel, Dorner, and others who adopt a somewhat similar view. In Ritschl and in many Modernists of the present day the view of Paul of Samosata reappears.

QUESTIONS FOR FURTHER STUDY

In what sense did the Scholastics regard the doctrine of the Trinity as a mystery? Why did Roscelinus deny the numerical unity of essence in God? How did the Church judge of his teaching? Why was Gilbert of Poitiers charged with Tetratheism? What was the nature of Abelard's Sabellianism? What was the attitude of the Church to his teaching? What was the generally accepted definition of a person in the Trinity, as given by Boethius? What criticisms were levelled against it? Did the Scholastics regard the divine essence of the Son or his personal subsistence as the object of generation? How did they distinguish between the generation of the Son and the procession of the Holy Spirit? What relation did they express by the term '*circumincessio*'? How did Calvin define a person in the Trinity? How did he conceive of the generation of the Son? Where do we find the doctrine of the Trinity developed along Arian lines? Where along Sabellian lines? And where along the line of a purely economical Trinity?

LITERATURE

Seeberg, *History of Doctrines*, II, cf Index; Otten, *Manual of the History of Dogmas*, II, pp 84–99; Sheldon, *History of Christian Doctrine*, I, pp 337–339; II, pp 96–103, 311–318; Cunningham, *Historical Theology*, II, pp 194–213; Fisher, *History of Christian Doctrine*, cf Index.

THE DOCTRINE
OF CHRIST

I: THE CHRISTOLOGICAL CONTROVERSIES

The Christological problem can be approached from the side of *Connection of* theology proper and from the side of soteriology. Though the *Christological and* early Church Fathers did not lose sight of the soteriological *trinitarian* bearings of the doctrine of Christ, they did not make these *problems* prominent in their main discussions. Breathing the air of the trinitarian controversies, it was but natural that they should approach the study of Christ from the side of theology proper. The decision to which the trinitarian controversy led, namely, that Christ as the Son of God is consubstantial with the Father and therefore very God, immediately gave birth to the question of the relation between the divine and the human nature in Christ.

The early Christological controversies do not present a very edifying spectacle. The passions were too much in evidence, unworthy intrigues often played an important part, and even violence occasionally made its appearance. It might seem that such an atmosphere could only be productive of error, and yet these controversies led to a formulation of the doctrine of the Person of Christ that is still regarded as standard in the present day. The Holy Spirit was guiding the Church, often through shame and confusion, into the clear atmosphere of the truth. Some claim that the Church attempted too much when it tried to define a mystery which from the nature of the case transcends all definition. It should be borne in mind, however, that the early Church did not claim to be able to penetrate to the depths of this great doctrine, and did not pretend to give a solution of the problem of the incarnation in the formula of Chalcedon. It merely sought to guard the truth against the errors of theorizers, and to give a formulation of it which would ward off various, palpably unscriptural, constructions of the truth.

The Church was in quest of a conception of Christ that would do justice to the following points: (a) His true and proper deity; (b) His true and proper humanity; (c) the union of deity and humanity in one person; and (d) the proper distinction of deity from humanity in the one person. It felt that as long as these requirements were not met, or only partly met, its conception of Christ would be defective. All the Christological heresies that arose in the early Church originated in the failure to combine all these elements in the doctrinal statement of the truth. Some denied wholly or in part the true and proper deity of Christ, and others disputed wholly or in part His true and proper humanity. Some stressed the unity of the person at the expense of the two distinct natures, and others emphasized the distinct character of the two natures in Christ at the expense of the unity of the Person.

I. FIRST STAGE OF THE CONTROVERSY

Rise of the Christological problem

[a] *The background.* This controversy also had its roots in the past. Ebionites, Alogi, and Dynamic Monarchians denied the deity of Christ, and Docetae, Gnostics, and Modalists rejected His humanity. They simply ruled out one of the terms of the problem. Others were less radical and denied either the full deity or the perfect humanity of Christ. The Arians denied that the Son-Logos, who became incarnate in Christ, was possessed of absolute Godhead. And on the other hand Apollinaris, bishop

Apollinarianism

of Laodicea (d. c.390), denied the true and proper humanity of Jesus Christ. He conceived of man as consisting of body, soul, and spirit, and sought the solution of the problem of the two natures in Christ in the theory that the Logos took the place of the human *pneuma* (spirit). In his opinion it would be easier to maintain the unity of the Person of Christ, if the Logos were simply regarded as taking the place of the higher rational principle in man. Over against Arius he defended the true divinity of Christ, and sought to safeguard His sinlessness by

[102]

substituting the Logos for the human *pneuma*, which he regarded as the seat of sin. According to him a complete human nature would naturally involve sinfulness. Moreover, he tried to make the incarnation intelligible by assuming an eternal tendency to the human in the Logos Himself as the archetypal man. But the solution of Apollinaris could not satisfy, because, as Shedd says, 'if the rational part be subtracted from man, he becomes either an idiot or a brute'. His purpose was praiseworthy, however, in that he sought to safeguard both the unity of the Person and the sinlessness of Christ.

There was considerable opposition to the solution of the problem offered by Apollinaris. The three Cappadocians and Hilary of Poitiers maintained that, if the Logos did not assume human nature in its integrity, He could not be our perfect Redeemer. Since the whole sinner had to be renewed, Christ had to assume human nature in its entirety, and not simply the least important parts of it. They also pointed to a docetic element in the teachings of Apollinaris. If there was no real human will in Christ, there could be no real probation and no real advance in His manhood. Even the opponents of Apollinaris, however, while stressing the complete humanity of Christ, conceived of this as overshadowed by His divinity. Gregory of Nyssa even says that the flesh of Christ was transformed and lost all its original properties by union with the divine. *Opposition to Apollinaris*

One result of this preliminary skirmish was that the Synod of Alexandria in 362 asserted the existence of a human soul in Christ. The word 'soul' was used by the Synod as inclusive of the rational element, which Apollinaris called *pneuma* or *nous*.

[b] The parties to the controversy

1. The Nestorian Party. Some of the early Church Fathers used expressions which seemingly denied the existence of two natures in Christ, and postulated a single nature, 'the incarnate and adorable Word'. From this point of view Mary was often called *theotokos*, mother of God. It was particularly the School of Alexandria that revealed this tendency. On the other hand the School of Antioch went to the other extreme. This appears

Theodore of Mopsuestia especially in the teachings of Theodore of Mopsuestia. He took his starting-point in the complete manhood of Christ and the perfect reality of His human experiences. According to him Christ actually struggled with human passions, passed through a veritable conflict with temptation, and came out victoriously. He owed the power to keep himself free from sin (a) to His sinless birth, and (b) to the union of His manhood with the divine Logos. Theodore denied the *essential* indwelling of the Logos in Christ, and allowed only for a mere moral indwelling. He saw no essential difference, but only a difference of degree, between the indwelling of God in Christ and that in believers. This view really substitutes for the incarnation the moral indwelling of the Logos in the man Jesus. Nevertheless, Theodore shrank from the conclusion to which his view would seem to lead inevitably, that there is a dual personality in Christ, two persons between whom a moral union exists. He said that the union was so close that the two might be spoken of as one person, just as husband and wife can be called one flesh.

Nestorius and Nestorianism The logical development of this Antiochian view is seen in Nestorianism. Following in the footsteps of Theodore, Nestorius denied that the term *theotokos* could properly be applied to Mary for the simple reason that she only brought forth a man who was accompanied by the Logos. Although Nestorius did not draw the inevitable conclusion that followed from this position, his opponent, Cyril, held him responsible for that conclusion. He pointed out (a) that, if Mary is not *theotokos*, that is, the mother of one person, and that person divine, the assumption of a single human being into fellowship with the Logos is substituted for the incarnation of God; and (b) that, if Mary is not *theotokos*, the relation of Christ to humanity is changed, and He is no more the effectual Redeemer of mankind. The followers of Nestorius did not hesitate to draw the conclusion.

Evaluation of Nestorianism Nestorianism is defective, not in the doctrine of the two natures in Christ, but in that of the one Person. Both the true and proper deity and the true and proper humanity are conceded, but they are not conceived in such a way as to form a real unity and to constitute a single person. The two natures are

[104]

also two persons. The important distinction between nature as substance possessed in common, and person as a relatively independent subsistence of that nature, is entirely disregarded. Instead of blending the two natures into a single self-consciousness, Nestorianism places them alongside of each other with nothing more than a moral and sympathetic union between them. The man Christ was not God, but God-bearer, *theophoros*, a possessor of the Godhead. Christ is worshipped, not because He is God, but because God is in Him. The strong point in Nestorianism is that it seeks to do full justice to the humanity of Christ. At the same time it goes contrary to all the scriptural proofs for the unity of the Person in the Mediator. It leaves the Church with an exalted example of true piety and morality in the human person of Jesus, but robs it of its divine–human Redeemer, the source of all spiritual power, grace, and salvation.

(2) The Cyrillian Party. The most prominent opponent of Nestorianism was Cyril of Alexandria. According to him the Logos assumed human nature in its entirety, in order to redeem it, but at the same time formed the only personal subject in the God-man. His terminology was not always clear, however. On the one hand he seemed to teach simply that the Logos assumed human nature, so that there are two natures in Christ, which find their indissoluble union in the one Person of the Logos, without any change in the natures themselves. But he also used expressions in which he stressed the unity of the two natures in Christ by means of a mutual communication of attributes, and spoke of the Person of Christ as if it were a *resultant* unity. His great significance lies in the fact that, over against Nestorianism, he stressed the unity of the Person of Christ. The three points which he emphasized above all were in perfect harmony with the catholic doctrine of the day, namely: (a) the inseparable conjunction of the two natures; (b) the impersonality and dependence of the manhood, which the Logos uses as His instrument; and (c) the unity and continuity of the Person in Christ. Occasionally he used expressions, however, which seemed to justify the later Eutychian error. He applied the term *phusis* (nature) to the Logos only, and not to the humanity of Christ, thus using it as a

Opposing view of Cyril

synonym of *hypostasis*. This gave some occasion to saddle on him the doctrine that, after the incarnation, there was only one divine-human nature in Christ, and made it possible for the Monophysites to appeal to him, when they wanted to prove that, as there was but one Person, so there was also only a single nature in the Mediator. They continued their appeal to him in spite of his strenuous denial of any mixture of the natures. The Council of Ephesus effected a sort of compromise by maintaining on the one hand that the term *theotokos* could be applied to Mary, and asserting on the other hand the doctrine of the two distinct natures of Christ.

(3) The Eutychian Party. Many of Cyril's adherents were dissatisfied. They did not take kindly to the doctrine of the two distinct natures. Eutyches, an aged monk of rather unbalanced *Eutichus and* convictions and with a strong anti-Nestorian bias, espoused the *Eutichianism* cause of the Alexandrian theology at Constantinople. According to Theodoret he maintained in effect, either an absorption of the human nature in the divine, or a fusion of the two natures, resulting in a sort of *tertium quid*. He was of the opinion that the human attributes were assimilated to the divine in Christ, so that His body was not consubstantial with ours and He was not human in the proper sense of the word. Condemned by the Council of Constantinople in 448, he appealed to Leo, the bishop of Rome. After Leo received a full report of the case from Flavian, bishop of Constantinople, and was urged to express his opinion, he addressed to Flavian his celebrated *Tome*. Because this *Tome* profoundly influenced the Chalcedonian formula, it may be well to note its main points, which are as follows: (a) There are two natures in Christ, which are permanently distinct. (b) The two natures unite in one Person, each one performing its own proper function in the incarnate life. (c) From the unity of the Person follows the communication of (*communicatio idiomatum*). (d) The work of redemption required a Mediator both human and divine, passible and impassible, mortal and immortal. The incarnation was an act of condescension on the part of God, but in it the Logos did not cease to be very God. The *forma servi* did not detract from the

forma dei. (e) The manhood of Christ is permanent, and its denial implies a docetic denial of the reality of the sufferings of Christ. This is really a compendium of western Christology.

[c] *The decision of the Council of Chalcedon.* After several local Councils had met, some favouring and some condemning Eutyches, the ecumenical Council of Chalcedon was convened in the year 451, and issued its famous statement of the doctrine of the Person of Christ. This reads as follows:

'We then, following the holy Fathers, all with one consent, teach men to confess one and the same Son, our Lord Jesus Christ, the same perfect in Godhead and also perfect in manhood; truly God and also truly man, of a reasonable soul and body; consubstantial with the Father according to the Godhead, and consubstantial with us according to the manhood; in all things like unto us, without sin; begotten before all ages of the Father according to the Godhead, and in these latter days, for us and for our salvation, born of the virgin Mary, the Mother of God, according to the manhood; one and the same Christ, Son, Lord, Only-begotten, to be acknowledged in two natures, inconfusedly (*asuggutos*), unchangeably (*atreptos*), indivisibly (*adiairetos*), inseparably (*achoristos*), the distinction of natures being by no means taken away by the union, but rather the property of each nature being preserved, and concurring in one Person and one subsistence, not parted or divided into two persons, but one and the same Son, the Only-begotten, God the Word, the Lord Jesus Christ; as the prophets from the beginning have declared concerning Him, and the Lord Jesus Christ Himself has taught us, and the Creed of the Holy Fathers has handed down to us.'

Deliverance of Chalcedon

The most important implications of this statement are the following: (1) The properties of both natures may be attributed to the one Person, as, for instance, omniscience and limited knowledge. (2) The suffering of the God-man can be regarded as truly and really infinite, while yet the divine nature is impassible. (3) It is the divinity and not the humanity that constitutes the root and basis of the personality of Christ. (4) The Logos did not unite with a distinct human individual, but with a human nature. There was not first an individual man, with whom the

[107]

Second Person in the Godhead associated Himself. The union was effected with the substance of humanity in the womb of the virgin.

2. SECOND STAGE OF THE CONTROVERSY

[a] *Confusion after the decision of the Council.* The Council of Chalcedon did not put an end to the Christological disputes any more than the Council of Nicaea terminated the trinitarian controversy. Egypt, Syria, and Palestine harboured many fanatical monks of Eutychian convictions, while Rome became ever-increasingly the centre of orthodoxy. In fact, the process of dogmatic development was fast passing from the East to the *Monophy-* West. After the Council of Chalcedon the adherents of Cyril and *sites* Eutichus were called Monophysites, because they conceded that after the union Christ had a *composite* nature, but denied that He had two *distinct* natures. As they saw it, two distinct natures would necessarily involve a duality of persons. There was a lengthy and rather unseemly struggle between the different parties. Even the Monophysites were not all agreed among themselves. They were divided into several sects, of which the names alone, says Dr Orr, 'are enough to give one a cold shiver'. There were the *Theopaschitists,* who emphasized the fact that God suffered; the *Phthartolatrists,* who came nearest to the formulation of Chalcedon, and stressed the fact that the human nature of Christ was, like ours, capable of suffering, and were therefore said to worship that which is corruptible; and the *Aphtharto-docetists,* who represented just the opposite view, namely, that the human nature of Christ was not consubstantial with ours, but was endowed with divine attributes, and was therefore sinless, imperishable, and incorruptible.

The ablest and most prominent defender of the Chalcedonian *Leontius of* theology was Leontius of Byzantium. He added an element to *Byzantium* the dogmatical construction of the doctrine of Christ, which was more fully worked out by John of Damascus. The point is this: The rejection of Nestorianism might lead to the idea of an independent impersonal existence of the human nature of Christ.

[108]

This idea was apt to be fostered by the use of the terms *anupostasis* and *anupostasia*. Therefore Leontius stressed the fact that the human nature of Christ is *enupostasia*, not impersonal but in-personal, having its personal subsistence in the Person of the Son of God from the very moment of the incarnation.

In 553 the emperor Justinian summoned the fifth oecumenical Council at Constantinople, which was favourable to the Monophysites in its condemnation of the writings of Theodore, but unfavourable to it in so far as it anathematized those who declared that the Council of Chalcedon countenanced the very errors which it condemned. This did not satisfy the Monophysites, but rather sealed their separation from the Church of the empire.

[b] *The Monothelitic controversy.* It soon became evident that the attempted settlement of the Monophysite controversy by the Council did not restore harmony. Several vital questions remained unanswered. Not only did the *how* of the two natures in Christ remain unsolved, but the additional question arose, How much is included in the person and how much in the nature? In this connection the very important question was raised, whether the will belongs to the former or to the latter. This is equivalent to asking, whether there is but one will in Christ or two? To say that there is but one seems to rob Christ of true human volition, and therefore to detract from the integrity of His humanity. On the other hand, to say that there are two seems to lead right into the Nestorian camp.

The result was that a new sect arose among the Mono- *Monothelites* physites, called Monothelites. As the name indicates, they started from the unity of the Person and asserted that there is but one will in Christ. This doctrine also took two forms: either the human will was regarded as merged in the divine, so that the latter alone acted; or the will was regarded as composite, resulting from the fusion of the divine and the human. The opponents of the Monothelites were called Duothelites. These took their stand on the duality of the natures and asserted the presence of two wills in Christ. The Monophysites charged them with the destruction of the unity of the personal life of Christ.

For a time the term *energeia* (energy) was used in this controversy in preference to *thelema* (will), but soon the latter, as the more definite term, prevailed. It should be borne in mind, however, that the word 'will' was used in a broad sense. Strictly speaking, we mean by 'will' the faculty of volition, of self-determination, and of choice. But the word is often used in a broader sense, as including the instincts, appetites, desires, and affections, with their corresponding aversions. All this was covered by the term 'will' in the ancient controversy, so that this included the question, whether Christ was capable of fear and of shrinking from suffering and death. The denial of the human will in Christ would therefore give His humanity a somewhat docetic character.

The sixth ecumenical Council of Constantinople (680), with the co-operation of the bishop of Rome, adopted the doctrine of the two wills and two energies as the orthodox position, but also decided that the human will must always be conceived as subordinate to the divine. The established opinion was that the human will by its union with the divine did not become less human, but was heightened and perfected by the union, the two always acting in perfect harmony.

[c] *The construction of the doctrine by John of Damascus.* In John of Damascus the theology of the Greek Church reached its highest development, and therefore it is of importance to notice his construction of the doctrine of the Person of Christ. According to him the Logos assumed human nature, and not *vice versa*, that is, the man Jesus did not assume the Logos. This means that the Logos is the formative and controlling agency, securing the unity of the two natures. The Logos did not assume a human individual, nor human nature in general, but a potential human individual, a human nature not yet developed into a person or hypostasis. Through the union of the Logos with this potential man in the womb of Mary, the latter acquired an individual existence. While the human nature of Christ has no independent personality of its own, it nevertheless has personal existence in and through the Logos. It is not non-hypostatic, but en-hypostatic. He illustrates the union of the two natures in Christ by

Christology of John of Damascus

[110]

the union of body and soul in man. There is a circumincession of the divine and the human in Christ, a communication of the divine attributes to the human nature, so that the latter is deified and we may also say that God suffered in the flesh. The human nature only is thus affected, and is therefore purely receptive and passive. The Son of God, now including His complete humanity, is an object of worship for the Church. Though there is a tendency to reduce the human nature of Jesus to the position of a mere organ or instrument of the Logos, it is admitted that there is a co-operation of the two natures, and that the one Person acts and wills in each nature. The will is regarded as belonging to the nature, but it is claimed that in Christ the human will has become the will of the incarnate God.

[d] *The Christology of the Western Church.* The Western Church remained comparatively unaffected by the controversies that were raging in the East. It seems that on the whole the western mind was not sufficiently familiar with all kinds of fine philosophical distinctions to take an active part in the discussion of questions that were so deep and subtle as those that divided the Eastern Church.

A new movement of Christological thought appeared in Spain, *Adoptionism* however, in the seventh and eighth centuries, called the Adoptionist Controversy. The term 'adoption' was already familiar in Spain, since a Council of Toledo declared in 675 that Christ was the Son of God by nature and not by adoption. The real champion of the Adoptionist doctrine was Felix, bishop of Urgella. He regarded Christ as to His divine nature, that is the Logos, as the only-begotten Son of God in the natural sense, but Christ on his human side as a Son of God by adoption. At the same time he sought to preserve the unity of the Person by stressing the fact that, from the time of his conception, the Son of Man was taken up into the unity of the Person of the Son of God.

This theory therefore makes a distinction between a natural and an adoptive sonship, the former predicated of the divinity and the latter of the humanity of Christ. Felix and his followers based their opinion: (1) On the distinction of natures in Christ, which, according to them, implied a distinction between two

[111]

modes of sonship. (2) On passages of Scripture which refer to the inferiority of Christ as man to the Father. And (3) On the fact that believers are sons of God by adoption, and are also called 'brethren' of Christ. This would seem to imply that Christ as to his human nature was a Son of God in the same sense. In order to explain their meaning still further they distinguished between a natural birth of Christ at Bethlehem and a spiritual birth, which had its inception at the time of baptism and was consummated in the resurrection. This spiritual birth made Christ the adopted Son of God.

While the opponents of this view did not charge the Adoptionists with the explicit error of teaching a dual personality in Christ, they asserted that this would be the logical result of a dual sonship. Alcuin, the noted scholar of the days of Charlemagne, took issue with Felix and charged him with dividing Christ into two sons. He maintained that no father could have a son, who was such both by nature and by adoption. Undoubtedly, the Adoptionists were in error, when they assigned to the human nature of Christ a sort of alien position until He was made to partake of divine sonship by a special act of adoption. This error was condemned by the Synod of Frankfort in AD 794.

QUESTIONS FOR FURTHER STUDY

Did the position of Apollinaris find any point of contact in Arianism? What interests did he seek to safeguard? What traces of Platonic and Manichæan influence are found in his theory? What was his peculiar view of the Logos as the archetype of humanity? What were the main objections to his theory? In what sense was Nestorianism a reaction against Apollinarianism? How many kinds of indwelling did Theodore distinguish? What led to the application of the term *theotokos* to Mary? Did Cyril really confuse the two natures? How can we account for a great deal of the misunderstanding current on this point? What was the strong point in Nestorianism? How did the Church meet its error? What was Cyril's view of the unity of the Person, and of the relation of the two natures in Christ? What was the particular interest of Eutychianism? In what respect did it err? How did Leo in his *Tome* construct the doctrine of Christ? What element did Leontius of Byzantium contribute to the construction of the doctrine of Christ? How did the Monothelite controversy arise? What did it involve and how was it settled? On what was the Adoptionist theory based? Were the Adoptionists really Nestorian in their view?

LITERATURE
Bruce, *The Humiliation of Christ*, pp 39–82; Ottley, *The Doctrine of the Incarnation*, pp 323–481; Mackintosh, *The Doctrine of the Person of Christ*, pp 175–229; Harnack, *History of Dogma*, IV, pp 138–267; Seeberg, *History of Doctrines*, I, pp 243–288; Loofs, *Dogmengeschiedenis*, pp 153–170; Thomasius, *Dogmengeschichte*, I, pp 287–378; Neander, *History of Christian Dogmas*, I, pp 316–339; Shedd, *History of Christian Doctrine*, I, pp 393–408; Cunningham, *Historical Theology*, I, pp 307–320; Fisher, *History of Christian Doctrine*, pp 148–160; Orr, *Progress of Dogma*, pp 173–206.

II: LATER CHRISTOLOGICAL DISCUSSIONS

1. IN THE MIDDLE AGES

During the Middle Ages the doctrine of the Person of Christ was not in the foreground. Other problems, such as those connected with the doctrines of sin and grace, and with the doctrine of the work of redemption, became the centre of attention. A brief indication of the most salient points of Thomas Aquinas' construction of the doctrine of Christ will be sufficient to indicate how the matter stood at the time of the Reformation.

Christology of Thomas Aquinas As to the hypostatic union in Christ, Thomas Aquinas adhered to the received theology. The Person of the Logos became composite after the union at the incarnation, and this union 'hindered' the manhood from arriving at an independent personality. A twofold grace was imparted to the human nature of Christ in virtue of its union with the Logos, namely: (a) the *gratia unionis* or the dignity that resulted from the union of the human nature with the divine, so that the human nature also became an object of worship; and (b) the *gratia habitualis*, the grace of sanctification which was vouchsafed to Christ as man, sustaining the human nature in its relationship to God. The human knowledge of Christ was twofold, namely, *scientia infusa* and *scientia acquisita*. In virtue of the former He could know all things that can be so known by men and all that is made known to them by revelation, a knowledge perfect in its kind but yet subject to creaturely limitations. And in virtue of the latter He knew all that can be known through the intellectual faculties. There is no communication of attributes between the natures in the abstract, but both human and divine attributes may be ascribed to the Person. The human nature of Christ was not omnipotent, but was subject to human affections, such as sorrow, sadness,

[114]

fear, wonder, and anger. There are two wills in Christ, but ultimate causality belongs to the divine will. The human will is always subject to the divine.

2. DURING THE REFORMATION

There is one peculiarity of Lutheran Christology which deserves special attention. Luther held firmly to the doctrine of the two natures and their inseparable union in the Person of the Logos. But his doctrine of the real presence in the Lord's Supper necessitated the view that, after the ascension, the human nature of Christ is omnipresent. This led to the Lutheran view of the *communicatio idiomatum*, to the effect 'that each of Christ's natures permeates the other (*peridhoresis*), and that His humanity participates in the attributes of His divinity.' Neve, *Lutheran Symbolics*, p 132. But while certain divine attributes, such as omniscience, omnipresence, and omnipotence, were ascribed to the human nature, there was considerable hesitation in ascribing human attributes to the divine nature, and in course of time this side of the matter was dropped altogether. According to the *Formula of Concord* the divine nature imparts its attributes to the human nature, but the exercise of these is dependent on the will of the Son of God. It should be noted, however, that the *Formula* is very ambiguous, if not actually inconsistent in its statements. Cf Schmid, *Doctrinal Theology*, p 340. Small wonder therefore that Lutheran theologians themselves do not agree on the subject.

Lutheran Christology: communication of attributes

The doctrine of the communication of attributes led to a controversy in the Lutheran Church. Lutheran theologians evidently realized that the logic of the case required a communication of attributes at the very time of the union of the two natures. But on this assumption they at once faced the question, how to explain the life of humiliation as it is pictured in the pages of the Gospel. This led to the dispute between the Giessen and the Tuebingen theologians. The former held that Christ laid aside the divine attributes received in the incarnation, or used them only occasionally; and the latter, that He always possessed

[115]

them, but concealed them, or used them only secretly. Chemnitz is the most important representative of the former, and Brenz of the latter opinion. The Formula of Concord on the whole leans to the side of the former, and his view gradually prevailed in the Lutheran Church. In the work of Quenstedt, at whose hands the doctrine received its final shape, the presence of strictly divine powers in the manhood of Christ becomes a mere potentiality. There is a noticeable tendency among some of the Lutherans today to discard their characteristic view of the *communicatio idiomatum*, and to conform to the Reformed view that the properties of each one of the natures can be ascribed to the Person. Cf. *Lectures on the Augsburg Confession*, p 91 f; Sprecher, *Groundwork of a System of Evangelical Lutheran Theology*, p 458.

Reformed Christology; Second Helvetic Confession

The most complete official deliverance on the Reformed position with respect to the doctrine of Christ is found in the Second Helvetic Confession, prepared in 1566. We quote some of the most pertinent statements:

'Therefore the Son of God is co-equal and consubstantial with the Father, as touching His divinity; true God, and not by name only, or by adoption, or by special favour, but in substance and nature.... We therefore do abhor the blasphemous doctrine of Arius, uttered against the Son of God ... We also teach and believe that the eternal Son of the eternal God was made the Son of Man, of the seed of Abraham and David; not by means of any man, as Ebion affirmed, but that He was most purely conceived by the Holy Spirit, and born of the virgin Mary ... Moreover, our Lord Jesus Christ had not a soul without sense or reason, as Apollinaris thought; nor flesh without a soul, as Eunomius did teach; but a soul with its reason, and flesh with its senses ... We acknowledge, therefore, that there be in one and the same Jesus Christ our Lord two natures – the divine and the human nature; and we say that these two are so conjoined or united that they are not swallowed up, confounded, or mingled together, but rather united or joined together in one person (the properties of each nature being safe and remaining still), so that we do worship one Christ, our Lord, and not two ... As, therefore, we detest the heresy of Nestorius, which makes two Christs of one and dissolved the union of the person, so do we abominate the madness of Eutyches and of the Monothelites and Monophysites, who overthrow the propriety of the human nature. Therefore we do not teach that the divine nature in Christ did suffer, or that Christ, according to His human nature, is yet in the world, and so in every place. For we do neither think nor teach that the body of Christ ceased to be a true body after His glorying, or that it was deified and so deified that it put off the properties, as touching body and soul, and became altogether a divine nature and began to be one substance alone; therefore we do not allow or receive the unwitty subleties, and the intricate, obscure, and inconsistent disputations of Schwenkfeldt, and such other vain janglers, about this matter; neither are we Schwenkfeldians.'

3. IN THE NINETEENTH CENTURY

During the eighteenth century a striking change took place in the study of the Person of Christ. Up to that time the point of departure had been prevailingly theological and the resulting Christology was theocentric. Scholars engaged in constructing the doctrine of Christ took their starting-point in the Logos, the Second Person in the Trinity, and then sought to interpret the incarnation so as to do justice to the unity of the Person of the Saviour, but also to the integrity and veracity of both natures. But in the course of the eighteenth century there was a growing conviction that this was not the best method, and that more satisfying results could be obtained by beginning closer at home, namely, with the study of the historical Jesus. A new Christological period was ushered in. For more than a century the attention *Christology* was focused on the picture of the Saviour presented to us in the *of the* Gospels, and many are so delighted with the results of this *century* study that they speak of it as the rediscovery of Jesus. The point of view was anthropological, and the result was anthropocentric.

Now the statement of Mackintosh may be true, that 'these adjectives need imply no serious difference of opinion as to ultimate conclusions', since 'anthropocentric must not be confused with humanitarian', but as a matter of fact the new method was employed in such a manner as to yield destructive rather than constructive results. Its application went hand in hand with a strong aversion to authority and the supernatural, and with an insistent appeal to reason and experience. Not what the Bible teaches us concerning Christ, but our own discoveries in investigating the phenomena of His life and our experience of Him, was made the determining factor in forming a proper conception of Jesus. A far-reaching and pernicious distinction was made between the historical Jesus, delineated by the writers of the Gospels, and the theological Christ, the fruit of the fertile imagination of theological thinkers from the days of Paul on, whose image is now reflected in the Creeds of the Church. The Lord of Glory was shorn of all that is supernatural – or nearly so – and the doctrine of (concerning) Christ gave way for the teachings of Jesus. He who had always been regarded by the Church as an object of divine worship now became a mere teacher of morality. Attempts were not wanting, however, to retain something of the religious significance of Jesus Christ, while yet conceiving of Him in a manner that conformed to the spirit of the age. We limit ourselves to a brief indication of some of the outstanding views respecting Christ.

[a] *The view of Schleiermacher.* In the Christology of Schleiermacher Jesus can hardly be said to rise above the human level. The uniqueness of His Person consists in the fact that He possesses a perfect and unbroken sense of union with the divine, and also realizes to the full the destiny of man in His character of sinless perfection. He was the second Adam, truly man like the first, but placed in more favourable circumstances and remaining sinless and perfect in obedience. He is the new spiritual head of the race, capable of animating and sustaining the higher life of all mankind. His transcendent dignity finds its explanation in a special presence of God in Him, in His supreme God-consciousness. He is the perfectly religious man, the fountain of all true religion; and through living faith in Him all men may become perfectly religious. The extraordinary character of

Christology of Schleiermacher

Christ points to the fact that He had an unusual origin, for there is no hereditary influence in Him that makes for sinful tendencies. It is not necessary to accept the virgin birth. His Person was constituted by a creative act which elevated human nature to the plane of ideal perfection.

[b] *The conceptions of Kant and Hegel*. The speculative Rationalism of Germany also claims a sympathetic appreciation of specifically Christian doctrines, and finds in them a large deposit of rational truth.

(1) The Kantian Christ. To Kant Christ was first of all merely an abstract ideal, the ideal of ethical perfection. What saves is faith in this ideal, and not in Jesus as a Person. The Church made a mistake when it applied to Him epithets and conceptions which rightly belong only to the ethical ideal, which He merely symbolizes. This ethical ideal, which hovered before the mind of God from the beginning and can be called the Son of God, came down from heaven and becomes incarnate in the measure in which it is realized on earth in a perfect humanity. It is revealed in the truths of reason, and is the content of a rational faith, of which Jesus was the most eminent preacher and pioneer. If truly appropriated, it will save man irrespective of any personal relation to Jesus Christ. This view eliminates the Gospel of the New Testament, robs us of our divine Lord, and leaves us only a preacher of morality. *Kant's view of Christ*

(2) The Hegelian Christ. For Hegel the beliefs of the Church respecting the Person of Jesus Christ are merely man's stammering utterances of ontological ideas – symbols expressive of metaphysical truth. He regards human history as the process of God's becoming, the self-unfolding of reason under conditions of time and space. This is the only sense in which the Word became flesh and dwelt among us. God becomes incarnate in humanity, and this incarnation expresses the oneness of God and man. Though students of Hegel differ as to the question, whether he conceives of the incarnation as purely racial, or regards the unique incarnation of Jesus Christ as its culminating point, the latter seems to be the correct interpretation. According to Hegel the historical manifestation of God in Christ is viewed in two different ways. *Hegel's view of Christ*

Humanity in general regards Jesus as a human teacher, bringing the doctrine of the Kingdom of God and a supreme code of morality, and giving us an example by living up to this teaching even unto death. But believers take a higher view. Faith recognizes Jesus as divine and as terminating the transcendence of God. All that He does becomes a revelation of God. In Him God Himself draws near unto us, touches us, and so takes us up into the divine consciousness. Here we meet with a pantheistic identification of the human and the divine in the doctrine of Christ. Of course, the Church expresses this idea only in a symbolical and imperfect way; philosophy, we are told, gives it more perfect expression.

[c] *The Kenotic theories.* A remarkable attempt was made in the so-called Kenosis doctrine to improve on the theological construction of the doctrine of the Person of Christ. The term *Kenosis* is derived from Philippians 2:7, which says that Christ 'emptied Himself, taking the form of a servant'. The Greek word here translated 'emptied' is *ekenosen*, the aorist of *kenoo*. A misinterpretation of this passage became the Scriptural basis for the Kenosis doctrine, along with II Cor 8:9. These passages were interpreted as teaching that Christ at the incarnation emptied or divested Himself of His divinity. But there are serious objections to this interpretation: (1) as Dr Warfield has shown, the rendering 'emptied Himself' is contrary to the usual meaning of the term 'to make oneself of no account' (*Christology and Criticism*, p 375); and (2) the implied object of the action expressed is not Christ's divinity, but His being on an equality with God in power and glory. The Lord of glory made Himself of no account by becoming a servant. However, the Kenoticists base on this passage and on II Cor 8:9 the doctrine that the Logos literally became, that is, was changed into a man by reducing (depotentiating) Himself, either wholly or in part, to the dimensions of a man, and then increased in wisdom and power until at last He again assumed the divine nature.

This theory evidently resulted from a double motive, namely, the desire (1) to maintain the reality and integrity of the manhood of Christ; and (2) to throw into strong relief the exceeding great-

Basis of kenosis doctrine

ness of Christ's humiliation in that He, being rich, for our sakes became poor. It assumed several forms. According to Thomasius *Thomasius'* the divine Logos, while retaining His immanent or moral attri- *view* butes of absolute power or freedom, holiness, truth and love, divested Himself temporarily of His relative attributes of omni- potence, omnipresence, and omniscience, but after the resurrec- tion resumed these attributes. The theory of Gess, which was *View of* more absolute and consistent, and also more popular, is to the *Gess* effect that the Logos at the incarnation literally ceased from His cosmic functions and His eternal consciousness, and reduced Himself absolutely to the conditions and limits of human nature, so that His consciousness became purely that of a human soul. It comes very close to the view of Apollinaris. Ebrard, a Reformed *Ebrard's* scholar, assumed a double life of the Logos. On the one hand the *view* Logos reduced Himself to the dimensions of a man and possessed a purely human consciousness, but on the other hand He also retained and exercised His divine perfections in the trinitarian life without any interruption. The same ego exists at once in the eternal and in the temporal form, is both infinite and finite. And Martensen postulates in the Logos during the time of His *View of* humiliation a double life from two non-communicating centres. *Martensen* As the Son of God, living in the bosom of the Father, He con- tinued His trinitarian and cosmic functions, but as the depotenti- ated Logos He knew nothing of these functions and knew Him- self to be God only in the sense in which such knowledge is possible to the faculties of manhood.

This theory, once very popular in one form or another, and *Objections* still defended by some, has now lost a great deal of its charm. *to kenosis* It is subversive of the doctrine of the Trinity, contrary to that *doctrine* of the immutability of God, and at variance with those passages of Scripture which ascribe divine attributes to the historical Jesus. In the most absolute and most consistent form it teaches what La Touche calls 'incarnation by divine suicide'.

[d] *Dorner's conception of the incarnation.* Dorner may be *Dorner on* regarded as the main representative of the Mediating School on *progressive* the doctrine of Christ. He stresses the fact that God and man are *incarnation* akin, and that there is in the essential nature of God an urge to

communicate Himself to man. In view of this fact the incarnation was transcendentally and historically necessary, and would have taken place even if sin had not entered the world. The humanity of Christ was a new humanity, in which the receptivity of the human for the divine was raised to the highest point. This was necessary, since Christ was destined to be the Head of the redeemed race. Now the Logos, the ante-mundane principle of revelation and self-bestowal in God, joined Himself to this humanity. But the bestowal of the Logos to the new humanity was not complete at once; the incarnation was of a progressive nature. The measure of it was at every stage determined by the ever-increasing receptivity of the human nature for the divine, and it did not reach its final stage until the resurrection. This theory is subversive of Scripture, since it represents the incarnation as the birth of a mere man, who gradually became the God-man in His conception and birth. It is really a new and subtle form of the old Nestorian heresy. Moreover, by making the union in Christ to consist of a union of two persons, it makes this even less intelligible than it is otherwise.

[e] *Ritschl's view of the Person of Christ.* With the single *Ritschl's* exception of Schleiermacher no one has exercised greater influ-
Christology ence on present-day theology than Albrecht Ritschl. In his Christology he takes his starting-point in the work of Christ rather than in His Person, and emphasizes the former far more than the latter. The work of Christ determines the dignity of His Person. Christ is a mere man, but in view of the work He accomplished and the service He rendered we rightly attribute to Him the predicate of Godhead. He who does the work of God can properly be described in terms of God. Christ, revealing God in His grace, truth, and redemptive power, has for man the value of God, and is therefore also entitled to divine honour. Ritschl does not speak of the pre-existence, the incarnation, and the virgin birth of Christ, because these have no point of contact in the believing experience of the Christian community. His view of Christ is in reality only a modern counterpart of the con-
Modern struction put on the historical Jesus by Paul of Somosata.
Christology [f] *Christ in modern theology.* On the basis of the modern

pantheistic idea of the immanence of God, the doctrine of the Person of Christ is today often represented in a thoroughly naturalistic way. The representations vary, but the fundamental idea is generally the same, that of an essential unity of God and man. Christ differed from other men only in that He was more conscious of the God immanent in Him, and consequently is the highest revelation of the Supreme Being in His word and work. Essentially all men are divine, because God is immanent in all, and they are all sons of God, differing from Christ only in degree. The latter stands apart only in view of His greater receptivity for the divine and of His superior God-consciousness.

QUESTIONS FOR FURTHER STUDY

What ancient errors were virtually revived by Roscellinus and Abelard? What was the Christological Nihilism in vogue among the disciples of Abelard? How did Peter the Lombard view Christ? Did the Scholastics bring any new points to the fore? What is the Boethian definition of personality, generally accepted by the Scholastics? Did Luther give occasion for the characteristically Lutheran view of the *Communicatio idiomatum?* Where do we find the official Lutheran Christology? How can we account for the seemingly inconsistent representations of the Formula of Concord? What Christological differences were there in the Lutheran Church? What objections are there to the Lutheran view that divine attributes may be predicated of the human nature? How did the Lutherans and the Reformed differ in their interpretation of Phil 2.5–11? How does the Reformed Christology differ from the Lutheran? What is the main difference between the Christological discussions of the last two, and those of the previous centuries? How do the Christologies of Kant and Hegel, and those of Schleiermacher and Ritschl differ? What objections are there to the Kenosis doctrine? What are the objectionable features of the Christology of Modernism?

LITERATURE

The Formula of Concord and *the Second Helvetic Confession;* La Touche, *The Person of Christ in Modern Thought;* Schweitzer, *The Quest of the Historical Jesus;* Ottley, *The Doctrine of the Incarnation,* pp 485–553, 587–671; Mackintosh, *The Doctrine of the Person of Jesus Christ,* pp 223–284; Bruce, *The Humiliation of Christ,* pp 74–236; Sanday, *Christologies Ancient and Modern,* pp 59–83; Heppe, *Dogmatik des deutschen Protestantismus,* II, pp 78–178; Dorner, *History of Protestant Theology,* pp 95 f, 201 f, 322 f; Seeberg, *History of Doctrines,* II, pp 65, 109 f, 154 f, 229 f, 321 f, 323 f, 374, 387; Hagenbach, *History of Doctrines,* II, pp 267–275; III, pp 197–209, 343–353; Thomasius, *Dogmengeschichte,* II, pp 380–385, 388–429; Otten, *Manual of the History of Dogmas,* II, pp 171–195.

THE DOCTRINE OF
SIN AND GRACE
AND RELATED
DOCTRINES

I: THE ANTHROPOLOGY OF
   THE PATRISTIC PERIOD

I. THE IMPORTANCE OF ANTHROPOLOGICAL
   PROBLEMS

While the Christological controversies were agitating the East, *Importance* other problems, such as those of sin and grace, of the freedom *of doctrines* of the will and divine predestination, were coming to the fore- *grace* ground in the West. Their importance can scarcely be over-rated from the point of view of practical Christianity. Their bearing on the work of redemption is even more directly apparent than that of the Christological questions. It is in this field that the chief lines of demarcation between the great divisions of Christianity are found. Says Dr Cunningham: 'There never, indeed, has been much appearance of true personal religion where the divinity of the Son of God has been denied; but there has often been a profession of sound doctrine upon this subject, long maintained, where there has been little real religion. Where-as, not only has there never been much real religion where there was not a profession of substantially sound doctrine in regard to the points involved in the Pelagian controversy, but also – and this is the point of contrast – the decay of true religion has always been accompanied by a large measure of error in doctrine upon these subjects; the action and reaction of the two upon each other being speedy and manifest.' *Historical Theology*, I, p. 321.

2. THE ANTHROPOLOGY OF THE GREEK FATHERS

The main interest of the Greek Fathers lay in the field of Theo- *Gre* logy and Christology, and while they discussed anthropological *anthropology's* questions, they touched these but lightly. There was a certain *sin* dualism in their thinking about sin and grace, which led to rather confused representations with a preponderant emphasis on doctrines which show a manifest affinity with the later teachings of Pelagius rather than with those of Augustine. In a measure, it may be said, they prepared the way for Pelagianism. In our brief discussion a bare indication of the main ideas prevalent among them must suffice.

Their view of sin was, particularly at first, largely influenced by their opposition to Gnosticism with its emphasis on the physical necessity of evil and its denial of the freedom of the will. They stressed the fact that Adam's creation in the image of God did not involve his ethical perfection, but only the moral perfectability of his nature. Adam could sin and did sin, and thus came under the power of Satan, death, and sinful corruption. This physical corruption was propagated in the human race, but is not itself sin and did not involve mankind in guilt. There is no original sin in the strict sense of the word. They do not deny the solidarity of the human race, but admit its physical connection with Adam. This connection, however, relates only to the corporeal and sensuous nature, which is propagated from father to son, and not to the higher and rational side of human nature, which is in every case a direct creation of God. It exerts no immediate effect on the will, but affects this only mediately through the intellect. Sin always originates in the free choice of man, and is the result of weakness and ignorance. Consequently infants cannot be regarded as guilty, for they have inherited only a physical corruption.

It should be noted, however, that there were some departures *Origen's* from this general view. Origen admitting that a certain hereditary *anthropology* pollution attached to every one at birth, found the explanation for it in a pre-natal or pre-temporal fall of the soul, and came very close to a doctrine of original sin. And Gregory of Nyssa came even nearer to teaching this doctrine. But even the great Athanasius and Chrysostom scrupulously avoided it.

Naturally the doctrine of divine grace that was prevalent in *Doctrine of* the teachings of the Greek Fathers was profoundly influenced *grace* and largely determined by their conception of sin. On the whole the main emphasis was on the free will of man rather than on the

[128]

operation of divine grace. It is not the grace of God, but the free will of man that takes the initiative in the work of regeneration. But though it begins the work, it cannot complete it without divine aid. The power of God co-operates with the human will, and enables it to turn from evil and to do that which is well-pleasing in the sight of God. These Fathers do not always make a clear distinction between the good which the natural man is able to do and that spiritual good which requires the enabling power of the Holy Spirit.

3. THE GRADUAL EMERGENCE OF ANOTHER VIEW IN THE WEST

This Greek anthropology also influenced the West more or less in the second and third centuries, but in the third and fourth centuries the seed of the doctrine that was destined to become prevalent in the West gradually made its appearance, especially in the works of Tertullian, Cyprian, Hilary, and Ambrose.

Latin anthropology

The traducianism of Tertullian was substituted for the creationism of Greek theology, and this paved the way for the doctrine of innate sin, in distinction from innate evil. His famous maxim was, *Tradux animae, tradux peccati*, that is, the propagation of the soul involves the propagation of sin. He wedded his doctrine of traducianism to a theory of realism, according to which God created generic human nature, both body and soul, and individualizes it by procreation. In this process the nature does not lose its distinctive qualities, but continues to be intelligent, rational and voluntary at every point and in every one of its individualizations, so that its activities do not cease to be rational and responsible activities. The sin of the original human nature remains sin in all the individual existences of that nature. Tertullian represents only the beginning of Latin anthropology, and some of his expressions still remind one of the teachings of the Greek Fathers. He speaks of the innocence of infants, but probably assumes this only in the relative sense that they are free from actual sins; and does not altogether deny the freedom of the will. And though he reduces human efficiency to a mini-

Tertullian's contributions

[129]

mum, he sometimes uses language that savours of the synergisti theory of regeneration, that is, the theory that God and man worl together in regeneration.

Cyprian, Ambrose, and Hilary

In the writings of Cyprian there is an increasing tendency towards the doctrine of the original sinfulness of man, and of monergistic renewal of the soul. He seems to hold that the guil of original sin is not as great as that of actual sin. The doctrin of a sinful, as distinguished from a corrupt, nature is even mor clearly asserted in the writings of Ambrose and Hilary. The clearly teach that all men have sinned in Adam, and are therefor born in sin. At the same time they do not hold to an entire cor ruption of the human will, and consequently adhere to the synergistic theory of regeneration, though they appear to b more uncertain and contradictory in this matter than some of the earlier Fathers. All in all we find in them a gradual preparatior for the Augustinian view of sin and grace.

QUESTIONS FOR FURTHER STUDY

Who were the principal representatives of early Greek theology? How di their opposition to Gnosticism influence their anthropology? Did Platonisn have any effect on it? How did they conceive of the original condition of man Does the fall receive due emphasis in their teachings? How do you account fo their conception of sin as corruption rather than guilt? How did they conceiv of the propagation of sin? Who were the principal representatives of early Latin theology? How did their anthropology differ from that of the East How do you account for the difference? How do creationism and traducianisn differ?

LITERATURE

Morgan, *The Importance of Tertullian in the Development of Christian Dogma,* Fairweather, *Origen and Greek Patristic Theology;* Moody, *The Mind of the Early Converts,* cf Index; Scott, *The Nicene Theology,* pp 209–219; McGiffert *A History of Christian Thought,* cf. Index under *Sin;* Neander, *History of Christian Dogmas,* I, pp 182–192; Moxon, *The Doctrine of Sin,* pp 17–46 Seeberg, *History of Doctrines,* I, pp 109–161; Sheldon, *History of Christian Doctrine,* I, pp 104–110.

II: THE PELAGIAN AND AUGUSTINIAN DOCTRINES OF SIN AND GRACE

I. AUGUSTINE AND PELAGIUS

Augustine's view of sin and grace was moulded to some extent *Augustine:* by his deep religious experiences, in which he passed through *early life* great spiritual struggles and finally emerged into the full light of the Gospel. He tells us in his *Confessions* that he wandered far from the path of morality and religion, sought escape in Manichaeism and almost fell into its snares, but finally turned to Christ. He was never quite at rest during the years of his wanderings, and Ambrose was instrumental in winning him back to the faith. His conversion took place in a garden at Milan after deep agitation, weeping, and prayer. He was baptized in 387, and became bishop of Hippo in 395. Some find traces of a Manichaean influence in his gloomy view of human nature as fundamentally evil, and in his denial of the freedom of the will. It is more likely, however, that it was exactly his sense of inherent evil and spiritual bondage that caused him to turn to Manichaeism temporarily, for he combats the Manichaeans on the very points in question, holding that human nature was not originally and necessarily evil, and insisting on a measure of freedom as a basis for human responsibility.

Pelagius was a man of an entirely different type. In comparing *Augustine* the two Wiggers says: 'Their characters were diametrically *and* opposite. Pelagius was a quiet man, as free from mysticism as *Pelagius* from aspiring ambition; and in this respect, his mode of thought *compared* and of action must have been wholly different from that of Augustine. . . . Both therefore thought differently, according to their totally different spiritual physiognomy; and both, moreover, must have come into conflict just as soon as an external occasion should be presented.' *Augustinianism and Pelagianism,* p 47. Pelagius was a British monk, a man of austere life, of a blameless character, and of an even temper, and perhaps partly for that very reason a stranger to those conflicts of the soul, those struggles with sin, and those deep experiences of an all-renewing grace, which had such profound influence in moulding Augustine's thought.

The question is sometimes raised, whether Augustinianism was not simply a reaction against Pelagianism and therefore largely determined by its antipode. It may be said, however, that in their original form the two views were developed independently before the authors became acquainted with each other's teachings. At the same time it cannot be denied that, when the two engaged in mortal combat, the formal statement of Augustinianism was determined in some of its details by Pelagianism and *vice versa.* Both represented elements that were already present in the writings of the early Church Fathers.

2. THE PELAGIAN VIEW OF SIN AND GRACE

Pelagius' view of sin

The most important questions in debate between Pelagius and Augustine were those of free will and original sin. According to Pelagius, Adam, as he was created by God, was not endowed with positive holiness. His original condition was one of neutrality, neither holy nor sinful, but with a capacity for both good and evil. He had a free and entirely undetermined will, which enabled him to choose with equal facility either of these alternatives. He could either sin or refrain from sinning, as he saw fit. His mortality could not depend on his choice, for he was created mortal in the sense that he was already subject to the law of death. Without any antecedent evil in his nature, which might in any way determine the course of his life, he chose to sin. His fall into sin injured no one but himself, and left human nature unimpaired for good. There is no hereditary transmission of a sinful nature or of guilt, and consequently no such thing as original sin. Man is still born in the same condition in which Adam was before the fall. Not only is he free from guilt but also from pollution. There are no evil tendencies and desires in his nature which inevitably result in sin. The only difference between him and Adam is that he has the evil example before him. Sin does not consist in wrong affections or desires, but only in the separate acts of the will. It depends in every case on the voluntary choice of man. As a matter of fact man need not sin. He is, like Adam, endowed with perfect freedom of the will, with a liberty of choice or of indifference, so that he can, at any given moment, choose either good or evil. And the very fact that God commands man to do what is good is proof positive that he is able to do it. His responsibility is the measure of his ability. If notwithstanding this, sin is universal – and Pelagius admits that it is – this is due only to wrong education, to bad example, and to a long-established habit of sinning. In turning from evil to good, man is not dependent on the grace of God, though its operation is undoubtedly an advantage and will help him to overcome evil in his life. But the grace of which Pelagius speaks in this connection does not consist in an inward-working divine energy, or, in other words, in the influence of the Holy Spirit, inclining the will and empowering man to do that which is good, but only in external gifts and natural endowments, such as man's rational nature, the revelation of God in Scripture, and the example of Jesus Christ. Though there would hardly seem to be any place for the baptism of infants in such a system, Pelagius holds that they should be baptized, but regards their baptism merely as a rite of consecration or an anticipation of future forgiveness. Rather illogically, he takes the position that children are excluded from the Kingdom of Heaven, though not from a lower state of blessedness, which is called eternal life.

Pelagius' view of grace

3. THE AUGUSTINIAN VIEW OF SIN AND GRACE

Augustine's view of sin and grace was undoubtedly influenced somewhat by his early religious experiences and by its opposite in the Pelagian system, but was primarily determined by his careful study of the Epistle to the Romans and by his general conception of the soul's relation to God. He regarded man, even

Augustine on man's dependence on God

in his unfallen state, as absolutely dependent on God for the realization of his destiny.

[a] *His view of sin.* In opposition to the Manichaeans Augustine strongly emphasizes the voluntary character of sin. At the same time he believes that the act of sin by which the soul cut loose from God brought it under an evil necessity. As a result of the entrance of sin into the world man can no more will the true good, which is rooted in the love of God, nor realize his true destiny, but sinks ever deeper into bondage. This does not mean that he has lost all sense of God for, as a matter of fact, he continues to sigh after Him.

Augustine's view of sin Augustine does not regard sin as something positive, but as a negation or privation. It is not a substantial evil added to man, but a *privatio boni*, a privation of good. He finds the root principle of sin in that self-love which is substituted for the love of God. The general result of man's defection is seen in concupiscence, in the inordinate power of sensuous desires, as opposed to the law of reason, in the soul. From sin and the disturbance it introduced death resulted. Man was created immortal, which does not mean that he was impervious to death, but that he had the capacity of bodily immortality. Had he proved obedient, he would have been confirmed in holiness. From the state of the *posse non peccare et mori* (the ability not to sin and die) he would have passed to the state of the *non posse peccare et mori* (the inability to sin and die). But he sinned, and consequently entered the state of the *non posse non peccare et mori* (the inability not to sin and die).

Through the organic connection between Adam and his descendants, the former transmits his fallen nature, with the guilt and corruption attaching to it, to his posterity. Augustine conceives of the unity of the human race, not federally, but realistically. The whole human race was germinally present in the first man, and therefore also actually sinned in him. The race is not constituted individually, that is, of a large number of relatively independent individuals, but organically, that is, of a large number of individualizations which are organic parts of that generic human nature that was present in Adam. And therefore the sin of the human nature was the sin of all its individualizations.

As the result of sin man is totally depraved and unable to do any spiritual good. Augustine does not deny that the will still has a certain natural freedom. It is still capable of acts that are civilly good, and from a lower standpoint even praiseworthy. At the same time he maintains that man, separated from God, burdened with guilt, and under the dominion of evil, cannot will that which is good in the sight of God. As he sees it, that only is good in the sight of God which springs from the motive of love to God.

[b] *His view of grace.* The will of man stands in need of renewal, and this is exclusively a work of God from start to finish – a work of divine grace. It is necessary to guard against a possible misunderstanding here. When Augustine ascribes the renewal of man to divine grace only, and in this connection speaks of 'irresistible grace', he does not mean to intimate that divine grace forces the will, contrary to the nature of man as a free agent, but rather that it so changes the will that man voluntarily chooses that which is good. The will of man is renewed and thus restored to its true freedom. God can and does so operate on the will that man of his own free choice turns to virtue and holiness. In this way the grace of God becomes the source of all good in man. *Augustine's view of grace*

From what has been said it follows that Augustine's doctrine of regeneration is entirely monergistic. The operation of the Holy Spirit is necessary, not merely for the purpose of supplying a deficiency, but for the complete renewal of the inner disposition of man, so that he is brought into spiritual conformity to the law. Says Shedd: 'Grace is imparted to sinful man, not because he believes, but in order that he may believe; for faith itself is the gift of God.' The divine efficiency in regeneration results in the conversion of the sinner, in which man may be said to co-operate. Augustine distinguishes several stages in the work of divine grace, which he calls 'prevenient grace', 'operative grace', and 'co-operative grace'. In the first the Holy Spirit employs the law to produce the sense of sin and guilt; in the second He uses the Gospel for the production of that faith in Christ and His atoning work which issues in justification and peace with God; and in the third the renewed will of man co-operates with Him in the life-long work of sanctification. The work of grace includes the entire renewal of man in the image of God and the spiritual transformation of the sinner into a saint. It is hardly in line with his main thought when he also represents the Church as a more or less independent dispenser of divine grace, and speaks of baptismal regeneration.

Augustine's view of predestination

Augustine's representation of the grace of God as the efficient cause of salvation led on to his doctrine of predestination. What God does in time for the gracious renewal of the sinner, He willed to do in His eternal plan. At first Augustine manifested a tendency to consider predestination as contingent on divine foreknowledge, and to represent God as electing those of whom He knew that they would believe. This really makes predestination conditional on the foreseen free action of man. He soon saw, however, that consistency and a fair interpretation of the relevant passages of Scripture, demanded that he should consider man's choice of the good and his faith in Christ as themselves the effect of divine grace; and therefore modified his doctrine of predestination accordingly. He usually views predestination in connection with the sinner's salvation, and even held that it might be called this salvation viewed *sub specie aeternitatis* (from the point of view of eternity). With reference to the non-elect, he conceives of the decree of God as one of pretermission only. Reprobation differs from election in this that it is not accompanied with any direct divine efficiency to secure the result intended. But while Augustine is a strict predestinarian, there is also here an element in his teachings that is foreign to his main thought, namely, the idea that the grace of regeneration can again be lost. He holds that only those who are regenerated *and persevere*, or in whom, after loss, the grace of regeneration is restored, are finally saved. There is a redeeming feature, however, in his assertion that the elect never die in an unregenerate condition.

4. PELAGIAN AND SEMI-PELAGIAN CONTROVERSIES

In the Pelagian controversy the views of Augustine on sin and grace were put to the test. Small wonder that his views met with opposition, since the problems involved had never yet been discussed in a thorough manner. The Eastern Church preferably emphasized the element of freedom in human nature, in opposition to the pagan idea of fate or destiny. It was admitted that the human will was corrupt, and had become subject to Satan, to sensuous temptations, and to death; and that the new life was communicated in baptism. On the whole the Greek Fathers were content with placing the grace of God and free will side by side.

In view of all this it was perfectly natural that Augustine's *Propagation* deriving everything, free will included, from divine grace, *and* collided with the opposite tendency, as represented in Pelagius. *of* The two systems were absolute antipodes. Pelagius advanced *Pelagianism* his views first at Rome from AD 409 to 411. His system was introduced into the North African Church by his pupil Celestius. At the same time Pelagius went to Palestine to propagate his views. The matter of his departure from the generally accepted teachings of the Church was brought up in several Councils. In 412 Celestius was adjudged heretical at Carthage, and was excommunicated when he refused to retract his opinions. Pelagius himself was accused of heresy before the Synods of Jerusalem and Diospolis (also in Palestine), but by specious explanations and by qualifying several of his statements he succeeded in satisfying his judges, and was acquitted, 414–416. In the year 416 Pelagianism was condemned as a heresy by the Synods of Mileve and Carthage, and this decision was finally endorsed by the vacillating bishop of Rome, Zozimus, who had first handed Pelagius a certificate of orthodoxy 418. Finally, in 431 the Council of Ephesus, which condemned Nestorianism, also passed a sentence of condemnation on Pelagianism.

Between the extremes of Augustinianism and Pelagianism a *Semi-* mediating movement arose, which is known in history as Semi- *Pelagianism* Pelagianism. As a matter of fact that halfway position served to bring out clearly – as nothing else could have done – that only a system like the Augustinian, with its strong logical coherence, could maintain its ground successfully against the onslaughts of Pelagius. Semi-Pelagianism made the futile attempt to steer clear of all difficulties by giving a place to both divine grace and human will as co-ordinate factors in the renewal of man, and by basing predestination on foreseen faith and obedience. It did not deny human corruption, but regarded the nature of man as weakened or diseased rather than as fatally injured by the fall. Fallen human nature retains an element of freedom, in virtue of which it can co-operate with divine grace. Regeneration is the joint product of both factors, but it is really man and not God that begins the work.

Semi-Pelagian views spread especially in Gaul. Their chief representative was Cassian, abbot of Massilia (Marseilles). They found able defenders also in Faustus of Rhegium and Gennadius of Massilia. But they lacked internal coherence, and could not hold out in debate against such a close-knit and compact system as Augustinianism. The system was condemned at the important Council of Orange, which vindicated a moderate Augustinianism.

Augustine's doctrine of sin and grace was adopted as the *Augustini-* anthropology of the Western Church, though its acceptance was *anism as* never general even there. Influential men, like Leo and Gregory, *accepted by* Bede and Alcuin, adhered to it, though they were not as strong *the Church* as Augustine in asserting the preterition and reprobation of the lost. They placed great emphasis on the enslavement of the human will, and on the absolute need of divine grace in renewal. It may be said that the most important leaders of the Church remained true to the most practical part of Augustinian anthropology for two or three centuries after Augustine. And the Synod of Orange adopted a moderate Augustinianism as the doctrine of the Church. Pelagianism and Semi-Pelagianism were both condemned as contrary to the orthodox faith. The Augustinian doctrine of salvation by grace only was victorious, but the doctrine of the irresistible grace of predestination was supplanted by that of the sacramental grace of baptism. And the doctrine of a double predestination – predestination also to evil – was abandoned in AD 529. Gradually the general decline in the Roman Catholic Church led to a drift in the direction of Semi-Pelagianism, which had long before secured a rather sure footing in the East. In course of time the Latin Church adopted the anthropology of the Greek Church and adhered to it ever since.

QUESTIONS FOR FURTHER STUDY

In what respect did the anthropology of the East differ from that of the West? Were the Pelagian and Augustinian tenets new in the Church? What was the fundamental error of Pelagius? How did his doctrine of free will affect the doctrines of sin and grace? Why did he stress the free will of man? Is his doctrine of free will psychologically tenable? Why is his explanation of the universality of sin insufficient? How did he conceive of the grace of God? What value did he ascribe to it? Did he altogether deny grace as an inward spiritual energy? What Scriptural basis did he have for his doctrine? How did Augustine conceive of the freedom of willing before and after the fall? Did he ascribe a voluntary character to sin or not? Did he regard concupiscence as sin or not? How do you account for his emphasis on sin as privation? Did his doctrine of original sin go beyond that of the earlier Fathers? If so, how? How did he conceive of the transmission of sin? How did his doctrine of sin and grace lead him to his doctrine of predestination? What was his conception of the decree of reprobation?

LITERATURE

Wiggers, *Augustinianism and Pelagianism;* Cunningham, *St. Austin;* Moxon, *The Doctrine of Sin,* pp 47–140; Cunningham, *Historical Theology,* I, pp 321–358; Harnack, *History of Dogma,* V, pp 61–261; Seeberg, *History of Doctrines,* I, pp 328–381; Loofs, *Dogmengeschiedenis,* pp 183–238; Thomasius, *Dogmengeschichte,* I, pp 437–557; Neander, *History of Christian Dogmas,* I, pp 345–356; Otten, *Manual of the History of Dogmas,* pp 357–386; Sheldon, *History of Christian Doctrine,* I, pp 222–243; Shedd, *History of Doctrine,* II, pp 26–110; Fisher, *History of Christian Doctrine,* pp 176–198; McGiffert, *A History of Christian Thought,* II, pp 71–143.

III: THE ANTHROPOLOGY OF
THE MIDDLE AGES

I. THE VIEWS OF GREGORY THE GREAT

Gregory the Great, born at Rome about AD 540, was a diligent
student of Augustine, Jerome, and Ambrose. His religious
disposition prompted him to renounce the world, and after the
death of his father he devoted his wealth to good works, and
particularly to the building of cloisters for the promotion of the
purely contemplative life. Unanimously elected Pope in 590,
he accepted the position only with great hesitation. Though not
an original thinker, he became an author of great repute and did
much to disseminate sound doctrine. Next to Augustine he was
the most influential authority in the Church. In fact, Augustine
was understood in the early Middle Ages, only as interpreted
by Gregory. For that reason the history of doctrine in the Middle
Ages must begin with him.

Anthropology of Gregory the Great The Augustinianism of Gregory was somewhat attenuated.
He explains the entrance of sin into the world by the weakness
of man. The first sin of Adam was a free act, in which he surren-
dered his love to God and became subject to spiritual blindness
and spiritual death. Through the sin of the first man all men
became sinners and as such subject to condemnation. This
sounds rather Augustinian, but Gregory did not carry these
ideas through consistently. He regarded sin as a weakness or
disease rather than as guilt, and taught that man had not lost
the freedom but only the goodness of the will. At the same time
he stressed the fact that without grace there can be no salvation
nor any human merits. The work of redemption is begun by the
grace of God. Prevenient grace causes man to will the good, and
subsequent grace enables him to do it. The change in man is
begun in baptism, which works faith and cancels the guilt of past

[140]

sins. The will is renewed and the heart is filled with the love of God, and thus man is enabled to merit something with God.

Gregory retained the doctrine of predestination only in a modified form. While he speaks of the irresistibility of grace, and of predestination as the secret counsel of God respecting the certain and definite number of the elect, this is after all only a predestination based on foreknowledge. God appoints a certain definite number unto salvation, since He knows that they will accept the Gospel. But no one can be certain of his own election or of that of any other person.

His view of predestination

2. THE GOTTSCHALKIAN CONTROVERSY

Augustine had occasionally spoken of a double predestination, and Isidore of Seville still wrote of it as being twofold. But many of the Augustinians in the seventh, eighth, and ninth centuries lost sight of this double character of predestination, and interpreted it as Gregory had done. Then came Gottschalk, who found rest and peace for his soul only in the Augustinian doctrine of election, and contended earnestly for a double predestination, that is, a predestination of the lost as well as of the saved. He was careful, however, to limit the divine efficiency to the redemptive line and the production of holiness, and to regard sin merely as the object of a permissive decree which nevertheless rendered it certain. He explicitly rejected the idea of a predestination based on foreknowledge, since this makes the divine decree dependent on the acts of man. Prescience merely accompanies predestination and attests the justice of it.

Gottschalk on predestination

He met a great deal of unwarranted opposition. His opponents did not understand him and lodged against him the familiar accusation that his teachings made God the author of sin. His doctrine was condemned at Mayence in AD 848, and the following year he himself was scourged and condemned to life-long imprisonment. A debate ensued, in which several influential theologians, such as Prudentius, Ratramnus, Remigius, and others, defended the doctrine of a double predestination as Augustinian, while especially Rabanus and Hincmar of Rheims

Opposition to Gottschalk

assailed it. But this controversy proved to be after all little more than a debate about words. Both the defenders and the assailants were at heart Semi-Augustinians. They expressed the same idea in different ways. The former spoke with Augustine of a double predestination, but based reprobation on foreknowledge, while the latter applied the term 'predestination' only to the election to life, and also based reprobation on prescience. Both subscribed to the idea of sacramental grace, and feared that the strict theory of predestination would rob the sacraments of their spiritual value and make them mere forms.

The decisions of the Councils of Quiercy and Valence were altogether in harmony with these views, the former reproducing the views of the assailants, and the latter those of the defenders. The statement of the Council of Valence reads as follows: 'We confess a predestination of the elect to life, and a predestination of the wicked to death; but that, in the election of those who are saved, the mercy of God precedes good merit, and in the condemnation of those who will perish, evil merit precedes the righteous judgment of God. But that in predestination God has determined only those things which He Himself would do, either from gratuitous mercy or in righteous judgment . . . But that in the wicked He foreknew the wickedness because it comes from them; and does not predestinate it, because it does not come from Him.' Quoted by Seeberg, *History of Doctrines*, II, p 33. These Councils met in 853 (Quiercy) and 855 (Valence).

3. THE CONTRIBUTION OF ANSELM

There was one great thinker during the Middle Ages who not only reproduced the Augustinian anthropology, but also made a positive contribution to it, namely, Anselm of Canterbury.

Anselm on original sin and its transmission

[a] *His doctrine of sin.* He emphasizes the doctrine of original sin, but stresses the fact that the term 'original' does not refer to the origin of the human race, but to that of the individual in the present condition of things. In his opinion original sin may also be called *peccatum naturale* (natural sin), though it does not belong to human nature as such, but represents a condition into

which it has come since creation. By the fall man became guilty and polluted, and both guilt and pollution are passed on from father to child. All sin, original as well as actual, constitutes guilt.

Since sin presupposes the exercise of free will, he raises the question, how sin can be ascribed to children, and why infants should be baptized for its remission. He finds the explanation in the fact that human nature apostatized after creation. Like Augustine he regards every child as an individualized part of that general human nature which Adam possessed, so that it has actually sinned in Adam and is therefore also guilty and polluted. If Adam had not fallen, human nature would not have apostatized, and a holy nature would have passed from father to son. In the present state of affairs, however, a sinful nature is propagated. Original sin therefore has its origin in a sin of nature, while later actual sin is altogether individual in character.

Anselm raises the question, whether the sins of the immediate ancestors are imputed to posterity as well as the sin of the first father. And his answer is negative, because these sins were not committed by the common nature in Adam. The sin of Adam was unique; there never was a second like it, because it was the transgression of an individual who included within himself the whole of humanity. This is undoubtedly a weak point in the system of Anselm, since all the following sins are committed by the same human nature, though individualized, and because it does not answer the question, why only the *first* sin of Adam is imputed to his posterity, and not his later sins. He further calls attention to the fact that in Adam the guilt of nature, that is, original sin, rests upon the guilt of the individual, while in his posterity the guilt of the individual rests upon the guilt of nature. In the person of Adam the whole human race was tried. At this point he approaches the later covenant idea.

[b] *His doctrine of the freedom of the will.* Anselm also discusses the problem of the freedom of the will and makes some valuable suggestions. He declares the popular definition of freedom as the power of sinning or not sinning, or as the *possibilitas utriusque partis*, to be inadequate. It does not hold with reference to the holy angels. They have perfect moral freedom, and yet are not

Anselm on the freedom of the will

able to sin. He held that the will which, of itself and without external compulsion, is so strongly determined to the right as to be unable to desert the path of rectitude, is freer than the will which is so feebly determined to the right as to be able to depart from the way of righteousness. But if this is so, the question arises, whether we can call the apostasy of the angels and of our first parents a free act. To this Anselm replies that the act of our first parents was certainly an act of spontaneity, of pure self-will, but not an act of genuine freedom. They sinned, not because of their freedom, but in spite of it, by virtue of the *possibilitas peccandi* (the possibility of sinning). The power to do otherwise than they were doing added nothing to their freedom, because they were voluntarily holy without it. He distinguishes between true freedom and the voluntary faculty itself. The former was lost, but the latter was not. The true end and destination of the will is not to choose *either* good or evil, but to choose the good. The voluntary faculty was intended by the Creator to will the right and nothing else. Its true freedom consists in its *self-determination to holiness*. This means the rejection of the idea that freedom is *caprice*, and that the will was created with the liberty of indifference. It is by creation shut up to the choice of but one object, namely, holiness. But the acceptance of this end must be a self-determination, and not a compulsion from without. The power to choose the wrong, when given for the purpose of probation, subtracts from the perfection of real freedom, because it exposes to the hazards of an illegitimate choice.

4. PECULIARITIES OF ROMAN CATHOLIC ANTHROPOLOGY

The Roman Catholic Church clearly harboured two tendencies, the one Semi-Augustinian and the other Semi-Pelagian, of which the latter gradually gained the upper hand. We cannot follow the discussions of all the Scholastics here, and therefore merely state the characteristic teachings that gradually emerged.

Rome on original righteousness The view gradually prevailed that original righteousness was not a natural but a supernatural endowment of man. Man, it was held, naturally consists of flesh and spirit, and from these diverse or contrary propensities there arises a conflict (concupiscence), which often makes right action difficult. To offset the disadvantages of this original languor of nature, God added to man a certain remarkable gift, namely, original righteousness, which served as a check to keep the inferior part of man in proper subjection to the superior, and the superior to God. This original righteousness was a supernatural gift, a *donum superadditum*, something added to the nature of man, who was created without positive righteousness, but also without positive unrighteousness.

With the entrance of sin into the world man lost this original righteousness. This means that the apostasy of man did not involve the loss of any natural endowment of man, but only the loss of a supernatural gift, which was foreign to the essential nature of man. Original righteousness was lost and man lapsed back into the condition of an unrestrained conflict between flesh and spirit. The supremacy of the higher over the lower element in his nature was fatally weakened. Man was brought back to the neutral condition, in which he was neither sinful nor holy, but from the very constitution of his nature subject to a conflict between the flesh and the spirit. *Its view of the loss of this righteousness*

Since Adam, the head of the human race, was constituted the representative of all his descendants, they all sinned in him and come into the world burdened with original sin. While the Scholastics differ very much as to the nature of original sin, the prevailing opinion is that it is not something positive, but rather the absence of something that ought to be present, particularly the privation of original justice, though some add a positive element, namely, an inclination to evil. By original justice some understand that original righteousness that was super-added to man, and others in addition to this also what is called the *justitia naturalis*. This sin is universal and is voluntary as derived from the first parent. It should not be identified with concupiscence, with the evil desires and lusts that are present in man, for these are not sin in the proper sense of the word. *Its view of original sin*

Roman Catholics reject the idea of man's spiritual impotence *Its synergism*

[145]

and his utter dependence on the grace of God for renewal. They adopt the theory of synergism in regeneration, that is, that man co-operates with God in the spiritual renewal of the soul. He prepares and disposes himself for the grace of justification, which is said to consist in infused righteousness. In the days of the Reformation the monergism of the Reformers was opposed by the Roman Catholic Church with greater vehemence than any other doctrine.

QUESTIONS FOR FURTHER STUDY

Why did the Church hesitate to accept strict Augustinianism? In what direction did the Church move at first, and what view gradually gained the upper hand? How did the views of Gregory the Great differ from those of Augustine? Did Gottschalk hold that God predestinated the reprobate to commit sin? What practical interests were thought to be endangered by his teaching? In what respect was Anselm's conception of original sin defective? Did he give an adequate explanation of the transmission of sin? How did his conception of the freedom of the will differ from that of Pelagius? What different views of original sin were current among the Scholastics? Do Roman Catholics believe that the fall of man affected the constitutional nature of man? How do they define original sin? How does it differ from concupiscence? Do they ascribe freedom to the will after the fall? In what sense?

LITERATURE

Moxon, *The Doctrine of Sin*, pp 142–165; Otten, *Manual of the History of Dogmas*, II, pp 129–170; Welch, *Anselm and His Work;* Seeberg, *History of Doctrines*, II, pp 21–23, 30–33, 114–118, and so on, cf Index; Neander, *History of Christian Dogmas*, II, pp 508–512; Sheldon, *History of Christian Doctrine*, I, pp 343–356; Thomasius, *Dogmengeschichte*, II, pp 115–121, 125–142; Shedd, *History of Christian Doctrine*, II, pp 111–151; Fisher, *History of Christian Doctrine*, cf Index.

IV: THE ANTHROPOLOGY OF THE PERIOD OF THE REFORMATION

1. THE ANTHROPOLOGY OF THE REFORMERS

Reformers on Adam's relation to his descendants

The Reformers followed Augustine and Anselm in their construction of the doctrine of sin and grace, though with some modifications. They gave a more exact definition of the relation of Adam's sin to that of his descendants by substituting for the realistic theory of Tertullian, Augustine, and Anselm, the covenant idea. It is true that they did not fully develop this idea; yet they utilized it in defining the relation between Adam and his descendants. Beza especially emphasized the fact that Adam was not only the natural head of the human race, but also its federal representative; and that consequently his first sin is imputed as guilt to all his descendants. And because all are guilty in Adam, they are also born in a polluted condition.

Their view of sin

Calvin stressed the fact that original sin is not merely a privation, but also a total corruption of human nature. And where Augustine sought this corruption primarily in the sensual appetites, Calvin pointed out that it has its seat in the higher as well as in the lower faculties of the soul, and that it operates through these as a positive evil. In opposition to the Roman Catholics the Reformers maintained that original sin is something more than a mere absence of original justice; and that also the first movements of the desires, which tend in the direction of sin, are actually sins, even before they are assented to by the will, and not merely the *fomes* or fuel of sin. They are indwelling sins, which make man guilty and worthy of condemnation. According to Calvin and the Reformers generally, original sin is a hereditary depravity and corruption of human nature, rendering man obnoxious to the divine wrath and producing in him the works of the flesh. We are by nature guilty and polluted in Adam, and stand justly condemned in the sight of God.

Their conception of total depravity

The generally prevailing view among the Reformers was that, as a result of the fall, man is totally depraved, incapable of doing any spiritual good, and therefore also unable to make the least advance toward his recovery. Luther and Calvin express themselves strongly on this point, and Zwingli is in general agreement with them here, though he seemingly regards original sin as a disease and a condition rather than as sin in the proper sense of the word. Even Melanchthon subscribed to this view at first, but in a later period modified his opinion. But while maintaining the doctrine of total depravity, the Reformers also held that the unregenerate could still perform civil righteousness, a righteousness which God approves in the social relations of men. Even Luther, who uses exceptionally strong expressions respecting the spiritual inability of man, clearly recognizes his ability to do good in secular affairs. Melanchthon went even further than Luther; and Calvin did more than anyone else to direct attention to the fact that there is a common grace of God, which enables man to perform civil righteousness.

Their view of the need of grace

The natural correlative of the doctrine of total depravity is that of the absolute dependence of man on the grace of God for renewal. Luther, Calvin, and Zwingli are a unit on this point, but Melanchthon, though at first in perfect agreement with Luther, under the stress of the opposition to the doctrine of the bondage of the will, ascribed a certain measure of material freedom or spiritual power to the will and taught a synergistic theory of regeneration.

Their doctrine of predestination

In view of all the preceding it was but natural that the Reformers should be strict predestinarians. Luther and Calvin both believed in a double predestination, though the former does not make the doctrine as prominent as the latter and sometimes manifests an inclination to deny the doctrine of reprobation or to make it dependent on foreknowledge. Zwingli also taught this doctrine in unmistakable terms, and was not as cautious as Calvin in describing the relation of the divine agency to sin, but insists on reprobation as an efficient decree. Melanchthon, of course, wavered here, as he did in his teaching on sin and regeneration. He avoided the subject of predestination as much as possible.

After the Reformation the covenant idea was more fully developed, especially in the writings of Bullinger, Polanus, Gomarus, Cloppenburg, and Cocceius. It became evident that Adam was not merely the natural head of humanity, but also its federal head, the moral and legal representative of all his descendants. As a result the idea that all men sinned in Adam literally and realistically gave way to the thought that they sinned in him representatively. Because the first man sinned as the legal representative of all his descendants, the guilt of his sin is imputed to them, and consequently they are also born corrupt. The realistic theory was abandoned, more generally in Reformed than in Lutheran circles, and the covenant idea was utilized in its stead to explain the transmission of sin.

2. THE SOCINIAN POSITION

Socinianism represents a reaction against the doctrine of the Reformation, and in the doctrines of sin and grace it is simply a revival of the old Pelagian heresy. According to it the image of God in which man was formed consisted merely in man's dominion over the lower creation, and not in any moral perfection or excellence of nature. Since Adam had no positive righteousness or holiness, he could not lose it as the result of sin. Though he sinned and incurred the divine displeasure, his moral nature remained intact, and is transmitted unimpaired to his posterity. Man dies, not because of the sin of Adam, but because he was created mortal. Men are even now by nature like Adam in that they have no proneness or tendency to sin, but are placed in somewhat more unfavourable circumstances because of the examples of sin which they see and of which they hear. While this increases their chances of falling into sin, they can avoid sin altogether, and some of them actually do. And even if they do fall in sin and are thus guilty of transgression, they do not therefore incur the divine wrath. God is a kind and merciful Father,

Socinian view of sin and deliverance

who knows their frailty and is quite ready to forgive them when they come to him with penitent hearts. They need no Saviour nor any extraordinary interposition of God to secure their salvation. No change in their moral nature is required, and no provision for effecting such a change was made. However, the teachings and example of Christ are helpful in leading them in the right direction.

3. ARMINIAN ANTHROPOLOGY

In the beginning of the seventeenth century the Calvinistic doctrine of sin and grace met with a determined opposition in the Netherlands, which centred in the great Arminian controversy. Arminius, a disciple of Beza, and at first a strict Calvinist, became a convert to the doctrine of universal grace and free will. He denied the decree of reprobation and toned down the doctrine of original sin. His successor at Leyden, Episcopius, and his other followers, such as Uytenbogaert, Grotius, Limborch, and others, departed still further from the accepted doctrine of the Church, and finally embodied their views in a remonstrance, consisting of five articles.

Arminian doctrine of sin

The position taken by the Arminians is practically that of Semi-Pelagianism. While they do believe that Adam's transgression had an evil effect on the spiritual condition of all his descendants, they reject the doctrine of original sin as it was taught by the Churches of the Reformation. They maintain that the guilt of Adam's sin is not imputed to his descendants, though its pollution is passed on from father to son. This pollution they do not regard as sin in the proper sense of the word but only as a disease or a weakness. It does not bring man under a sentence of condemnation, but weakens his nature, so that he is incapable of attaining to eternal life, either by re-establishing himself in the favour of God or by discovering for himself a way of salvation. They do not believe in the total depravity of human nature, though they occasionally express themselves as if they do, but leave room for the free will of man in the material sense of the word, that is, as a natural power or ability in man to do something that is spiritually good, so that he can also in some measure prepare himself for turning to God and doing His will.

They also propose a theory of grace which differs essentially *Arminian view of grace* from that of the Confessions, distinguishing three different degrees in grace, namely, (a) prevenient or common grace; (b) the grace of evangelical obedience; and (c) the grace of perseverance. The Holy Spirit confers on all men sufficient grace to counteract the effect of the inherited depravity and to enable them to co-operate with the Spirit of God in regeneration. If some are not regenerated, it must be due to the failure of the human will to co-operate with the divine. He who makes proper use of this sufficient or enabling grace becomes the object of God's efficient grace. He receives the higher grace of evangelical obedience, and in the way of obedience may become a partaker of the still higher grace of perseverance.

This theory of sufficient grace is supposed to safeguard the doctrine of human responsibility. Since original sin cannot be imputed to man as a fault, God cannot demand faith of him irrespective of the bestowal of enabling grace. But if He bestows a grace on him, as He does, which removes his spiritual inability, He also has the perfect right to demand faith. If man resists this grace of God and refuses to co-operate with it, he is naturally responsible for the fact that he is not regenerated.

In harmony with these views the Arminians naturally did not *Arminian view of predestination* believe in absolute election or reprobation, but based election on foreseen faith, obedience, and perseverance, and reprobation on foreseen unbelief, disobedience, and persistence in sin. In that respect they were far less consistent than the Socinians, who clearly saw that, if they rejected predestination, they had to reject foreknowledge as well.

4. THE POSITION OF THE SYNOD OF DORT

This Synod was summoned by the States General of the Netherlands in 1618, and was indeed an august assembly, consisting of eighty-four members and eighteen political delegates. Forty-eight of these were Hollanders, and the rest foreigners, representing England, Scotland, the Palatinate, Hesse, Nassau, Bremen, Emden, and Switzerland. The delegates of France and Brandenburg did not appear. The Arminians were not seated as members, but appeared only as defendants. One hundred and fifty-four sessions were held, and a large number of conferences. It was the most representative body that ever met. The Synod was uncompromising in the doctrinal matters that were brought before it: it rejected the five Articles of the *Remonstrance*, and adopted five thoroughly Calvinistic Canons, in which the doctrines of the Reformation, and particularly of Calvin, on the disputed points are set forth with clearness and precision, and the Arminian errors are exposed and rejected.

Synod of Dort on predestination

The Synod affirmed the doctrine of a double predestination, based on the good pleasure of God, and not on foreseen faith and unbelief. Both election and reprobation are therefore absolute. Election is from the fallen race subject to condemnation on account of the sin of Adam; and reprobation consists in preterition, the passing by of a certain number of the fallen race, leaving them in their ruin and condemnation on account of their sin.

On original sin and human depravity

It asserted the doctrine of original sin in the strict sense of the word. Since Adam was the legal representative of all his descendants, the guilt of his first sin is imputed to them, and in consequence the corruption of human nature is also propagated to them. They are totally corrupt, that is, corrupt in every part of their being and so corrupt that they cannot do any spiritual good and cannot make a single effort to restore the broken relationship with God. At the same time the Canons also say: 'There remain, however, in man since the fall, the glimmerings of natural light, whereby he retains some knowledge of God, of natural things, and of the difference between good and evil, and discovers some regard for virtue, good order in society, and for maintaining an orderly external deportment. But so far is this light of nature from being sufficient to bring him to a saving knowledge of God, that he is incapable of using it aright even in things natural and civil.' III and IV, Art 4.

On regeneration

Regeneration is regarded as strictly monergistic, and not at all as the work of God and man. Without regenerating grace no one can turn to God, and none can accept the offer of salvation apart from an efficient act of God founded on election. Yet salvation is offered in all seriousness to all who hear the Gospel on condition of faith and repentance. They who are lost will have only themselves to blame.

The decisions of the Synod of Dort were of great importance for various reasons: (a) They were deliverances on some of the most important points of Reformed theology, which up to that time had not received such careful consideration. (b) They were to all intents deliverances of an Ecumenical Council, composed of many of the ablest theologians of the day, the most representative body that ever met. (c) They terminated the uncertainty that prevailed in the churches of the Netherlands, an uncertainty that was also felt in other countries, and warded off a great danger that threatened the Reformed faith. (d) They had a determining influence on the composition of the later Westminster Confession.

5. THE POSITION OF THE SCHOOL OF SAUMUR

The School of Saumur made an attempt to tone down the Calvinism of the Synod of Dort especially on two points. *Hypothetical universalism* Amyraldus distinguished between a universal and conditional, and a limited and unconditional decree. In the former God decreed to provide a universal salvation through the mediation of Jesus Christ, to be offered to all alike on condition of faith, and in the latter He, seeing that of himself no man would believe, elected some to eternal life and decided to give them the necessary grace of faith and repentance. And Placaeus, another representa- *Mediate imputation* tive of the School, denied the immediate imputation of Adam's sin to his posterity. Men are not accounted guilty in Adam and therefore born corrupt, but derive from him the corruption of nature, and this is now imputed to them as guilt. Placaeus calls this mediate and consequent imputation.

The case of Amyraldus was brought up at three Synods, which did not condemn him, but found it necessary to guard against the misconceptions to which his view might lead, while the Synod of Charenton in 1644 rejected the theory of Placaeus. In opposition to both, the *Formula Consensus Helvetica* was drawn up by Heidegger, Turretin, and Geneler, which gave a clear statement of the Reformed position and was for a time honoured in Switzerland as an official standard. The Articles bearing on the position of Amyraldus and Placaeus are quoted by Shedd, *History of Doctrine* II, pp 472, 473.

QUESTIONS FOR FURTHER STUDY

How do Calvin and Luther differ with respect to the doctrine of predestination? What advantage has the covenant idea in the explanation of original sin? Is the total depravity taught by the Reformers the same as absolute depravity? What is the Arminian view of sin and grace? Does it differ in any way from Semi-Pelagianism? How do the Wesleyan Arminians differ from the original Arminians on these doctrines? Does the position of the Synod of Dort differ from that of the Heidelberg Catechism on these points? What objections are there to the position of Amyraldus? What is the difference between mediate and immediate imputation?

LITERATURE

Calvin, *Institutes of the Christian Religion*, Books II and III; Luther, *The Bondage of the Will; Canons of Dort;* Cunningham, *The Reformers and the Theology of the Reformation*, pp 413–470; Koestlin, *The Theology of Luther*, cf Index; Dorner, *History of Protestant Theology*, 2 vols, cf Index; Cunningham, *Historical Theology*, II, pp 371–513; Seeberg, *History of Doctrines*, II, pp 227–272, 398–408; Sheldon, *History of Christian Doctrines*, II, pp 117–133; Neander, *History of Christian Dogmas*, II, pp 653–660; Shedd, *History of Christian Doctrine*, II, pp 111–196.

V: ANTHROPOLOGICAL VIEWS OF POST-REFORMATION TIMES

It is not necessary to discuss the anthropology of the Post-Reformation period at length. There have been no controversies that brought new elements to the foreground, and no Synods or Councils that formulated new dogmas. It may be well, however, to notice a couple of divergences from the teachings of the Reformation, and to give a brief description of the most important theories of sin that were advanced by individual theologians during the last two centuries.

I. DIVERGENT VIEWS

There are especially two that deserve consideration.

[a] *Modification of the Arminian view in Wesleyan Arminianism.* It is a well-known fact that Arminius himself did not depart as far from Scripture truth and from the teachings of the Reformers as did his followers at the time of the Synod of Dort. Moses Stuart even thought it possible to prove that Arminius was not an Arminian. Now Wesleyan Arminianism, which originated in the middle of the eighteenth century, claims the parentage of Arminius himself rather than that of later Arminianism, though it differs in some respects even from Arminius. 'Its theology', says Sheldon, 'was shapen by a warm evangelical piety, and bears the impress at once of a deep sense of dependence upon God, and of an earnest, practical regard for human freedom and responsibility.' *History of Christian Doctrine*, II, p 263. It differs from the doctrine of sin and grace of the earlier Arminians in the following points: (1) It stresses the fact that original sin is not merely a disease or a pollution of nature, which cannot be called sin in the strict sense of the word, but is really and truly sin and

Wesleyan Arminianism on original sin

[155]

renders man guilty in the sight of God. The guilt of Adam's sin is indeed imputed to his descendants. But at the same time it holds that this original guilt was cancelled by the justification of all men in Christ. This means that the idea of original guilt has after all only a theoretical place in this system, since its cancel-lation is one of the universal benefits of the atonement. (2) It denies that man, as he is by nature, has any ability whatsoever to co-operate with the grace of God, and admits his entire moral depravity, so that he is absolutely dependent on the grace of God for salvation. But at the same time it holds that no man actually exists in that state of inability. In view of the universal bearing of the redemption through Christ God graciously endows every man with sufficient enabling grace, so that he can turn to God in faith and repentance. The original Arminians held that it was only just that God should thus enable men to believe and repent, since they could not be held accountable without some spiritual ability. The Wesleyan Arminians, how-ever, regard this as a matter of free grace on the part of God.

Wesleyan Arminianism on total depravity

[*b*] *A modification of the Reformed views in New England.* The anthropology of the New England theologians differs in some respects from that of the Reformers and of the Reformed Churches in general. The most important of these departures are the following:

(1) That on the relation of God's will to the fall of man. Jonathan Edwards ruled out the category of efficiency from God's connection with the fall of man, and used the ordinary Calvinistic phraseology. But some of his followers were not so careful, and either implied or stated explicitly that there is a divine efficiency in connection with the production of evil. Hopkins seems to imply this in some of his statements, and Emmons teaches it explicitly. In later New England or New Haven theology, represented by such men as Timothy Dwight and N. W. Taylor, there was a strong tendency to reduce the divine connection with the entrance of sin into the world to the lowest possible point consistent with an all-inclusive providence. The general view seems to be that God's determination to create a moral universe naturally included the creation of free moral

New England theology on fall of man

[156]

agents with the power of contrary choice, and thus rendered sin possible, but hardly certain. At the same time sin is also regarded as 'necessarily incidental to the best system'.

(2) That in connection with the free will of man. Jonathan Edwards somewhat over-emphasized the determinate character of the will, and thus exposed himself to the charge of determinism. He was perfectly right, however, in emphasizing the fact that freedom has its laws, known to God, and that in view of this fact it is perfectly consistent with certainty. Man as he was created by God possessed moral freedom and possesses it still; and it was in the exercise of this freedom that he brought sin into the world. He also possessed real freedom, however, that is, his will was determined in the direction of goodness and holiness by the original constitution of his nature. This real freedom he lost by sin. Later New England theologians stressed the fact that the power of contrary choice must be predicated of a free and responsible moral being. They approached the Arminian standpoint, but yet subscribed to the theory that given antecedents will be followed by given consequents, that the power to vary the result is never used, and that the divine foreknowledge is dependent on this variable, but non-necessitated succession of consequents from antecedents. *New England theology on free will*

(3) That respecting the transmission of sin. Edwards adopted the realistic theory. We are connected with Adam as the branches are with a tree, and consequently his sin is also our sin and is imputed to us as such. This theory is not peculiar to him, however. It finds great favour among the Lutherans, and is also advocated by such Reformed scholars as H. B. Smith and W. G. T. Shedd. Some New England theologians, such as Woods and Tyler, defended the Placaean theory of mediate imputation. Through his natural connection with Adam man inherits moral depravity, and this is imputed to him as guilt and makes him worthy of condemnation. *New England theology on transmission of sin*

2. SOME MODERN THEORIES OF SIN

[a] *Philosophical.* Some prominent philosophers of the eighteenth and nineteenth centuries expressed themselves on the *Leibnitz and Kant on sin*

nature and origin of sin, and in a measure influenced theological thought. Leibnitz looked upon the evil of the world as something metaphysical rather than ethical, regarding it as the simple and natural result of the necessary limitation of the creature. Kant struck a discordant note in his day by postulating a radical evil in man, a fundamental inclination to evil that cannot be eradicated by man. It precedes all empirical acts, but is nevertheless rooted in an autonomous will, and therefore involves guilt. He does not identify this 'radical evil' with what is generally called original sin, for he rejects the historical account of the origin of sin and also the idea of its physical inheritance. To him sin is *Hegel on sin* something that defies explanation. Hegel regarded sin as a necessary step in the evolution of man as a self-conscious spirit. The original condition of man was one of naive innocence – a state almost resembling that of the brute – in which he knew nothing of good or evil, and merely existed in unity with nature. That state, however natural for animals, was not natural for man, and was therefore not ideal. Man was destined to separate himself from it and to become a self-conscious spirit. The transition from the natural to the moral state was effected by knowledge. The eating of the tree of knowledge caused man to fall out of his state of paradisaical bliss. With the awakening of the self-conscious life, the beginning of the ego-sense, man involuntarily begins to follow his natural desires and makes the new-found self the centre of these, that is, he becomes selfish and thus evil. This is a stage, however, through which he must necessarily pass in his self-development. While this selfishness is sinful, it cannot really be ascribed to man as guilt until he wilfully chooses it even after he has awakened to the consciousness that he must rise above it, and that the selfish man is not what he ought to be. The struggle against this selfishness is the path to virtue.

[b] *Theological.* Schleiermacher regards sin as the necessary *Schleier-* product of man's sensuous nature – a result of the soul's connec-*macher on sin* tion with a physical organism. It is found where the bodily appetites prevent the determining power of the spirit from performing its proper function, and the sensuous nature exercises a

dominating influence. He denies the objective reality of sin, however, and ascribes to it only a subjective existence, that is, he regards it as existing only in our consciousness. The sense of sin, the consciousness of strife within man is due to the inadequacy of his God-consciousness as long as the sensuous nature predominates. God has so ordained that man should ascribe guilt to this feeling of deficiency, not because it is really sin, but so that there might be occasion for redemption. 'Original sin' is simply an acquired habit that has gradually been formed, and that is now the source of all actual sin.

Julius Mueller, a disciple of Kant and a representative of the *Mueller on sin* Mediating School, wrote an important monograph on the doctrine of sin. He agrees with Kant in regarding sin as a free act of the will in disobedience to the moral law. He went beyond Kant, however, in an attempt to explain the origin of sin. The Koenigsberg philosopher found it impossible to shed any light on this. Mueller saw that the 'radical evil' of which Kant spoke was present in human nature from birth, or at least prior to any conscious decision of the will, apart from which there is no sin. Since he could not discover the origin of sin in time, he sought it in a non-temporal or pre-temporal determination of the will. In some previous existence the choice was made, and therefore man is born guilty and depraved. This theory is so extremely speculative and so utterly beyond the possibility of verification that it has found little acceptance.

Ritschl agrees with Hegel in regarding sin as a species of *Ritschl on sin* ignorance and as a necessary stage in man's moral development. Like Schleiermacher he holds that man knows sin only from the point of view of the religious consciousness. Man must seek the Kingdom of God as the highest good, but in his ignorance of the perfect good does the opposite. Actual sin – and this is the only sin which Ritschl recognizes – sets itself in opposition to the Kingdom of God. Increasing knowledge of the ideal carries with it the consciousness of sin, which man imputes to himself as guilt. In reality, however, as Orr says, 'The guilt attaching to these acts is but a feeling in the sinner's own consciousness, separating him from God, which the revelation of God's fatherly love in the Gospel enables him to overcome.' *The Christian View of God and the World*, p 179. God does not impute sin as guilt because of the ignorance in which we now live. It is purely imaginary to think that He is angry with the sinner.

Tennant on sin

Tennant in his Hulsean Lectures on '*The Origin and Propagation of Sin*' develops the doctrine of sin from the point of view of the evolutionary theory. He denies that the impulses, desires, and qualities which man inherited from the brute can be called sinful. These constitute only the *material* of sin, and do not become actual sin until they are indulged in contrary to ethical sanctions. In the course of his development man gradually became an ethical being with an indeterminate will (Tennant does not explain how such a will is possible in a being subject to the law of evolution), and this will is the only cause of sin. Sin is defined as 'an activity of the will expressed in thought, word or deed contrary to the individual's conscience, to his notion of what is good and right, his knowledge of the moral law and the will of God'. In the measure in which the race develops the ethical standards become more exacting and the heinousness of sin increases. Tennant recognizes the universality of sin, and admits that our nature and environment are of such a kind that they make the realization of our better self a 'stupendously difficult task'.

QUESTIONS FOR FURTHER STUDY

What theories were advanced respecting the origin of the human soul? In what circles is traducianism favoured? Why do the Reformed Churches favour creationism? Was the covenant idea generally utilized to account for the transmission of sin? Where do you meet with a realistic explanation? What extremes do we meet in New England respecting God's connection with the fall? Can we conceive of sin as a necessity in human life, and yet maintain man's responsibility? What objections are there to the view that the guilt of sin is merely a matter of our subjective consciousness? Does the doctrine of evolution allow for a fall of man? Can it consistently find a place for sin as guilt?

LITERATURE

Girardeau, *Calvinism and Evangelical Arminianism;* Boardman, *New England Theology,* pp 61–130; Foster, *History of New England Theology,* cf Index; Taylor, *Moral Government,* I, pp 302–325; Mackintosh, *Christianity and Sin,* pp 119–147; Moxon, *The Doctrine of Sin,* pp 176–219; Orchard, *Modern Theories of Sin,* pp 30–46, 49–58, 65–88, 94–103; Tennant, *The Origin and Propagation of Sin,* especially Lecture III; Sheldon, *History of Christian Doctrine,* II, pp 324–347; Fisher, *History of Christian Doctrine,* pp 381–423, 502–528.

THE DOCTRINE OF
THE ATONEMENT
OR OF THE
WORK OF CHRIST

I: THE DOCTRINE OF THE ATONEMENT BEFORE ANSELM

I. IN GREEK PATRISTIC THEOLOGY

The Apostolic Fathers speak in general, usually Scriptural terms, of the work of Christ. The most significant statement is found in the Epistle to Diognetus. It combines the ideas of man's sin as deserving punishment, of God as giving His Son as a ransom for sin, and of the resulting covering of sin by the righteousness of Christ. The Apologists contain very little on the subject that is of importance. In so far as Christ is represented as a Redeemer, it is usually as a Redeemer from the power of the devil. In the Gnostic systems the redemption wrought by Christ is a redemption from the kingdom of darkness, the world of matter. In Marcion the death of Christ is the price at which the God of love purchased men from the creator of the world.

Apostolic Fathers on work of redemption

Irenæus, who stands mid-way between the East and the West, agrees with the Apologists in contemplating man as enslaved by the powers of darkness, and looks upon redemption partly as deliverance from the power of Satan, though he does not look upon it as a satisfaction due to Satan. His idea is rather that the death of Christ satisfied the justice of God and thus liberates man. At the same time he gives great prominence to the *recapitulation theory*, the idea 'that Christ recapitulates in himself all the stages of human life, and all the experiences of these stages, including those which belong to our state as sinners'. (Orr). By His incarnation and human life he thus reverses the course on which Adam by his sin started humanity and thus becomes a new leaven in the life of mankind. He communicates immortality to those who are united to him by faith and effects an ethical transformation in their lives, and by his obedience compensates for the disobedience of Adam.

Irenæus on the atonement

[165]

Clement of Alexandria and Origen on the atonement   In the Alexandrian School we find several representations. In one of his minor works Clement of Alexandria represents the death of Christ as a payment of man's debt and as a ransom; but in his main works he gives more prominence to the thought that Christ as Teacher saves men by endowing them with true knowledge and inspiring them to a life of love and true righteousness. Origen presents several different views without combining them into a synthetic whole. Christ saves by deifying human nature through the incarnation; by giving the supreme example of self-sacrifice, thus inspiring others to a similar sacrifice; by laying down his life as a sacrifice for the expiation of sin; and by redeeming men from the power of Satan. In connection with the idea of man's redemption from the power of the devil Origen introduces a new idea, namely that Satan was deceived in the transaction. Christ offered Himself as a ransom to Satan, and Satan accepted the ransom without realizing that he would not be able to retain his hold on Christ because of the latter's divine power and holiness. Satan swallowed the bait of Christ's humanity, and was caught on the hook of His divinity. Thus the souls of all men – even of those in hades – were set free from the power of Satan.

Athanasius on the atonement   The first systematic treatise on the work of the atonement was Athanasius' *De Incarnatione*. This work also contains several different ideas. The Logos became incarnate to restore to man the true knowledge of God, which had been lost by sin. The incarnate Logos is also represented as man's substitute, who pays his debt for him by enduring the penalty of sin. The necessity of this satisfaction is based on the veracity rather than on the justice of God. It is not said that the price was paid to Satan. The idea of Irenæus that the Logos assumed flesh in order to deify and immortalize it, however, is made particularly prominent. At the same time the representation of Athanasius differs from that of Irenæus on two points: (a) the incarnation is connected up more directly with the death and resurrection of Christ in the saving process; and (b) the emphasis is on the ethical rather than on the physical element in the process. Christ operates by His word and example on the hearts of man.

The true successors of Athanasius are the three Cappadocians.

[166]

Basil contributed little to the doctrine of the atonement. His younger brother, Gregory of Nyssa, is of far greater importance as the author of the second important systematic treatment on the work of Christ, the *Great Catechism*. He repeats the idea of the deceit practised on Satan, and justifies the deceit on two grounds: (a) the deceiver simply received his due when he was deceived in turn; and (b) Satan himself benefits by it in the end, since it results in his salvation. The underlying thought of the *Great Catechism* is the idea, borrowed from Athanasius, that in the incarnation God joined himself to our nature, in order to free it from death. It is pointed out, however, that not only death but sin also was destroyed. Gregory of Nazianzus repudiates with scorn and indignation the idea of a ransom paid to Satan. But he also rejects the idea that God the Father required a ransom. For the rest he virtually repeats the teachings of Athanasius. John Chrysostom and Cyril of Alexandria stress the immense value of the death of Christ. The main contribution of the latter lies in his emphasis on the infinite value of the death of Christ as the death of a divine Person. Baur finds that in him we have practically the full concept of satisfaction, except the express reference of it to God and the divine righteousness.

Gregory of Nyssa and Gregory of Nazianzus on the atonement

Greek patristic theology culminates in John of Damascus. He gathers up the previous thoughts on the work of Christ, but adds no distinctive contribution of his own. In summing up the development thus far, we may say that the doctrine of the work of Christ appears under two main aspects in Greek theology. (a) On the one hand salvation is contemplated as the direct result of the incarnation, as a new divine revelation given to man, or as (along with Christ's death and resurrection) communicating new life to mankind. (b) On the other hand it is viewed as the result of the fulfilment of certain objective conditions, such as that of a sacrifice to God, or of a satisfaction to the divine justice, or of a ransom paid to Satan. If we were to name any theories that are characteristic of the Greek patristic period, we would point to what Mackintosh calls 'the great *exoteric* doctrine of atonement in the Greek Church', the doctrine of a ransom paid to the devil; and to what he styles 'the *esoteric* theory of *recapitulatio*'.

John of Damascus on the work of redemption

2. IN LATIN PATRISTIC THEOLOGY

Tertullian's view of redemption Though the doctrine of the work of Christ in Latin patristic theology has several points in common with that of early Greek theology, yet even in this early period important differences begin to emerge. The distinctively Latin type of theology begins with Tertullian. To a certain extent he adopts Irenaeus' recapitulation theory, but conceives of the incarnation as affecting mankind chiefly through precept and example. Yet this whole idea recedes somewhat into the background. He stresses far more than Irenaeus the central significance of the death of Christ on the cross, regarding it as the culminating point in, and as the real end of, the mission of Christ. It cannot be said that he went far beyond Irenaeus in the definite formulation of the doctrine of the death of Christ. His real significance lies in the fact that he introduced the use of several legal terms into theology, such as 'guilt', 'satisfaction', 'merit', and so on, which were destined to play a great part in the theological development of the doctrine of the work of Christ. It should be noted, however, that he did not yet apply these terms to the sacrificial work of Christ, but to the repentance and good works that should follow sins committed after baptism. He laid the foundation for the development of the doctrine of penance in the Roman Catholic Church.

Hilary and Ambrose on work of redemption From Tertullian we pass on to Hilary of Poitiers and Ambrose, who interpreted Greek thought to the West. The former represents more than any other the Greek conception of the restoration of humanity by the incarnation. But this does not prevent him from ascribing the most definite significance to the death of Christ. In distinction from Tertullian he even views it as a satisfaction rendered to God. Christ died voluntarily, in order to satisfy a penal obligation. He infers the necessity of this satisfaction, like Athanasius, from the veracity rather than from the justice of God. Ambrose also shares the view of Irenaeus, and in addition repeats the idea of Origen that Christ paid a ransom to Satan and practised deceit on him. At the same time he strongly stresses the fact that the death of Christ was a sacrifice to God, and regards this sacrifice as a satisfaction of the divine sentence of death pronounced on sinful humanity. However, he does not explain why this sacrifice was necessary.

We naturally feel inclined to expect that Augustine, the greatest Church Father of the West, added greatly, both materially and formally, to the doctrine of the work of Christ. But this is not the case; his main accomplishments lie elsewhere. Summing up in himself the previous development, he presents a variety of views. There is the idea of the deification of human nature by the incarnation, though only in an ethical manner; and there is also the notion that Satan had a claim on man, complemented, however, by the thought that the claim of Satan was annulled by the death of Christ. But in what may be considered as his main line of thought Augustine is far removed from Greek theology. Both his presuppositions and his conclusions are different. The central ideas are those of original sin, of justification by grace, and of reconciliation by the sacrifice of Christ. The new Western type of thought is asserting itself and we find ourselves moving in a Pauline circle of ideas. Man is contemplated as subject to the wrath of God, and the sacrifice of Christ as placating this wrath and reconciling man to God. Augustine does not work out these thoughts into a complete system; his statement falls far short of Anselm's well articulated theory of the atonement. He does not sharply distinguish between the judicial and the renovating side of redemption. Justification is sometimes made to rest, not upon the removal of the guilt of sin by Jesus Christ, but on the sanctifying influence of the Holy Spirit. Again, he sometimes teaches that, though the atonement by Christ was the most suitable way of salvation, God might have saved sinners in some other way, thus making the atonement only relatively necessary. This really means that God's power might have gone against His wisdom.

Augustine on work of redemption

Of the theologians that were strongly influenced by Augustine only one calls for special mention, namely, Gregory the Great. His writings contain a passage which has been called 'the completest synthesis of ancient Latin theology on the atonement'. Its thought runs as follows: Man voluntarily fell under the dominion of sin and death, and only a sacrifice could blot out

Gregory the Great on work of redemption

such sin. But where was the sacrifice to be found? An animal could not serve the purpose; only a man would do, and yet no man could be found without sin. Therefore the Son of God became incarnate, assuming our nature, but not our sinfulness. The Sinless One became a sacrifice for us, a victim that could die in virtue of His humanity, and could cleanse in virtue of His righteousness. He paid for us a debt of death which He had not deserved, that the death which was our due might not harm us. This statement of Gregory may be regarded as a distinct advance in the development of the doctrine of the atonement.

QUESTIONS FOR FURTHER STUDY

At what points did the philosophy of the day affect the doctrine of the work of Christ? In what sense did the early Church Fathers speak of the deification of human nature? How is it to be understood that man becomes immortal through the work of Christ? Is there any scriptural basis for Irenæus' recapitulation theory? Is the idea that the incarnation saves man fundamentally Johannine? Does Origen have the same conception of deification as Irenæus? How can we explain the origin of the idea that a ransom had to be paid to Satan? Did all the early Fathers conceive of salvation by the incarnation in the same way? Did they have a clear conception of the death of Christ as rendering satisfaction to the justice of God? How did Tertullian apply the concepts of guilt, satisfaction, and merit? What Pauline ideas do we meet with in Augustine? How did Gregory the Great conceive of the atonement?

LITERATURE

Franks, *A History of the Doctrine of the Work of Christ*, I, pp 34–140; Scott, *The Nicene Theology*, pp 219–245; Fairweather, *Origen and Greek Patristic Theology;* Morgan, *The Importance of Tertullian in the Development of Christian Dogma;* Mozley, *The Doctrine of the Atonement*, pp 94–125; Mackintosh, *Historic Theories of the Atonement*, pp 80–116; Thomasius, *Dogmengeschichte*, I, pp 379–395; Shedd, *History of Christian Doctrine*, II, pp 203–272; Sheldon, *History of Christian Doctrine*, I, pp 115–125, 251–258; Orr, *Progress of Dogma*, pp 209–220; Histories of Harnack, Seeberg, Loofs, Neander, Fisher, cf Index.

The theological discussions in the five centuries between Gregory the Great and Anselm were of such a nature that they did not contribute much to the development of the doctrine of the atonement. With Anselm the systematic study of the doctrine of the atonement began. He opens a new era in the history of this doctrine.

I. THE DOCTRINE OF THE ATONEMENT IN ANSELM

Anselm of Canterbury made the first attempt at a harmonious and consistent representation of the doctrine of atonement. His *Cur Deus Homo* is an epoch-making book, a masterpiece of theological learning, in which the author combines metaphysical depth with clearness of presentation. The opening portion of the work testifies to the fact that at the time of its writing many minds were occupied with the question of the nature and necessity of the atonement. It also indicates that the problem of the atonement was generally approached from the Christological side as a question respecting the necessity of the incarnation. Several questions were raised at the time, such as the following: Could not God have saved man by a mere act of His omnipotence, just as easily as He could create the world? Could not He, the merciful God, simply have pardoned the sin of man, without demanding satisfaction? And if a mediator was necessary, why did He choose His only-begotten Son for the work of mediation, and not some other rational being? Once the incarnation was admitted, it was felt that it could only find its explanation in some stupendous exigency. This question respecting the incarnation explains the title of Anselm's work.

Anselm on the atonement

The alpha and omega of the position of Anselm is the absolute necessity of the atonement for the redemption of man. He deliberately rejects as unsatisfactory the Recapitulation Theory, the Ransom-to-Satan Theory, and the idea that the death of Christ was merely a manifestation of the love of God to man, since these do not explain the necessity of the atonement adequately. In his opinion the absolute necessity of the atoning sacrifice of Jesus Christ must be grounded in an immanent and necessary attribute of the divine nature. He finds the ultimate ground for it in the honour of God.

The exact position of Anselm can be understood only in the light of his conception of sin and satisfaction. As a creature of God man was under obligation to subject his will absolutely and entirely to the divine will, and when he refused this in a spirit of revolution, he dishonoured God and thus contracted a debt. God was robbed of His honour and this must be restored in some way. His mercy could not simply overlook sin, for this would be an irregularity and an injustice. There were two and only two ways in which the divine honour could be vindicated, namely by punishment or by satisfaction. God did not pursue the way of punishment, since this would have spelled ruin for the human race and would have defeated His very purpose. He chose the way of satisfaction, which included two things: (a) that man should now render to God the willing obedience which he owed Him; and (b) that he should make amends for the insult to God's honour by paying something over and above the actual debt. But since even the smallest sin, as committed against an infinite God, outweighs the whole world and all that is not God, and the amends must be proportionate, it follows that these are beyond the power of man. A gift – and Anselm looks upon satisfaction as a gift rather than as a punishment – surpassing all that is not God can only be God. God only could make true reparation, and His mercy prompted Him to make it through the gift of His Son. It was not sufficient that the one rendering satisfaction should be God; He had to be man as well, one of the human race that contracted the debt of sin, but a man without sin, who was not himself burdened with debt. Only the God-man could satisfy these requirements and thus do justice to the honour of God.

It was necessary for the God-man to render the obedience which man failed to render to God. But this was not sufficient to maintain the honour of God, for in doing this He did nothing more than His duty as man, and this could not constitute merit on His part. However, as a sinless being He was not under obligation to suffer and die. This was entirely voluntary on His part, and by submitting to bitter sufferings and a shameful death in the faithful discharge of His duty to His Father, He brought infinite glory to God. This was a work of supererogation, which could accrue to the benefit of mankind, and which more than counter-balanced the demerits of sin. Justice required that such a free gift should be rewarded. But there is nothing which the Father can give the Son, for He needs nothing. Therefore the reward accrues to the benefit of man and assumes the form of the forgiveness of sins and of future blessedness for all those who live according to the commandments of the Gospel.

The theory of Anselm marks an important advance in the development of the doctrine of the atonement. Its real value lies in the fact that it establishes the objective character of the atonement and bases its necessity on the immutable nature of God, which makes it impossible that He should permit the violation of His honour to go unpunished. It is defective, however, as compared with the later penal substitutionary doctrine, in several points: (a) It erroneously represents punishment and satisfaction as alternatives from which God could choose. (b) It has no place for the idea that in His suffering Christ endured the penalty of sin, since it regards the sufferings of Christ as a voluntary tribute to the honour of God, a superfluous merit which served to compensate for the demerits of others. This is really the Roman Catholic idea of penance applied to the work of Christ. (c) It is inconsistent in so far as it starts out with the principle of 'private law' or custom, according to which the injured party may demand whatever satisfaction he sees fit, and then, in order to establish the absolute necessity of the atonement passes over to the standpoint of public law. (d) It is one-sided in basing redemption exclusively on the death of Christ, and denying the

Evaluation of Anselm's contribution

atoning significance of His life. And (e) it represents the application of the merits of Christ to the sinner as a merely external transaction. There is no hint of the mystical union of Christ and believers.

2. ABELARD'S THEORY OF THE ATONEMENT

Abelard on the atonement

Abelard's theory has little in common with that of Anselm, except the denial that a price was paid to Satan. The death of Christ is not regarded as a ransom, not even as a ransom offered to God. Abelard rejects the Anselmian view that God was reconciled by the death of His Son. God could not take such pleasure in the death of His only-begotten Son as to make it the ground for the forgiveness of sins. Moreover, no such ground was needed, since God is love and is quite ready to forgive irrespective of any satisfaction. All He requires is penitence in the sinner; and He is ready and even eager to pardon the penitent. At the same time it may be said that we are justified and reconciled to God by the blood of Christ. Christ revealed the love of God by assuming our nature and by persevering as our teacher and example even unto death. This great love calls for and awakens a responsive love in the heart of the sinner, and this is the ground for the forgiveness of sins, Luke 7:47. The newly awakened love redeems us by liberating us from the power of sin and by leading us into the liberty of the sons of God, so that we obey God freely from the motive of love. Thus the forgiveness of sins is the direct result of the love kindled in our hearts, and only indirectly the fruit of the death of Christ.

This theory brought Abelard into difficulty in connection with the common doctrine of the forgiveness of sins through baptism. If the love that is kindled in our hearts by the death of Christ justifies us, why is baptism still necessary unto salvation? To this question Abelard replies that, unless baptism or martyrdom follows the kindling of this love, it must be concluded that perseverance has been lacking. This means that the remission of sins does not really take place until baptism is administered, even though love was kindled before. Particularly in the case of children Abelard had to admit that the remission of sin was independent of the love kindled in the heart. Loofs correctly remarks that Abelard's new view could not be maintained without more changes than he was prepared to make. It is probably due to this fact that he sometimes speaks of Christ as having borne our sins, and of His death as a sacrifice for sin.

In distinction from Anselm's doctrine of the atonement, this theory of Abelard is thoroughly subjective. It is sadly lacking in that moral depth and inner coherence that is so characteristic of Anselm's view. We have in it a typical representation of what is today called the Moral, or Moral Influence Theory of the atonement. It proceeds on the false principle that love is the central and all-controlling attribute in God, and ignores the demands of His justice and holiness. Moreover, it furnishes no adequate reason for the sufferings of Christ. If God could have forgiven sins without demanding satisfaction, why did He give up His Son to bitter sufferings and a shameful death? Was this not a very dubious revelation of love, seeing that He could have awakened the sinner's love in many other ways? This theory robs the sufferings of Christ of their redemptive significance and reduced Him to a mere moral teacher, who influences men by His teachings and by His example. *Evaluation of Abelard's view*

3. REACTION TO ABELARD IN BERNARD OF CLAIRVAUX

Bernard of Clairvaux criticized Abelard's theory, but did not present one of his own. Neither did he accept the view of Anselm. He took Abelard to task especially for his rationalistic interpretation of Christianity, and maintained that the example of Christ makes us saints just as little as the example of Adam made us sinners. He was quite willing to admit the greatness and importance of the example of the love of Christ, but only as founded in His redemptive work. In fact, it may be said that he had this in common with Abelard, that he stressed the love of Christ manifested in His human life and passion; but he saw in this not merely a revelation of the love of God, but the saving manifestation of Christ's own divinity. *Bernard of Clairvaux on the atonement*

This idea of Bernard may be regarded as the Western counter-part of the doctrine of Irenæus and Athanasius, that the incarna-tion was the transforming entrance of God into humanity. It should be observed, however, that he did not emphasize the physical result of the incarnation, as bringing life and immor-tality, but its psychological effect, as inspiring a patience and love similar to that of Christ. At the same time he did not rest satisfied with this purely subjective idea, but firmly believed in an objective redemption as the basis for the subjective. The Father did not require the death of His Son, but accepted it as an oblation; and now it serves to redeem us from sin, death, and the devil, and to reconcile us to God.

4. SYNCRETISTIC VIEWS OF THE ATONEMENT

In such Schoolmen as Peter the Lombard, Bonaventura, and Thomas Aquinas, we find traces of the influence of both Anselm and Abelard. They adopt elements from both, but do not suc-ceed in combining them into an inner unity.

Peter the Lombard on the atonement

[a] *Peter the Lombard.* Peter the Lombard takes his starting-point in the merits of Christ. By His pious life Christ merited for Himself freedom from suffering and glorification, and when he entered into sufferings and death, He did it voluntarily, not for Himself but for sinners. He thereby merited for them redemption from sin, punishment, and the devil, and admittance to paradise. Up to this point the train of thought is Anselmian. But when the question is asked, how the death of Christ effects this deliverance, the answer is that it reveals to us the love of God. By so great a pledge of love to us, we are moved and prompted to love God, and are thus released from sin and made righteous. And when we are free from sin, we are also free from the devil.

Bonaventura on the atonement

[b] *Bonaventura.* According to Bonaventura it was the re-quired satisfaction that made the incarnation necessary. A simple creature was not able to make satisfaction for the whole human race, and it was not proper that a creature of another race should be taken for that purpose. Hence it was necessary that the person

rendering satisfaction should be both God and man. This satisfaction was rendered by the merits of Christ, which He won by acting and suffering. To make satisfaction is to pay the honour that is due to God, and this is done by the sufferings of Christ as the most appropriate means for placating God. Thus the righteousness as well as the mercy of God is displayed. With this Anselmian idea, however, the Abelardian is combined, that the passion of Christ was also the most fitting means, since it was best suited to arouse in man a responsive love to God. By developing the thought of Christ's relation to the Church as that of the Head to the members of the body, Bonaventura explains far better than Anselm had done, how the blessings of Christ are transferred to believers.

[c] *Thomas Aquinas.* The greatest of the Schoolmen was Thomas Aquinas. He absorbed the thoughts of his predecessors more completely than any other mediæval theologian. In view of this it is not surprising that we find in him traces of both the Anselmian and Abelardian views, and that there is no unity in his representation of the work of Christ. *Thomas Aquinas on the atonement*

There is a representation that reminds us of both Irenæus and Abelard. The fullness of all grace dwells in the human nature of Christ, and because He is now the Head of the human race, His perfection and virtue overflow to the members of the body in so far as they are willing to belong to the head. Christ as the new man is the principle and the leaven of the new humanity. The work of redemption is thus considered from the point of view that makes Christ the teacher and pattern of the human race by His teachings, acts, and sufferings. These sufferings reveal more particularly the love of God and awaken a responsive love in the hearts of men.

However, there is also a more Anselmian line of thought, and this is generally followed in the Roman Catholic Church. Aquinas maintains that redemption was not absolutely necessary, since God might have permitted mankind to perish in its sins; yet he regards it as most fitting in view of all the attributes of God. Again, he is of the opinion that God could have redeemed man without demanding any adequate satisfaction. He admits that a human judge could not simply overlook a violation of the law, but asserts that God could do this in the case of sinful humanity, since He is Himself the source of justice and also the injured party in the case under consideration. He Himself determined by an act of His will what was right in this case, and could very well have remitted sin without satisfaction, since this would have wronged no one. God chose to demand satisfaction, however, and this made the incarnation of the Son of God necessary, because a mere man could not atone for sin committed against an infinite God.

The merits of Christ extended throughout the whole time of His earthly existence, so that every action of His life contributed to the atonement of man's sin. And this was really all that was necessary to render to God condign satisfaction. The passion and death of Christ were, strictly speaking, not needed. There were special reasons of congruity, however, why God wanted full redemption to be wrought by the passion and death of Christ, namely, that this was in keeping with both His mercy and justice, and at the same time ensured the greatest possible effect. The death of Christ reveals the great love of God, sets man an example of obedience, humility, constancy, and so on; it not only delivers from sin, but also merits justifying grace and eternal bliss, and offers a strong motive for refraining from sin.

The passion of Christ effects the salvation of sinners in four different ways: (a) by meriting the blessings of salvation, which are passed on to sinners; (b) as a superabundant satisfaction well-pleasing to God, the benefits of which are communicated to the faithful in virtue of the mystical union; (c) as a voluntary sacrifice with which God was delighted; and (d) by redeeming sinners from slavery and punishment. Though man was reduced to spiritual slavery by the devil, the latter had no rightful claims, and therefore did not receive the ransom. The superabundant satisfaction of Christ does not save man, however, apart from baptism and penance; and the reason for this lies in the necessary 'configuration' of the members to the Head in the mystical body of Jesus Christ.

While these views of Thomas Aquinas reveal considerable

similarity to those of Anselm, they are in some respects *Evaluation* inferior and in others superior to them. They are inferior, *of Thomas* since they do not manifest the same logical coherence and fail to *view* ground the necessity of the atonement in the divine nature, making it dependent simply on the will of God, which might have chosen another way and might even have dispensed with satisfaction altogether. This element of arbitrariness readily became a bridge to the acceptilation theory of Duns Scotus. They are superior, however, in their approach to the idea of penal satisfaction, that is, of satisfaction through punishment; in their greater emphasis on the merits of Christ, in which the later distinction between the active and passive obedience of Christ is anticipated; and in the introduction of the idea of the mystical union to account for the transmission of the merits of Christ to believers.

5. DUNS SCOTUS ON THE ATONEMENT

While Aquinas represents the Dominican theology, which is *Duns Scotus* the official theology of the Church of Rome, Duns Scotus may *on the* be regarded as the founder of the Franciscan theology. His work *atonement* is primarily critical and negative. He wrote no *Summa* like Aquinas, but incorporated his views on the atoning work of Christ in his *Commentaries* on the *Sentences of Lombardus*. We may proceed on the assumption that he shares the views of Lombardus where he does not correct them. In this way it is possible to obtain a somewhat more positive construction of his view of the atonement than would otherwise be available. He differs in some important points from his predecessors.

He makes the atonement itself, the character it assumes, and the effect which it has, depend altogether on the arbitrary will of God. He asserts that there was no inherent necessity for rendering satisfaction. This was necessary only because God willed it; but it was not necessary that He should will it; this was altogether a contingent act of God. Furthermore, he holds that, even if the necessity of satisfaction were granted, it would not follow that it had to assume the exact form which it actually took. It was not necessary that the one rendering it should be God, or should be greater than the whole creation. One pious act of Adam might have served to atone for his first sin. Again, he does not consider it capable of proof that satisfaction had to be rendered by a man. God might have accepted the deed of an angel as a sufficient atonement. It all depended on the arbitrary will of God.

However, God foreordained from eternity the passion of Christ as the means for the salvation of the predestinated. This passion has a peculiar value and a special efficacy only because it was foreordained as the means of salvation, and because God was willing to accept it as effectual. Duns denies the infinite value of the merits of Christ, because they were merits of the human nature, which is after all finite. By an act of His will, however, God determined to accept them as sufficient. A merit that is not at all commensurate with the debt owed is willingly accepted by God. This theory is generally called the *Acceptilation Theory*, but according to Mackintosh (*Historic Theories of the Atonement*, p 110 f) should really be called the *Acceptation Theory* of the atonement.

QUESTIONS FOR FURTHER STUDY

Does the Roman Catholic Church follow Anselm in maintaining the absolute necessity of the atonement? How do you account for it that Anselm represents the honour rather than the penal justice of God as demanding satisfaction? What was his conception of sin? Where did he get the idea that sin must be followed by either punishment or satisfaction? How can it be accounted for that he centres his thought of merit exclusively on the death of Christ? Why is his theory sometimes called the 'Commercial Theory'? In what sense did Abelard regard the atonement as necessary? Why is his theory called subjective? Is it proper to speak of the so-called subjective theories as theories of *atonement*? Does Abelard give a sufficient explanation of the sufferings and death of Christ? What is the great objection to the view of Duns Scotus? What remains of the merits of Christ in his view? What is the difference between *acceptilation* and *acceptation*? In what respect does the view of Thomas Aquinas mark an advance on that of Anselm?

LITERATURE

Mackintosh, *Historic Theories of the Atonement*, pp 117–148; Mozley, *The Doctrine of the Atonement*, pp 125–140; Franks, *A History of the Doctrine of the Work of Christ*, I, pp 147–328; Welch, *Anselm and His Work*, particularly pp 172–184; Otten, *A Manual of the History of Dogmas*, II, pp 201–213; McGiffert, *A History of Christian Thought*, II, pp 185–305; Seeberg, *History of Doctrines*, II, pp 66–74, 110–114, 156–160; Loofs, *Dogmengeschiedenis*, pp 260–264; Thomasius, *Dogmengeschichte*, II, pp 95–115; Neander, *History of Christian Dogmas*, II, pp 514–521, 580–584; Shedd, *History of Christian Doctrine*, II, pp 273–320; Sheldon, *History of Christian Doctrine*, I, pp 361–370; Orr, *Progress of Dogma*, pp 220–233; Fisher, *History of Christian Doctrine*, pp 216–228.

III: THE DOCTRINE OF THE ATONEMENT IN THE PERIOD OF THE REFORMATION

The doctrine of the atonement did not constitute one of the subjects of debate between the Reformers and the Roman Catholic Church. Both regarded the death of Christ as a satisfaction for sin, and a satisfaction of infinite value. Their differences concerned primarily the subjective application of the work of Christ. Yet there was a difference of emphasis even in connection with the atonement. The Reformers moved along definite lines in fundamental agreement with Anselm, though differing from him in some details, while the Roman Catholic Church reflected the uncertainty and indeterminateness of the scholastic era, though in the main agreeing with Thomas Aquinas.

1. THE REFORMERS IMPROVE ON THE DOCTRINE OF ANSELM

The Reformers on the atonement There is substantial agreement between the Reformers and Anselm. Both maintain the objective nature of the atonement and both regard it as a necessity. They differ, however, as to the nature of this necessity. Anselm speaks of this as absolute, while some of the Reformers regard it as relative or hypothetical. Speaking of the requirement that the Mediator should be both God and man, Calvin says: 'If the necessity be inquired into,' (the very question of Anselm), 'it was not what is commonly termed simple or absolute, but flowed from the divine decree on which the salvation of mankind depended. What was best for us, our most merciful Father determined.' *Institutes* II. 12. 1 They are all agreed, however, that the atonement through the sufferings and death of Christ is most in harmony with divine wisdom and highly appropriate. And it is certainly unfair to say

[182]

that Calvin, like Duns Scotus, makes the atonement dependent on the arbitrary will of God. He knows of no indeterminate will in God, but only of a will that is determined by the whole complex of His attributes, and duly emphasizes the fact that the atonement in Christ fully satisfies the justice of God.

In several points the doctrine of the atonement, as developed by the Reformers, is superior to its Anselmian form. While Anselm regards sin primarily as an infringement on the honour of God, the Reformers look upon it first of all as transgression of the law of God and therefore as guilt rather than as an insult. And while the former views the atonement in the death of Christ as a superabundant gift to God in vindication of His honour, the latter think of it as a penal sacrifice to satisfy the justice of God. Thus the atonement is lifted out of the sphere of private rights into that of public law.

This means that the Reformers also rejected the Anselmian alternative 'satisfaction or punishment', and pointed out that the one does not exclude the other, but that the satisfaction rendered through the sacrifice of Christ was satisfaction through punishment. In other words, they stressed the fact that the sufferings of Christ were *penal* and *vicarious*.

Again, they went beyond Anselm in distinguishing clearly between active and passive obedience in the mediatorial work of Christ, and in recognizing the former as well as the latter as a part of the atoning work of Christ. The God-man satisfied the demands of the divine justice, not merely by His sufferings and death, but also by obedience to the law in its federal aspect. His atonement consisted not only in making amends for past transgressions, but also in keeping the law as the condition of the covenant of works. As the last Adam He did what the first Adam failed to do.

Finally, they also surpassed Anselm in their conception of the manner in which the merits of Christ were passed on to sinners. Anselm's view of this had a rather external and commercial aspect. Aquinas improved on this by stressing the significance of the mystical union as the means of transferring the blessings of salvation to those who stood in living relationship to Jesus Christ.

He failed, however, to give due prominence to the receptive activity of faith. The Reformers shared his opinion respecting the great importance of the mystical union, but in addition directed the attention to that conscious act of man by which he appropriates the righteousness of Christ – the act of faith. They were very careful, however, not to represent faith as the meritorious cause of justification.

2. THE SOCINIAN CONCEPTION OF THE ATONEMENT

Socinus'
conception
of the
atonement
A formidable attack was made on the doctrine of the Reformers by Socinus. He began with an attempt to remove the very foundation on which it was based, namely, the idea of justice in God as understood by Anselm and the Reformers. He denied the presence of any such justice in God 'as requires absolutely and inexorably that sin be punished'. That perpetual and constant justice by which He is characterized is merely His moral equity and rectitude, by virtue of which there is no depravity or iniquity in any of His works. The justice which is commonly so called and which is opposed to mercy is not an immanent attribute of God, but only the effect of His will. This also holds for that mercy of God which is opposed to justice. It is not an internal quality in God, but is merely an effect of His free choice. Such mercy does not prevent Him from punishing anyone; neither does such justice keep Him from pardoning whom He pleases, and that without satisfaction of its claims.

The burden of Socinus' criticism is to the effect that it is inconsistent to combine the grace of God and the merits of Christ as the ground of forgiveness and reconciliation. It is possible to maintain one of two things: either that God forgives freely, or that He forgives for the sake of Christ; but you cannot say both, for they are mutually exclusive. Of the two alternatives he chooses the former, namely, that God forgives freely. He also holds that, since guilt is personal, substitution in penal matters is impossible; and that, even if it were allowable, it cannot be said that Christ bore the exact penalty of the law, since this would mean that He died as many eternal deaths as there are sinners.

And yet He did not even suffer one endless death, but only finite pain. Moreover, Socinus maintains that the idea of satisfaction and imputation are self-contradictory. If Christ rendered complete satisfaction, that settles the matter by setting the world free. It is inconsistent to make the enjoyment of its fruits dependent on divine imputation and on the faith of man.

Socinus never tires of saying that the forgiveness of sins is an act of pure mercy, simply on the basis of repentance and obedience. The only conditions are sorrow for sin and an earnest desire to obey the law. He realized, however, that he had to give some explanation of the unique significance of Jesus, whose saving work was really excluded by his system. He says that Christ saves sinners by revealing to them the way of faith and obedience as the way to eternal life; by giving them an example of true obedience both in His life and in His death and by inspiring them to a similar life; by giving a concrete representation of obedience as the way of life in an obedience unto death followed by the resurrection; and by bestowing eternal life, by virtue of the power received at the resurrection, on all those that attach themselves to Him in faith. God gave Him this power as a reward for His obedience. This theory establishes no direct connection between the death of Christ and the salvation of sinners. The death of Christ did not atone for our sin, neither did it move God to pardon sin. The forgiveness of sins depends exclusively on the mercy of God. But because Christ received the power to bestow eternal life on believers immediately after His death, Socinus considers it possible to maintain that this death expiated our sins.

The Socinian doctrine is really nothing but a concoction of several heresies condemned by the early Church; a revival of ancient Pelagianism with its belief in the inherent goodness and spiritual ability of man; of the old Adoptionist doctrine, making Christ as to His human nature a Son of God by adoption; of the Moral Influence theory of the atonement with its emphasis on the exemplary life of Christ; and of the Scotist doctrine of an arbitrary will in God. It found little favour even among those who opposed the penal substitutionary doctrine of the atonement. *Evaluation of Socinus' view*

And this is no wonder in view of the fact that it is thoroughly rationalistic, a mere abstract play of human logic that fails altogether to do justice to the facts revealed in the Word of God and experienced in the lives of the redeemed.

3. THE GROTIAN THEORY OF THE ATONEMENT

Grotius on the atonement This theory really represents a middle course between the doctrine of the Reformers and the Socinian view. Grotius himself evidently did not so consider it, for he entitled his work, *Defence of the Catholic Faith Concerning the Satisfaction of Christ Against Faustus Socinus of Siena*. It is the work of an able jurist who, on the basis of Roman law, to which Socinus appealed, points out several flaws in the latter's arguments. At the same time he fails to meet the most important criticism of Socinus on the doctrine of the Reformers, namely, that Christ did not and could not really bear the penalty of the law imposed on sinners. In fact, he himself abandons this idea and broaches a new theory. He maintains that there is no dominant quality of distributive justice in God which demands that the requirements of the law be met *in every particular*, and which, in case of transgression, makes *full satisfaction* by punishment imperative. The law with which the sinner is concerned is not a transcript of the inherent righteousness of God, but a positive law (as opposed to natural law), a product of the divine will, by which God is in no way bound and which He can alter or abrogate as He pleases. Both the law itself and its penalty can be modified or even abolished altogether by the Ruler of the universe.

While God certainly intended this law to be valid and binding, He reserved the right to *relax* it, if He should deem this best for some important reason. This is the fundamental idea which Grotius applies in his theory of the atonement. In strict justice the sinner deserved death, even eternal death; but as a matter of fact that sentence is not strictly executed, for believers are free from condemnation. A relaxation takes place: the penalty is dispensed with, and that without strict satisfaction. Grotius indeed speaks of Christ as rendering satisfaction, but this should

[186]

not be understood in the strict sense of an exact equivalent of the penalty due to man. It is only a nominal equivalent, something which God is pleased to accept as such. 'This act of the Father,' says Grotius, 'so far as it relates to the law is *relaxation*, but so far as it relates to the criminal is *remission*.' According to the doctrine of the Reformers there is such a relaxation on the part of the Supreme Judge in the adoption of the principle of vicarious substitution, but not in the substitution that is made; this is a *real* and not a mere *nominal* equivalent. Grotius extends the principle to both. The sufferings of Christ were only a nominal equivalent for the sufferings due to the human race. Grotius disclaims that his theory is a theory of *acceptilation*, for this, according to him, denotes an act by which a creditor, without any compensation whatsoever, absolutely remits an indebtedness.

But now the question naturally arises, Why did not God simply abrogate the law, seeing that this was within His power? Why was it necessary at all that Christ should suffer? Why was not the penalty remitted outright? Grotius answers that God as the Ruler of the universe had to maintain order in His great realm. It would not have been safe for Him to remit without revealing in some way the inviolable nature of the law and His holy displeasure against sin. Says Shedd: 'The sufferings and death of the Son of God are an exemplary exhibition of God's hatred of moral evil, in connection with which it is safe and prudent to remit that penalty, which as far as God and the divine attributes are concerned, might have been remitted without it.' The necessity of the atonement is therefore based on the interests of the moral government of the universe. Hence the theory is called the Governmental Theory of the Atonement.

On the one hand the theory of Grotius shows some leanings *Evaluation* to the doctrine of the Reformers. It has at least some appearance *of Grotius'* of teaching an objective atonement, and maintains that the *view* atonement was necessary to safeguard the moral government of the universe, a consideration which occupies a secondary place in the doctrine of the Reformers. On the other hand it also has affinity with the Socinian theory. Both deny that the satisfaction of Christ was required by the nature and attributes of God, and

[187]

was a full equivalent for the penalty of sin. It is perfectly evident that, according to Grotius, the death of Christ is merely exemplary and not at all retributive, while the Reformers claim that it is both. And finally, on this theory the sufferings of Christ merely serve the purpose of preventing future sins, and do not really atone for past sin.

4. THE ARMINIAN VIEW OF THE ATONEMENT

Arminian view of the atonement This took shape after Grotius had published his work, and the two theologians that were most active in its construction were Curcellæus and Limborch. They did not adopt the Grotian scheme, though they joined him in the attempt to sail in between the Scylla of the Socinians and the Charybdis of the Church doctrine. In line with the Reformers they based the necessity of the atonement on the divine nature rather than on the interests of the moral order, though they failed to carry the idea through with logical consistency.

It is quite characteristic of the Arminian view that it represents the death of Christ as a *sacrificial offering*, but at the same time maintains that this sacrifice should not be regarded as the payment of a debt, nor as a complete satisfaction of justice. It is rather somewhat of a concomitant or a *conditio sine qua non* of the forgiveness of sins. In both the Old Testament and the New God sees fit to connect the manifestation of His pardoning grace with the antecedent death of a sacrifice. The sufferings and death of Christ are regarded as penal and judicial, and therefore as of the nature of punishment. This does not mean, however, that He endured what man deserved to endure, but only that by a divine appointment His sacrificial death took the place of a penalty, and as such had the effect of reconciling God to man and procuring the forgiveness of sins. This means that the death of Christ is not regarded as a substituted penalty which is a strict equivalent (the view of the Reformers), but as a substitution for a penalty which may be of inferior worth. It is spoken of as a satisfaction of *benevolence*. On this point the Arminians are quite in agreement with Grotius.

[188]

They have several objections to the officially adopted doctrine of the atonement, the most important of which may be stated as follows: (a) Christ did not endure the full penalty of sin, since He did not suffer eternal death, either in time or in degree. There was no endless suffering in His case, neither was there absolute despair. (b) If Christ *completely* atoned for sin, there is nothing left for divine grace to accomplish. If justice is satisfied, the remission of sin can no longer be a matter of divine compassion. And (c) if Christ rendered full satisfaction, God has no right to demand faith and obedience, nor to punish the sinner, if he fails to obey, for it is unjust to exact double punishment for one and the same sin.

Moreover, they regard the atonement of Christ as general or universal, which means that he 'made an atonement for the sins of mankind in general, and of every individual in particular'. God sent Christ into the world, and Christ offered Himself willingly for the purpose of saving every individual of the human race. But while the atonement is universal in the divine intention, it is not universally effective, since many are lost. This partial failure is ascribed to the obstinacy of the sinner in refusing the offered atonement and defeating the divine intention. The effective application of the atonement depends ultimately on the sinner's will, which can and does in many cases defeat the very purpose of God.

In opposition to this Arminian error the Synod of Dort took the position that the atonement of Christ, though quite sufficient for the salvation of all men, was nevertheless intended only for those to whom it is effectively applied, in other words, for the elect. Moreover, it maintained that the effectual application of the atonement does not, ultimately, depend on the sinner's decision, but on the divine determination to exert special grace. By the power of the Holy Spirit the atonement of Christ is made effective in the hearts and lives of all those for whom Christ shed His blood. They are all saved, and they owe their salvation exclusively to the grace of God.

Synod of Dort on limited atonement

5. THE COMPROMISE OF THE SCHOOL OF SAUMUR

School of Saumur on the atonement The School of Saumur represents an attempt to tone down the rigorous Calvinism of the Synod of Dort, and to avoid at the same time the error of Arminianism. This is seen especially in the work of Amyraldus, who boldly taught a hypothetical universalism, which was really a species of universal atonement. God willed by an antecedent decree that all men should be saved on condition of repentance and faith in Jesus Christ. He therefore sent Christ into the world to die for all men. But seeing that, left to themselves, none would repent and believe, He by a subsequent decree elected some as the objects of the saving operation of His grace. These and these only are actually saved.

The outcome proved this to be an untenable position. Of the followers of this school some emphasized the first decree and the universal offer of salvation based on it, with the result that they landed in the Arminian camp; and others stressed the second decree and the necessity of effectual grace, and thus returned to the Calvinistic position. The views of the School of Saumur were practically shared by Davenant, Calamy, and especially Richard Baxter, in England. Its peculiar opinions gave occasion for the construction of the *Formula Consensus Helvetica* by Turretin and Heidegger, in which these views are combated.

QUESTIONS FOR FURTHER STUDY

Did the Reformers agree with Anselm on the absolute necessity of the atonement? What was Calvin's view on this point? Are the Reformed theologians of the seventeenth century in agreement with him? Do they base the necessity of the atonement on the honour or on the justice of God? Did the Lutheran and the Reformed theologians agree on the extent of the atonement? Are they agreed in their view of the active obedience of Christ? What is your criticism of the Socinian system? Did Socinus regard Christ as a priest during His earthly life? In what sense did he regard the death of Christ as a means of redemption? How did Grotius seek to escape the Socinian position? What criticism would you offer on the Governmental Theory? Does the universalism of the Arminians imply that the atonement of Christ is universally efficacious? Why did the Synod of Dort insist on the limited nature of the atonement? On what grounds did Piscator deny that the active obedience of Christ was part of his satisfaction? Wherein lies the weakness of the Amyraldian position?

LITERATURE

Franks, *A History of the Doctrine of the Work of Christ*, I, pp 353–444; II, pp 1–120; Mackintosh, *Historic Theories of the Atonement*, pp 149–187; Mozley, *The Doctrine of the Atonement*, pp 141–158; Cunningham, *Historical Theology*, II, pp 237–370; Seeberg, *History of Doctrines*, cf Index; Shedd, *History of Christian Doctrines*, II, pp 348–386; Sheldon, *History of Christian Doctrines*, II, pp 138–152; Fisher, *History of Christian Doctrines*, pp 317–325; 337–346; Orr, *Progress of Dogma*, pp 236–239.

IV: THE DOCTRINE OF THE ATONEMENT AFTER THE REFORMATION

I. THE MARROW CONTROVERSY IN SCOTLAND

Neono-mianism on the atonement An interesting controversy arose in Scotland in the beginning of the eighteenth century. Neonomianism, very prevalent in England in the seventeenth century, also made its appearance in Scotland. The name is due to the fact that it practically changed the Gospel into a new law. According to this view Christ atoned for all men in the sense that He made salvation possible for all, and thus brought them all into a salvable state. He met all the conditions of the covenant of works, and thereby abrogated the old law of that covenant, so that His work can be called our *legal righteousness*. Having met all the conditions of the covenant of works, He then introduced a new law, the law of the Gospel, which requires faith and conversion. These constitute the *evangelical righteousness* of the believer which, however imperfect it may be, is the ground of his justification rather than the imputed righteousness of Jesus Christ. Thus the covenant of grace was changed into a covenant of works. This is simply Arminianism under a new name.

The Neonomian position was opposed in England by Fisher's *Marrow of Modern Divinity*, published in 1645. On the appearance of Neonomianism in Scotland this work was republished in that country under the care of James Hogg in 1718, and found ardent admirers in Thomas Boston and the two Erskines. These men, together with Hogg, were soon called the Marrow-men, and were in course of time accused of teaching antinomianism (which was not true; they were anti-neonomians), and also of *Marrow-men on the atonement* sponsoring a doctrine of universal atonement and universal pardon. Though this charge did not do them justice, yet it must be said that their desire to establish firmly the warrant of the

[192]

universal offer of salvation led them to use dubious language, by which they laid themselves open to the charge in question. They heartily endorsed the soundly Calvinistic principle that Christ died, in pursuance of the covenant of redemption, to secure the salvation of the elect. But at the same time they insisted on a general reference of the atonement. They said that, while Christ did not die for all, that is, to save all, yet He is available for all, was dead for all, if they will but receive Him. The giving love of God made a gift of Christ and of the benefits of redemption to all men, to be claimed on condition of faith. This is the basis for the universal offer of salvation. At the same time only the elect are the objects of God's elective love, and they alone secure salvation. Their position was condemned in 1720, and this gave rise to the separation of 1733.

2. SCHLEIERMACHER AND RITSCHL ON THE ATONEMENT

[a] *Schleiermacher*. We meet with a comparatively new line of thought in Schleiermacher. He rejects altogether the doctrine of penal satisfaction. His constructive work on the doctrine of the atonement reveals little resemblance to earlier theories, except when, in dwelling on the sympathetic sufferings of Christ and its effect on men, it recalls the view of Abelard. His main line of thought may be said to echo somewhat the thoughts of those early Church Fathers who stress the incarnation as the great redemptive act of Christ, though they certainly did not share his pantheistic notions. Under the influence of Hegel the idea that the incarnation was the central fact of redemption was rejuvenated; and it was adopted by Schleiermacher, though with a slightly different emphasis.

Schleiermacher on the atonement

Schleiermacher regards Christ as the archetypal man, the perfect prototype of humanity, whose uniqueness consisted in the fact that He possessed a perfect and unbroken sense of union with God, and also realized to the full the destiny of man in his character of sinless perfection. He was the second Adam, like the first, truly man, but placed in more favourable circumstances and remaining perfect and sinless in obedience. He was the

[193]

spiritual Head of humanity, capable of animating and sustaining the higher life of all mankind, the perfectly religious man and the fountain of true religion, through living faith in whom others may also become perfectly religious. This transcendent dignity finds its explanation in a peculiar presence of God in Him. He entered into the life of humanity as a new leaven, making those who come in contact with Him receptive for higher things and communicating to them an inner experience of God-consciousness similar to His own. His activity is of a creative kind, an inspiring and life-giving influence of spirit upon spirit. His voluntary sufferings and death served to reveal His love to mankind and His devotion to His task, and to intensify the influence which He brings to bear on souls that were previously alienated from God. This view is called the Mystical Theory of the atonement. It is thoroughly subjective and is therefore, strictly speaking, no theory of atonement at all. It takes no account of the guilt of sin, but only seeks to explain how man is delivered from its pollution, which in his theory is really no sin at all. It also fails to explain how the Old Testament saints were saved.

Ritschl on the atonement

[b] *Ritschl.* The influence of Ritschl in modern theology is second only to that of Schleiermacher and is still potent in present-day theological thought. Ritschl views Christ as a man who has for us the value of a God and to whom the predicate of Godhead can be ascribed on account of His work. He denies the fact and even the possibility of a vicarious atonement, declares that reconciliation consists exclusively in the sinner's change of attitude to God, and maintains that the work of redemption pertains primarily to a community, and only secondarily to individuals in so far as they become members of the redeemed community and thus share its benefits. Christ wrought redemption, according to him, as the bearer of the perfect and final revelation of God, and as the founder and sustainer of the Christian community – the Kingdom of God. He founded the Christian community by living His life in perfect trust and obedience, and by exhibiting the same qualities when fidelity to His vocation made it necessary for Him to endure sufferings and death. However, this death had no significance as a propitiation

for sin. Its value lies in the fact that it is a power which continues to awaken steadfast faith in God's love, a spirit of obedience unto death, and a sense of victory over the world. Yet God pardons sin on the basis of the work of Christ in founding the Kingdom, or for the sake of the Kingdom. In distinction from the Moral Influence Theory, therefore, Ritschl posits an objective ground for the forgiveness of sin. Sometimes he seems to regard Christ merely as an exemplar, but this is only apparent. He traces the influence of Christ primarily through the collective spirit and life which passes from the Lord to the community which He founded.

3. SOME OF THE MORE RECENT THEORIES OF THE ATONEMENT

In the English-speaking countries we meet with reproductions of most of the typical theories considered in the preceding, though often with variations. The following are the most important.

[a] *The governmental theory in New England theology.* The history of New England theology reveals a downward trend in the doctrine of the atonement. At first the penal substitutionary doctrine of the atonement found a congenial soil there. But even as early as 1650 William Pynchon, a prominent layman, attacked the doctrine that Christ suffered the very torments of the lost, and the doctrine of imputation founded on it. He was answered by Norton in 1653. Bellamy introduced what was afterwards known as the New England doctrine of the atonement, and was in essence simply a reproduction of the Governmental Theory of Grotius. He also denied the limited, and asserted the universal design of the atonement. Hopkins was in agreement with him, and maintained that Christ did not suffer the exact penalty for sin, but something that was substituted for it. Moreover, it was generally denied that Christ merited anything by His active obedience; only the sufferings of Christ were regarded as having redemptive significance. The Governmental Theory became the dominant view of the atonement in New England theology.

Atonement in New England theology

[195]

Emmons tried to improve upon it by the introduction of a moral element. He stressed the fact that the government of God is a moral government, actuated by love. And Horace Bushnell went still further by introducing the Moral Influence Theory.

[b] Different types of the Moral Influence theory.

Bushnell on the atonement

(1) Bushnell. Horace Bushnell rejected both the penal and the governmental theories, but considered the former as superior to the latter, since it does not lose sight of the justice of God. He does not understand how a spectacle revealing God's abhorrence of sin can ever issue in the forgiveness of sin. But he objects to both theories on the score that they are too legal and external and fail to do justice to the ethical element in the atonement. In his *Vicarious Sacrifice* he rejects the idea that God had to be propitiated, and maintains that the only requirement was that man should be reconciled to God and manifest a new spirit of love and obedience. God Himself went forth in Christ to save man and even suffered in the Son of His love. Christ came to lead man to repentance and thus to reconcile him to God. In order to do this, He had to reveal God to man and to gain a new power over him, by which He could lead him away from sin. So He came on earth and actually entered into the lot of man, suffered from man's opposition and sin, served him in every way, healed his diseases, sympathized with him in his troubles, and thereby revealed God to him in all His holiness and suffering love. By doing this He broke man's opposition and gained his love. This was the atonement. Christ is not only man's exemplar, but also a power of righteousness in the life of man.

Later on Bushnell received new light, and then saw that God had to be propitiated. Consequently, in his *Forgiveness and Law* he retracted the last part of his former publication, and substituted for it the idea of self-propitiation by self-sacrifice. He laid down the principle that neither God nor man can forgive a sinner until he has sought to do him good and has suffered under his repulses. When man contemplates the forgiveness of one who has wronged him, he feels a resentment that hinders him; but

[196]

he can overcome this resentment by sacrificing something or by suffering for the culprit. So God by His self-sacrifice overcame His resentment to forgiveness, and thus made objective atonement. Bushnell evidently did not realize that he made God inferior to good men, who often forgive freely and gladly without resorting to such unusual methods.

(2) Frederick Denison Maurice. Maurice takes his starting-point in true Alexandrian fashion in Christ as the Logos, and regards Him as the archetype or root of humanity. As such Christ stands in a unique and original relation to the race – an eternal second Adam. In the incarnation He becomes the Mediator between God and man, bringing man into union with God through fellowship with Himself. He is not a substitute for, but the representative of the human race. His sufferings and sacrifice are those due to God from the humanity of which He is the Root and Head, and are accepted by God as a perfect satisfaction. Thus in Christ all men are redeemed, irrespective of their faith, and they need only to be brought to the consciousness of this redemption. The basis of this theory is a realistic union of Christ with mankind. It can be called a Moral Influence Theory in so far as it holds up Christ's offering of obedience as an example for us to follow. Evidently, Maurice's view is also related to that of Schleiermacher.

Maurice on the atonement

(3) McLeod Campbell. The theory of Campbell is sometimes described as the theory of vicarious repentance. Campbell examined the doctrine of the atonement as taught by Owen and Edwards and had great respect for this type of theology. Yet he regards their view of the atonement as defective in that it is too legal and does not sufficiently reflect the love of God. In the admission of Edwards that a perfect repentance would have availed as an atonement, if man had only been capable of adequate repentance, he finds a hint of the true theory of the atonement. He maintains that Christ offered to God, on behalf of humanity, the requisite repentance, and by so doing fulfilled the conditions of forgiveness. The work of Christ really consisted in the vicarious confession of sins in behalf of man. The question naturally arises, how the death of Christ is related to this vicarious

Campbell on the atonement

confession. By His sufferings and death Christ entered sympathetically into the Father's condemnation of sin, brought out the heinousness of sin, and condemned sin; and this was viewed by the Father as a perfect confession of our sins. This condemnation of sin is calculated to produce in man that holiness which God demands in sinful humanity. The great trouble with this theory is that it has no scriptural basis whatsoever, and that it is hard to conceive of vicarious repentance in a sinless being. Moreover, it falls short woefully in its conception of the seriousness of sin.

Irving on the atonement

[c] *The mystical theory of the atonement.* There is another theory that is popular in some circles, namely, the mystical theory that was first taught by Schleiermacher. Bruce speaks of it in its later development as the 'theory of redemption by sample'. It is also known as the *Irvingian Theory*, or the *Theory of Gradually Extirpated Depravity*. We conclude our sketch by calling attention to the views of Edward Irving, the great English preacher and contemporary of Thomas Chalmers. According to him Christ assumed human nature as it was in Adam after the fall, that is, human nature with its inborn corruption and predisposition to moral evil. But through the power of the Holy Spirit, or of His divine nature, He was able to keep this corrupt human nature from manifesting itself in any actual or personal sin, gradually purified it through His sufferings, completely extirpating the original depravity by death, and thus reunited it to God. This purifying of human nature in the person of Jesus Christ constitutes His atonement. Consequently, men are saved, not by any objective propitiation, but by becoming partakers of Christ's new humanity by faith.

QUESTIONS FOR FURTHER STUDY

How did the Marrow-men expose themselves to the charge of universalism? Is it correct to say that Christ is dead for all men, or is available for all? What type of theory did Schleiermacher advocate? Did he conceive of sin as a reality? Does a theory of atonement have a logical place in his system? Does the Ritschlian theology do more justice to the doctrine of the atonement? Do these systems do justice to the death of Christ in the work of redemption? Was Jonathan Edwards in any way responsible for the introduction of the Governmental Theory in New England? What advantage has this theory over the Moral Influence Theories? Why is it, strictly speaking, incorrect to call the latter theories of atonement? Why are these theories so much more popular than the theory of vicarious atonement? Does the theory of Irving do justice to the holiness of Christ? Do his followers still teach it in its original form?

LITERATURE

Franks, *A History of the Doctrine of the Work of Christ*, II, pp 225–259, 329–370, 387–414; Bruce, *The Humiliation of Christ*, pp 309–326; Mackintosh, *Historic Theories of the Atonement*, pp 207–258; Crawford, *The Atonement*, pp 297–381; Sheldon, *History of Christian Doctrine*, II, pp 353–362; Orr, *Progress of Dogma*, pp 338–345; Fisher, *History of Christian Doctrine*, pp 411–413, 437–445, 477–479; Mozley, *The Doctrine of the Atonement*, pp 165–201; Park, *The Atonement* (In New England Theology).

THE DOCTRINE OF
THE APPLICATION
& APPROPRIATION
OF DIVINE GRACE

I: THE SOTERIOLOGY OF
   THE PATRISTIC PERIOD

It is natural to pass from the doctrine of the atonement, or of
the objective work of redemption through Christ, to a discussion
of the method in which believers obtain a share in its benefits,
or of the subjective application of the merits of Christ through
the operation of the Holy Spirit.

I. THE SOTERIOLOGY OF THE FIRST THREE CENTURIES

It would be unreasonable to look for a common, definite, well
integrated, and fully developed view of the application of the
work of redemption in the earliest Church Fathers. Their
representations are naturally rather indefinite, imperfect, and
incomplete, and sometimes even erroneous and self-contradictory. Says Kahnis: 'It stands as an assured fact, a fact knowing
no exceptions, and acknowledged by all well versed in the matter,
that all of the pre-Augustinian Fathers taught that in the
appropriation of salvation there is a co-working of freedom and
grace.'

In harmony with the New Testament statement, that man *Faith in the
obtains the blessings of salvation by 'repentance toward God, early Fathers*
and faith in our Lord Jesus Christ', the early Fathers stressed
these requirements. This does not mean, however, that they at
once had a full and proper conception of faith and repentance.
Faith was generally regarded as the outstanding instrument for
the reception of the merits of Christ, and was often called the
sole means of salvation. It was understood to consist in true
knowledge of God, confidence in Him, and self-committal to
Him, and to have as its special object Jesus Christ and His
atoning blood. This faith, rather than the works of the law, was

[203]

regarded as the means of justification. These ideas are repeatedly expressed by the Apostolic Fathers, and re-occur in the Apologetes alongside of the idea that the new knowledge of wisdom revealed by the Logos has saving significance. Later Fathers, such as Irenæus and Origen, share the idea that man can be saved by faith, while the Latin Fathers, Tertullian, Cyprian, and Ambrose, even surpass them in stressing the utter depravity of man and the necessity of justification by faith. It cannot be said, however, that a clear conception of faith emerged in the thinking of the first three centuries. In their emphasis on faith the Fathers largely repeated what they found in the Bible. It is not altogether clear just what they meant when they spoke of faith. The prevalent idea seems to be that of a merely intellectual assent to the truth, but in some cases it apparently includes the idea of self-surrender. Yet it generally falls far short of the full and rich conception of it as saving trust in Jesus Christ. The Alexandrians sometimes contrast faith and knowledge, representing the former as the initial stage, the acceptance of the truth in a general way, and the latter as the more perfect stage in which its relations and bearings are fully understood.

Moreover, in spite of all their emphasis on the grace of God and on faith as the appropriating organ of salvation, the early Fathers reveal a moralism that is not in harmony with the Pauline doctrine of salvation. The Gospel is frequently described as a new law (*nova lex*). Faith and repentance are sometimes represented as being simply dependent on the will of man. Salvation is made to depend now on the grace of God, and anon on the voluntary co-operation of man.

Alongside of faith repentance was also regarded as a preliminary condition of salvation. There is some doubt as to the exact connotation of the term 'repentance', as it is found in the early Fathers. It is uncertain, whether they conceived of it merely as an act or condition of the mind, or regarded it as including amendment of life. At the same time it is quite evident that, when they speak of it in the former sense, they attach great importance to its external manifestations in penitential deeds. These deeds are even regarded as having expiatory value in atoning for sins

Repentance in the early Fathers

committed after baptism. There is a tendency to stress the necessity of good works, especially works of self-denial, such as liberal almsgiving, abstinence from marriage, and so on, to attach special merit to these, and to co-ordinate them with faith as a means of securing the divine favour. The view taken of good works is legal rather than evangelical. This moralistic perversion of New Testament Christianity found its explanation in the natural self-righteousness of the human heart, and opened a doorway through which a Judaistic legalism entered the Church.

There is another point that deserves notice. The Church Fathers of the first three centuries already reveal an initial drift towards ceremonialism. The idea is widely prevalent among them that baptism carries with it the forgiveness of previous sins, and that pardon for sins committed after baptism can be obtained by penance. Moreover, the thought is gradually gaining ground that the good works of some, and especially the sufferings of martyrs, may serve to atone for the sins of others. Towards the end of this period an excessive value is ascribed to the intercessions of confessors and martyrs, though some of the Church Fathers discourage this idea. Sohm finds the explanation for this departure from the teachings of Scripture in the fact that 'the natural man is a born Catholic'. It was inevitable that in course of time these two fundamentally different types of thought should come into conflict with each other.

Ceremonialism and work-righteousness in the early Fathers

2. THE SOTERIOLOGY OF THE REMAINING CENTURIES OF THE PATRISTIC-PERIOD

Pelagius deviated much further from the Scriptural representation of the application of redemption than any of the earlier Church Fathers. It may even be said that he forsook the biblical foundation which was sacred to them, and re-asserted the self-sufficient principle of heathen philosophy. His conception of sin and its results led him to deny the absolute necessity of the grace of God in Christ unto salvation, and to consider it quite possible for man to obtain salvation by keeping the law. He did not altogether despise the 'help of grace' or 'divine assistance',

Pelagius on grace of God

[205]

but even considered this desirable 'in order that what is commanded by God may be *more easily* fulfilled'. But the grace of which he speaks is not the *gratia interna*, the regenerating grace of God by which the mind is enlightened and the will is inclined to goodness and holiness. It consists only in: (a) 'the good of nature', that is, man's endowment with a free will, so that he can do either good or evil; and (b) the preaching of the Gospel and the example of Christ, both of which are directed to the mind of man and teach the way of salvation. The grace of nature is universal and absolutely essential or necessary, but the grace of the Gospel is neither universal nor necessary, though rendering it easier for men to obtain salvation. It is given only to those who make a proper use of their natural powers. This grace does not operate *directly* and *immediately* on the *will* of man, but only on his *understanding*, which it illuminates, and through this on the will. Moreover, it is quite possible for man to resist its operation. Christianity is regarded as a new law and, in comparison with the Old Testament, as an enlarged law. The real Christian is one who knows God, believes that he is accepted by God, obeys the precepts of the Gospel, and imitates the holiness of Christ rather than the sin of Adam.

Augustine on grace of God Augustine takes his starting-point in a radically different view of man's natural condition. He regards the natural man as totally depraved and utterly unable to perform sprititual good. He also speaks of grace in the objective sense, consisting in the Gospel, baptism, the forgiveness of sins, and so on, but realizes that this is not sufficient, and that sinful man has need of an internal, spiritual grace, a supernatural influence of the Spirit of God by which the mind is enlightened *and the will is inclined to holiness*. This grace, which is the fruit of predestination, is freely distributed according to the sovereign good pleasure of God, and not according to any merits in man. It is a gift of God that precedes all human merits. It renews the heart, illuminates the mind, inclines the will, produces faith, and enables man to do spiritual good. Up to the time of man's renewal its operation is strictly monergistic. Augustine at one time thought it was in the power of man to believe, but was taught otherwise by Paul in 1 Cor 4:7.

He distinguishes between a *gratia operans* and a *gratia co-operans*. The former 'goes before man when unwilling, that he may will'; the latter 'follows him when willing, that he may not will in vain'. This grace is irresistible, not in the sense that it constrains man against his will, but in the sense that it inevitably renews the heart, so that the will voluntarily chooses the right. Man receives the first blessings of grace through baptism, namely, regeneration or the initial renewal of the heart and the forgiveness of sins. Both of these blessings can be lost; in fact, neither of them can be retained unless the grace of perseverance is also received.

Great significance is attached to faith as marking the beginning of the Christian life and as the source of all good works. Augustine conceives of faith primarily as an intellectual assent to the truth, though in some passages he evidently rises to a higher conception. He distinguishes between faith in general and Christian faith, between believing Christ and believing *in* Christ. One really believes in Christ only when one loves Him and fixes one's hope on Him. Christian faith is a faith that works by love. His conception of faith does not yet give due prominence to that childlike trust in Christ which is the crowning element of saving faith. He does regard faith as functioning in the justification of the sinner, for he says that man is justified by faith, that is, obtains justification by faith. But he does not conceive of justification in a purely forensic sense. While it includes the forgiveness of sins, this is not its main element. In justification God not merely *declares* but *makes* the sinner righteous by transforming his inner nature. He fails to distinguish clearly between justification and sanctification and really subsumes the latter under the former. The notable feature of Augustine's doctrinal system is that he refers everything to the grace of God. *Augustine on faith*

The Semi-Pelagians took an intermediate position, denying the total inability of man to do spiritual good, but admitting his inability to perform really *saving* works without the assistance of divine grace. The grace of God illuminates the mind and supports the will, but always in such a manner that the free will of man is in no way compromised. In fact, the two co-operate in the work *Semi-Pelagians on grace of God* of redemption. While the grace of God is universal and intended for all, it becomes effective in the lives of those who make a proper use of their free will. Strictly speaking, it is really the will of man that determines the result. It is up to man to believe and to continue in faith, and grace is needed only for the strengthening of faith. There is no such thing as irresistible grace. Pelagianism was condemned by the Synod of Carthage, by the Council of Ephesus, and again by the Synod of Orange, which also rejected Semi-Pelagianism; and, in a fashion, Augustinianism appeared triumphant in the Church.

Modification of Augustine's views This does not mean, however, that the doctrine of Augustine did not undergo certain modifications. The teachings of this great Church Father himself contained some elements that were in conflict with the idea of man's absolute dependence on the grace of God, and pointed in the direction of ceremonialism and work-righteousness. The following points may be mentioned: (a) Participation in the grace of God is sometimes made dependent on the Church and its sacraments. (b) It is considered regeneration may be lost again. (c) The doctrine of justification by faith, so vital to a true conception of the way of salvation, is ~~faith, so vital to a true conception of the way of salvation, is~~ represented in a way that can hardly be reconciled with the doctrine of free grace. The grace of God freely given, does not consist primarily in the forgiveness of sins – which is in fact a minor point in Augustine's system – but in regeneration, in the infusion of a grace which enables man to do good works and to merit everlasting life. Faith justifies, not because it appropriates the righteousness of Jesus Christ, but because it works by love. Man, it is true, has no merits antecedent to the operation of grace and the gift of faith, but when the grace of renewal and faith is wrought in the heart, his works are indeed meritorious. Fundamentally, therefore, grace merely serves the purpose of making it possible for man once more to merit salvation.

Now these elements are certainly foreign to Augustine's main line of thought, but were eagerly seized upon by some in the Church and gave countenance to teachings that were more Semi-Pelagian than Augustinian. There was a protracted struggle between Augustinianism and Semi-Pelagianism, which revealed a strong opposition to the doctrines of predestination, the total inability of man to do spiritual good, and irresistible grace. And the position that was finally sanctioned by the Church was that of a moderate Augustinianism. Seeberg says that 'the doctrine of "grace alone" came off victorious; but the doctrine of predestination was abandoned. The irresistible grace of predestination was driven from the field by the sacramental grace of baptism. The doctrine of grace was hereby brought into closer relationship with the popular Catholicism, as also by the exaltation of good works as the aim of the divine impartation of grace.' *History of Doctrines*, I, p 382.

There were influences at work in the Church that were contrary to the doctrine of grace as the source of all spiritual blessings and of faith as the principle from which good works proceed; influences which induced many to exalt outward works, to insist on their meritorious character, and to stress them at the expense of the great subjective conditions of salvation. The following should be noted particularly: (a) There was a tendency to confound faith with orthodoxy in the assumption that to believe was simply to hold an orthodox creed. The attention was focused on a list of doctrines that required assent, and was diverted from faith as an attitude of the soul to God, productive of the fruits of righteousness. (b) Works of mercy and self-discipline were highly commended and often described as the proper way of making satisfaction for the sins of believers. (c) Many Church Fathers distinguished between divine commands and evangelical counsels, of which the former were absolutely binding on all Christians, while compliance with the latter was a matter of choice, but brought greater reward to those who observed them. This distinction was made in the interest of monasticism, and tended to make eminent holiness the prerogative of a class that was diligent in the performance of certain externals. (d) The increasing practice of saint-worship and dependence on the intercession of saints, and especially of the virgin Mary, proved detrimental to spiritual conceptions of salvation. It led to externalism and to reliance on the works of

Contrary influences in the Church

[209]

man. The underlying idea was that the saints had a super
abundance of good works, and could simply transfer some o
them to others. (e) There was a growing tendency to make salv
ation dependent on baptism, which marked the entrance int
that Church outside of which there is no salvation. In the Eas
the possibility of being saved without baptism was doubted
and in the West it was absolutely denied. Even Augustin
taught that children which die unbaptized are lost.

QUESTIONS FOR FURTHER STUDY

What accounts for the emphasis on faith from the very beginning? Doe
Scripture justify the special prominence given to repentance? Does th
patristic conception of repentance agree with the scriptural idea of it? Hov
does penance differ from repentance? What led to the conception of Chris
tianity as a new law? How can it be explained that faith was primarily under
stood as intellectual assent to the truth? Do the early Fathers relate faith i
justification? Have they a proper conception of this relation? Do they regar
good works merely as the fruits of faith, or as meritorious performances
How do they conceive of the forgiveness of sins after baptism? What di
Cyprian mean, when he wrote, 'There can be no salvation to any except i
the Church'? How far does Augustine regard divine grace as operating in
purely monergistic manner? Did he consider regeneration as a sure sign c
election? Did he regard it as possible that some of the elect are finally lost?

LITERATURE

Means, *Faith, An Historical Study*, pp 80–176; Scott, *The Nicene Theology*
Lecture IV; Buchanan, *The Doctrine of Justification*, pp 77–98; Swete, *Th
Forgiveness of Sins*, pp 87–116; Bavinck, *Gereformeerde Dogmatiek*, III, p
573–586; Wiggers, *Augustinianism and Pelagianism*, pp 177–228; Otten
Manual of the History of Dogmas, I, pp 89–98, 180–189, 368–381; Sheldon
History of Christian Doctrine, I, pp 125–132, 258–267; Crippen, *History o
Christian Doctrine*, pp 146–153; Seeberg, *History of Doctrines*, I, cf Inde
under 'grace', 'faith', justification', 'baptism', 'penance', 'good works', an
so forth.

II: THE SOTERIOLOGY OF THE
SCHOLASTIC PERIOD

When we come to the scholastic period, we meet with a variety of opinions respecting the main elements of the saving process, such as grace, faith, justification, merit, and good works. On the whole the position of the Church was that of a mild Augustinianism, though there appears in the Schoolmen a drift in the direction of Semi-Pelagianism. We shall briefly consider some of the main concepts.

I. THE SCHOLASTIC CONCEPTION OF GRACE

There was one point on which the prevailing opinion among the Scholastics was in agreement with Augustinianism rather than with Pelagianism and Semi-Pelagianism. While the latter asserted that it lay in the power of the natural man to originate and increase faith, the Scholastics generally maintained that man could not do this without the aid of *sufficient* grace. But this is about as far as the agreement with Augustine went. And even here the agreement was not complete, for Augustine asserted the necessity of *efficient* grace. There was no general agreement on the subject of grace among the Schoolmen. The views of Peter the Lombard, which show an unmistakable affinity with those of Augustine, were rather widely accepted. He considered it difficult to define the exact nature of grace, but preferred to think of it as a supernatural quality or power wrought in man, and distinguished between a *gratia operans*, which enables man to turn to God in faith, and a *gratia co-operans*, which co-operates with the will and is effective in bringing about the desired result. Only the former, and this merely as it is first bestowed on man, is wrought in him without any action on his part, and is purely

The Scholastics on grace

a gift of gratuitous mercy. All further communication of grace to man is dependent on the active consent and co-operation of the will. The free will of man acts, but divine grace assists it as a co-operating principle, and thus secures the desired effect.

The representation of Alexander of Hales is in general agreement with that of Peter the Lombard, but he introduced another division, which is characteristic of scholastic theology, when he spoke of a *gratia gratis dans*, a grace *giving* freely (referring to the gracious activity of God), a *gratia gratis data*, a grace *given* freely (designating all actual graces and infused virtues), and a *gratia gratum faciens*, a grace making gracious (grace as a permanent quality of the soul, making it well-pleasing to God). Thomas Aquinas uses these terms in a somewhat different sense, and thereby determined their later usage. While he employs the term *gratia gratum faciens* as a designation of all the supernatural helps intended for the recipient's own sanctification, he restricts the term *gratia gratis data* to those gratuitous gifts that aim at the good of others rather than at that of the recipient. In connection with the *gratia gratum faciens* he distinguishes between prevenient or operating and subsequent or co-operating grace. The former renews the will, and the latter assists it in its operations; the former may be called *sufficient* and the latter *efficacious*.

2. THE SCHOLASTIC CONCEPTION OF FAITH

The Scholastics on faith There was a general tendency in the scholastic period to distinguish between faith as a form of knowledge, a mere assent to the truth, and faith as a spiritual affection, productive of good works. Peter the Lombard makes a threefold distinction here, namely, *Deum credere*, *Deo credere*, and *in Deum* or *Christum credere*. The first two mean practically the same thing, that is, to accept as true what God says; but the last denotes faith in a deeper sense, by which we enter into communion with God. He says that it is one thing to believe God, to believe that what He says is true, and quite another to believe in God, that is, to believe so as to love Him, to go to Him, to cleave to Him, and to be joined to the members of the body of Christ. He also makes a distinction between the faith which is believed, that is, the creed or dogma, and the faith by which one believes and is justified.

After his day it became customary to distinguish between a *fides informis*, consisting in a mere intellectual assent to the truth, and a *fides formata* (*charitate*), a faith which is augmented, vivified, and determined by the power of love, and of which love is therefore the formative principle. Moreover, it was emphatically declared that, while the *fides informis* was one of the preparations for justification, only the *fides formata*, which includes the right inward disposition and works by love, is the faith that justifies. At the same time the priesthood considered it advantageous to stress the idea that unquestioning submission to the authority of the Church was the main characteristic of faith, and some of the theologians rather encouraged that notion.

3. THE SCHOLASTIC CONCEPTION OF JUSTIFICATION AND MERIT

Augustine's confusion of justification and sanctification was not rectified but rather intensified by the Schoolmen. Their common teaching is that justification is effected through the infusion of sanctifying grace into the soul by God. It includes on the part of God the infusion of sanctifying grace and the forgiveness of sins, and on the part of man the turning of his free will to God through faith and contrition. Naturally, the last elements are not included in the case of infants, for in them justification is entirely the work of God, and as such comprises only the infusion of grace and the remission of original sin.

The Scholastics were generally agreed as to what was included *The* in justification, and never conceived of it as a mere imputation *Scholastics* of the righteousness of Christ to the sinner. They differed, how- *on* ever, in their determination of the logical order of the various *justification* elements in justification. According to Thomas Aquinas there is first of all the infusion of grace, then the turning of the free will to God, next the turning of the free will against sin, and, finally, the remission of guilt. Alexander of Hales and Bonaventura, however, contend for a different order, namely, attrition or

[213]

turning from sin, infusion of grace, remission or expulsion of sin, and the turning of the free will to God. The moment grace is infused, however, attrition becomes contrition, and then sin is expelled by grace.

Duns Scotus has an altogether different opinion. He conceives of justification as consisting of two divine operations, namely, the forgiveness of sins and the renovation of the soul through sanctifying grace. While the two are simultaneous in time, in the order of nature the forgiveness of sin precedes the infusion of grace.

The Scholastics speak of justification as an instantaneous act, but the Council of Trent makes mention of a progressive increase of justification. With respect to the assurance of possessing the grace of justification, Aquinas maintains that this is not the common privilege of believers in general. These must be satisfied with a reasonable conjecture, based upon the signs of grace. Absolute assurance is given only to those who have accomplished or suffered much for the sake of religion, and then by means of a special revelation.

Alongside of the doctrine of free grace, and in connection with *The* that of justification, the doctrine of merit came to the foreground. *Scholastics* The meritoriousness of virtue, especially as expressed in good *on merit* works, was generally taught in the Middle Ages, and was hardly opposed by any scholastic theologian of note. Thomas Aquinas distinguished between two kinds of merit, namely, 'merit of condignity', which in strict justice deserves reward and belongs to Christ alone, and 'merit of congruity', which is fit to be rewarded and can be acquired by men. However, his followers, the Thomists, went so far as to assert that *after* justification a man may by the aid of divine grace acquire a merit of condignity, that is, can do something that gives him a claim on God. The followers of Duns Scotus denied this, but maintained that good works done *before* justification might obtain a merit of congruity and on this basis receive an increase of grace. They held that the perfection of the divine character would impel God to bestow on man the grace thus merited.

The Roman Catholic doctrine of the application and appropriation of divine grace finally assumed the following form. Children born within the pale of the Church receive the grace of regeneration, including an infusion of grace and forgiveness of sin, in baptism. Others, however, who come under the influence of the Gospel in later years, receive sufficient grace, that is, an illumination of the understanding and a strengthening of the will by the Holy Spirit. They can resist but also yield to this work of God and follow the promptings of the Spirit. By yielding to it and co-operating with God they prepare themselves for the grace of justification (*gratia infusa*). This preparation consists of the following seven elements: (a) Assent to the truth taught by the Church; (b) insight into one's sinful condition; (c) hope in the mercy of God; (d) the beginnings of love to God; (e) an abhorrence of sin; (f) a resolution to obey the commandments of God; and (g) a desire for baptism.

Final form of Roman Catholic soteriology

It is quite evident that faith does not occupy a central place here, but is co-ordinated with the other preparations. It is merely an intellectual assent to the doctrines of the Church (*fides informis*), and acquires its justifying power only through the love that is imparted in the *gratia infusa*, by which it becomes a *fides caritate formata*. It can be called justifying grace only in the sense that it is the first of the seven preparations, and in that sense the basis and root of justification.

After this sevenfold preparation justification itself follows in baptism. It consists in the infusion of grace (super-natural virtues), followed by the forgiveness of sins. The measure of this forgiveness is commensurate with the degree in which sin is actually overcome. It is given freely and is not merited by the preceding preparations. And it is preserved by obeying the commandments and by doing good works. In the *gratia infusa* man receives the supernatural strength to do such works, and thus to merit with a merit of condignity all following grace and everlasting life. The grace of God, therefore, serves the purpose of enabling man once more to merit salvation. But it is not certain that the precious gift of justification will be retained. It may be lost, not only through unbelief, but by any mortal sin. It may be regained, however, by the sacrament of penance, consisting in contrition (or attrition), confession, together with absolution, and works of satisfaction. Both the guilt of sin and eternal punishment may be removed by absolution, but the temporal penalties of sin can only be cancelled on the basis of works of satisfaction.

QUESTIONS FOR FURTHER STUDY

What factors contributed to the externalization of religion in the Middle Ages? Did the Scholastics emphasize external or internal grace? What was their conception of divine grace, and how does their view compare with that of Augustine? How did their representations of the *gratia gratis dans* differ? How does Aquinas' use of the terms *Gratia gratis data* and *gratia gratum faciens* differ from that of the earlier Scholastics? What was the most prevalent conception of faith in the scholastic period? Did they conceive of faith as excluding merit? Did they have the Pauline conception of justification by faith? What did justification include? How is faith related to justification in the Roman Catholic system? How do you account for the Roman Catholic position that ordinary believers cannot have an assured faith?

LITERATURE

Means, *Faith, An Historical Study*, pp 177–226; Buchanan, *The Doctrine of Justification*, pp 87–99; Swete, *The Forgiveness of Sins*, pp 117–127; Ritschl, *History of the Christian Doctrine of Justification and Reconciliation*, pp 73–120; McGiffert, *History of Christian Thought*, II, pp 185–312; Bavinck, *Gereformeerde Dogmatiek*, III, pp 580–586; Otten, *Manual of the History of Dogmas*, II, pp 234–271, 338–360; Sheldon, *History of Christian Doctrine*, I, pp 370–380; Crippen, *History of Christian Doctrine*, pp 153–158; Histories of Seeberg and Fisher, cf Index.

III: REFORMATION AND POST-REFORMATION SOTERIOLOGY

1. THE LUTHERAN ORDER OF SALVATION

It was especially the system of penances as developed in the Roman Catholic Church and the traffic in indulgences closely connected with it, that prompted Luther to take up the work of reformation. He himself was deeply engaged in works of penance, when from Rom 1:17 the truth flashed upon him that man is justified by faith only, and he learned to understand that the repentance demanded in Matt 4:17 had nothing in common with the Roman Catholic works of satisfaction, but consisted in real inner contrition of the heart and was a fruit of the grace of God only. It dawned upon him that the really important thing in repentance was not the private confession before a priest, which has no foundation in Scripture, nor any satisfaction rendered by man, since God freely forgives sin; but a heartfelt sorrow on account of sin, an earnest desire to lead a new life, and the forgiving grace of God in Christ. Therefore he made the doctrine of sin and grace central once more in the doctrine of salvation, and declared that the doctrine of justification by faith alone was 'the article of a standing or falling Church'. The result was that the Reformation rejected all that was most distinctive in mediæval theology, such as indulgences, expiatory penances, priestly absolution in the Roman Catholic sense, works of supererogation, and the doctrine of human merit.

Scholars differ as to the relation in which Luther placed repentance and faith to each other. Ritschl holds that he first regarded repentance as a fruit of faith, but afterwards placed it before faith as wrought by the law; but Lipsius denies this change and maintains that the great Reformer always regarded *poenitentia* as including contrition, wrought by the law, and

Luther on faith and repentance

THE DOCTRINE OF THE APPLICATION

faith as a believing acceptance of Jesus. Both are instrumental
in leading the sinner to Christ, and therefore do not yet presup-
pose a union with Him. At the same time it can be said that in
the earlier period of his life his opposition to Roman Catholic
work-righteousness prompted him to stress the fact that *true
repentance* is the fruit of faith, and that in a later period he met
antinomianism with the assertion that true faith is preceded
by a deep feeling of penitence. But he always conceived of the
way of salvation as consisting in *contritio* (penitence in the
limited sense, that is sorrow on account of sin), *fides*, and *bona
opera*, a life consecrated to God. This order is retained by the
early Lutheran theologians, and is also that of the confessional
standards of the Church.

The Lutheran *ordo salutis*, which at first comprised only
Lutheran three elements, became far more elaborate in the writings of
ordo salutis the great Lutheran theologians of the seventeenth century. It
was based rather artificially on Acts 26:17, 18, and made to
include calling, illumination, conversion, regeneration, justification, renovation and glorification. In the doctrine that all who
live under the Gospel receive sufficient grace, either in baptism
or through the preaching of the word, whereby they are enabled
to not-resist the grace of God in regeneration, the germ of
synergism made its appearance in Lutheran soteriology, and the
process of salvation was conceived of as follows: Children born
of Christian parents, who cannot yet resist the grace of God, are
regenerated in baptism and receive the gift of faith. Others,
however, are called in later life with a *vocatio sufficiens*, which is
alike in all cases, and which by illumining the mind and strengthening the will enables them to not-resist the grace of God. If
they do not resist the work of the Holy Spirit in calling, they are
brought to contrition (penitence in the limited sense), are regenerated, and are endowed with the gift of faith. By faith they
are then justified, receive the forgiveness of sins, are adopted
as children of God, are incorporated into Christ, are renewed
by the Holy Spirit, and are finally glorified.

Such is the process in all those in whom it is completed; but
its beginning does not yet ensure its completion. The grace of

[218]

God is always resistible, can be resisted all along the line, can always be lost no matter how far its work has progressed, and that not merely once but several times. Notwithstanding the strong assertions that man owes his salvation entirely to God, it is held that man can frustrate the divine operation effectively, so that the decision really lies with him.

Furthermore, the Lutheran *ordo salutis* centres in faith and justification. Strictly speaking, calling, repentance, and regeneration, are merely preparatory and serve the purpose of leading the sinner to Christ. It is not until he by faith accepts the righteousness of Christ, that God pardons his sin, sets him free from the law, adopts him as His child, and incorporates him into the mystical body of Jesus Christ. Everything, therefore, depends on faith. With it man enters increasingly on the possession of the blessings of salvation, but without it he loses all. Hence it is of the utmost importance to retain this faith. While this is the *ordo salutis* as it is usually represented, it does not always reveal exactly the same form in later Lutheran theology.

2. THE REFORMED ORDER OF SALVATION

In Reformed theology the *ordo salutis* acquired a somewhat different form. This is due to the fact that Calvin consistently took his starting-point in an eternal election and in the mystical union established in the *pactum salutis*. His fundamental position is that there is no participation in the blessings of Christ, except through a living union with the Saviour. And if even the very first of the blessings of saving grace already presupposes a union with Christ, then the gift of Christ to the Church and the imputation of His righteousness precedes all else. In the Council of Peace a union was already established between Him and those who were given unto Him by the Father, and in virtue of that union, which is both legal and mystical, all the blessings of salvation are ideally already the portion of those who are of Christ. They are ready for distribution and are appropriated by them through faith.

From this fundamental position several particulars follow.

Calvin's ordo salutis

The salvation of the elect is not conceived atomistically, since they are all eternally in Christ, and are born out of Him, who is the Head, as members of His mystical body. Regeneration, repentance, and faith are not regarded as mere preparations, altogether apart from any union with Christ, nor as conditions to be fulfilled by man, either wholly or in part, in his own strength. They are blessings of the covenant of grace, which already flow from the mystical union and the grant of Christ to the Church. Penitence assumes a different place and character than in the Lutheran order. Calvin recognized a repentance preceding faith, but saw in it merely an initial fear, a legal repentance that does not necessarily lead to faith and cannot be regarded as an absolutely essential preparation for it. He stresses the repentance that flows from faith, that is possible only in communion with Christ, and that continues throughout life. Moreover, he does not regard it as consisting of *contritio* and *fides*. He recognises the close connection between repentance and faith, and did not consider the former possible without the latter, but also pointed out that Scripture clearly distinguishes the two, and therefore ascribed to each of them a more independent significance in the order of salvation.

But however Calvin may have differed from Luther as to the order of salvation, he quite agreed with him on the nature and importance of the doctrine of justification by faith. In their common opposition to Rome they both describe it as an act of free grace, and as a forensic act which does not change the inner life of man but only the judicial relationship in which he stands to God. They do not find the ground for it in the inherent righteousness of the believer, but only in the imputed righteousness of Jesus Christ, which the sinner appropriates by faith. Moreover, they deny that it is a progressive work of God, asserting that it is instantaneous and at once complete, and hold that the believer can be absolutely sure that he is for ever translated from a state of wrath and condemnation to one of favour and acceptance.

Lutheran theology did not always remain entirely true to this position. Faith is sometimes represented as a work that is basic for regeneration; and the mediating theologians base justification on the infused righteousness of Jesus Christ.

3. THE ARMINIAN ORDER OF SALVATION

The Arminians teach that God bestows a universal grace on man, which is sufficient to enable the sinner to believe and obey the Gospel; and that the call which comes to man through the preaching of the Word exerts a merely moral influence on his understanding and will. If he assents to the truth, trusts in the grace of God and obeys the commandments of Christ, he receives a greater measure of divine grace, is justified *on account of his faith* and, if he perseveres to the end, becomes a partaker of life eternal. *Arminian ordo salutis*

The School of Saumur moved in the same general direction. Cameron teaches that the will of man always follows the final dictate of the understanding, and that therefore in regeneration and conversion an effective illumination of the mind is all that is required and all that actually takes place. There is no supernatural operation of the Holy Spirit *directly on the will of man*. And Pajon holds that a special internal operation of the grace of God is unnecessary, and that the efficacy of the divine calling depends on its congruity with the external circumstances in which it comes to man. *Views of the school of Saumur*

These Arminian teachings led to that representation of the *ordo salutis*, which was known in England as Neonomianism. According to the Neonomians Christ atoned for the sins of all men, that is, made salvation possible for all and brought them all into a savable state. He did this by meeting the demands of the old law, the law of the covenant of works, and by substituting for it a new law, a law of grace which is satisfied with faith and conversion, and a true, albeit imperfect, obedience of the repentant sinner. This work of Christ may be called the sinner's legal righteousness, since it was instrumental in satisfying and abrogating the old law. But evangelical righteousness, consisting in obedience to the new law, that is, faith and conversion, constitutes the ground of the sinner's justification. This rationalistic ten- *Neonomian views* dency finally resulted in that liberalism which recognizes Christ only as a great prophet and teacher, who proclaimed the truth of God and sealed it with His death, and whose example man has but to follow, in order to obtain eternal salvation.

Wesleyan view

Methodism is another, more pietistic, form of Arminianism. It is averse to the idea of gradual conversions, and knows of no lengthy period of contrition, followed by a period in which the darkness is dispelled and the light breaks through, and a still later season when doubt turns into the glad assurance of salvation. It concentrates all efforts in the preaching of the Gospel on a single point: casting the sinner down by the preaching of the law, dragging him, as it were, to the very brink of the abyss, filling his heart with fear and trembling; and then placing him at once before the glorious Gospel of redemption, and pleading with him to accept Jesus Christ by faith and be saved from eternal damnation. The sinner who does so accept Christ passes in a single moment from the greatest misery into the most rapturous ecstasy, and from the deepest gloom into the most transcendent joy. This sudden transition carries with it an immediate assurance of being saved. Many Methodists hold that a second radical change is necessary, and is actually wrought in man, for entire sanctification.

4. MINOR CONCEPTIONS OF THE ORDER OF SALVATION

Antinomian soteriology

[a] *Antinomian.* The Antinomians really leave no room for a subjective application of the redemption wrought by Christ. They do not distinguish between the work of Christ in procuring, and that of the Holy Spirit in applying the blessings of saving grace; but speak as if Christ did all there is to be done, as if He took upon Himself not only our guilt but also our pollution, so that we are justified, regenerated, and sanctified – in short, are perfect in Him. In view of the fact that man is subjectively righteous and holy in Christ, the only thing required of him is to believe, that is, to become conscious of that fact. He may rest assured that God can see no sin in him as a believer. His so-called sins are not really sins, but merely works of the old

man, which are not reckoned to the believer, since he is free from the law, is perfect in Christ, and glories in the grace of God. Sometimes the Antinomian will go even further than that, and claim that Christ did not really merit salvation, since this was eternally ready in the counsel of God, but merely revealed the love of God. To believe, is simply to lay aside the false notion that God's anger is kindled against us. Such ideas as these prevailed among some of the Anabaptists, the Libertines, the Hattemists, and certain sects both in England and in New England.

[b] *Mystical.* In Germany, England, and the Netherlands a large number of preachers arose who sought the essential thing of the Christian life in experience, and emphasized the fact that true faith is experience. They enlarged on what one must needs experience before one can be considered as a true believer, and in doing this were primarily guided, not by the representations of Scripture, but by the experiences of those who were reputed to be 'oaks of righteousness'. They held that the law should be preached to all, but the Gospel only to certain 'qualified' sinners. Before men might really believe themselves to be children of God, they had to be brought under the terrors of the law, had to pass through agonizing struggles, had to feel the accusing pangs of conscience, and had to writhe in the throes of a fearful anticipation of eternal damnation. They were not permitted to believe without some special warrant of the Holy Spirit and even then their faith could at first be only a faith that flees for refuge to Jesus Christ, a hungering and thirsting for righteousness. This faith precedes and is the condition of justification; in it the sinner entrusts himself to Christ, in order to be justified. This refuge-seeking faith does not at once turn into an assured faith. There is a great distance between the two, and it is only after many ups and downs, after all kinds of doubts and uncertainties, and through many spiritual struggles, that the believer passes into the assurance of salvation – the privilege of but a select few. This assurance often comes to him in a very special way, by a voice, a vision, a word from Scripture, and other similar means.

Mystical soteriology

QUESTIONS FOR FURTHER STUDY

What were the three usual stages of the *ordo salutis* in the theology preceding the Reformation? Should the *ordo salutis* stress the application or the appropriation of the work of redemption? How do Lutherans, Reformed, and Arminians differ on this point? What elements do the Lutherans consider as the most important in the *ordo salutis*? How do the Reformed differ from them in this respect? What views did Schwenkfeld, Agricola, Osiander, and the Dutch Mennonites hold as to faith and justification? How do the Lutherans and the Anglicans conceive of regeneration by baptism? Do the Reformed connect the grace of regeneration with baptism in any way? What is the Wesleyan doctrine of entire sanctification? What views did the Reformed, the Arminians, and the Wesleyans hold as to the assurance of salvation?

LITERATURE

Bavinck, *Gereformeerde Dogmatiek* III, pp 587–690; Buchanan, *The Doctrine of Justification*, pp 100–219; Swete, *The Forgiveness of Sins*, pp 128–141; Heppe, *Geschichte des Pietismus;* ibid, *Dogmatiek*, II, pp 262–395; Pope, *Christian Theology*, II, pp 439–451; Bavinck, *Roeping en Wedergeboorte;* Kramer, *Het Verband van Doop en Wedergeboorte;* Sheldon, *History of Christian Doctrine*, II, pp 153–181; Crippen, *History of Christian Doctrine*, pp 158–169; Seeberg, *History of Doctrines*, II, cf Index.

THE DOCTRINE
OF THE CHURCH
AND THE
SACRAMENTS

I: THE DOCTRINE OF THE CHURCH

I. IN THE PATRISTIC PERIOD

The doctrine of the Church also has its roots in the earliest *The Church* literature of the Christian era. In the Apostolic Fathers and in *in the early* the Apologetes the Church is generally represented as the *Fathers* *communio sanctorum*, the people of God, which He has chosen for a possession. While it is spoken of as the true Israel, its relation to its historic preparation in Israel was not always well understood. But even in the second century a perceptible change came about in the conception of the Church. The rise of heresies made it necessary to designate some external characteristics by which the true Catholic Church could be known. The result was that the Church began to be conceived as an external institute, ruled by a bishop as a direct successor of the apostles, and in possession of the true tradition. The idea became prevalent that the universal Church was the historical 'prius' of all local churches. The local churches were not conceived as so many separate units, but as parts of the universal Church with the episcopacy; and they were regarded as true churches only as long as they were loyal and subject to the catholic Church as a whole.

In the sects, however, another tendency manifested itself, *The Church* namely, to make the holiness of its members the real mark of *in the sects* the true Church. It was represented by Montanism in the middle of the second, by Novatianism in the middle of the third, and by Donatism in the beginning of the fourth century. These sects were born of a reaction against the gradual secularization and the increasing worldliness and corruption of the Church. The Montanist leaders inveighed with prophetic authority against the laxity and worldliness of the churches, and insisted on ascetic practices. They spoke of gross sins committed after baptism as being unpardonable; but also of the possibility of atoning for mortal sins by martyrdom. The Novatians did not share the prophetic claims of the Montanists, but followed their example in striving for the purity of the Church. They held that the Church had no power to forgive those who had denied the faith during the Decian persecution and sought readmission to the Church. Finding that many bishops readmitted such members, and that the churches in general were lax in discipline, they rebaptized those who joined their circle. The Donatists represented the same tendency during the persecution of Diocletian. They insisted on rigorous ecclesiastical discipline and pure church-membership, rejected unworthy ministers, and protested against State interference in religious matters; but at the same time themselves courted the favour of the emperor.

Cyprianic conception of the Church

The Church Fathers took issue with all these sectaries and emphasized ever increasingly the episcopal institution of the Church. Cyprian, the disciple of Tertullian, has the distinction of being the first to develop the doctrine of the episcopal Church. He regarded the bishops, chosen by the Lord Himself, as the real successors of the apostles, and maintained on the basis of Matt 16:18, that the Church was founded on the bishops. The bishop was regarded as the absolute lord of the Church. It was up to him to decide who could belong to the Church and who might be restored to its fellowship. He conducted the worship of the Church as a priest of God, and in that capacity offered sacrifices. Cyprian was the first one to teach an actual priesthood of the clergy *in virtue of their sacrificial work.* According to him the bishops constituted a college, called the episcopate, and as such represented the unity of the Church. He based the unity of the Church on the unity of the bishops. At the same time he maintained the parity of the bishops and ascribed no primacy to the bishop of Rome. Rebellion against the bishop was regarded as rebellion against God. Anyone who refused to submit to the rightful bishop thereby forfeited his fellowship with the Church and consequently also his salvation. True members will always obey and remain in the Church, *outside of which there is no possibility of being saved.* This conception of the Church logically caused Cyprian to deny the validity of baptism administered by heretics. To him it was perfectly evident that one who was himself outside the Church could not induct others into it. Moreover, he believed that only the leaders who received the Spirit – and He was received only in the Church – could impart the forgiveness of sins. Thus Cyprian was the first to bring out clearly and distinctly the idea of a catholic Church, comprehending all true branches of the Church of Christ, *and bound together by a visible and external unity*. This is what Cunningham calls 'Cyprian's grand contribution to the progress of error and corruption in the Church'. *Historical Theology*, I, p 169.

Augustine moved in the same general circle of thought. It was his struggle with the Donatists that compelled him to reflect more deeply on the essence of the Church. Sad to say, his conception of the Church does not altogether harmonize with his doctrine of sin and grace. As a matter of fact there is a certain dualism in his idea of the Church. On the one hand he is the predestinarian who conceives of the Church as the company of the elect, the *communio sanctorum*, who have the Spirit of God and are characterized by true love. The really important thing is to belong to the Church so conceived, and not to be in the Church in a merely outward sense and to partake of the sacraments. It is through the intercession of this community that sins are forgiven and that gifts of grace are bestowed. The real unity of the saints and therefore of the Church is an invisible one. At the same time it exists only within the catholic Church, for it is there only that the Spirit works and that true love dwells. *Augustine on the Church*

On the other hand he is the Church-man, who holds to the Cyprianic idea of the Church, at least in its general aspects. The true Church is the catholic Church, in which the apostolic authority is continued by episcopal succession. It is spread throughout the world, and outside of it there is no salvation, for it is only within its pale that one is filled with love and receives the Holy Spirit. Its sacraments are not merely symbols, but are also accompanied with an actual exertion of divine energy. God really forgives sins in baptism, and in the Lord's Supper actually gives spiritual refreshment to the soul. For the present this

Church is a mixed body, in which good and evil members are present, but it is destined for perfect purity in the future.

The Donatists criticized Augustine by saying that he split the Church into two Churches, the mixed Church of the present and the pure Church of the future in heaven. In answer to them he maintained the purity of the one catholic Church also in the present, but sought it more particularly in the objective institution with its offices, sacraments, and ministrations. In addition to that, however, he also defended a certain subjective purity. While he admitted that good and evil members were commingled in the Church, he held that these two were not in it in exactly the same sense. While the wicked cannot be outwardly excluded, they are nevertheless inwardly separated from the pious: they belong to the house, but are not in the house; they are the evil tumours in the body of Christ that are destined to be sloughed off. Thus Augustine effected in thought the purity which the Donatists sought to realize in actual life.

Another point to be taken into consideration here, is Augustine's doctrine of the Kingdom of God. The earlier Church Fathers used the term 'Kingdom of God' to describe the result and goal of the Church's development, that is, as the designation of the eschatological Kingdom. But Augustine says: 'The Church is even now the Kingdom of Heaven.' By this he means primarily that the saints constitute the Kingdom of God, though he also applies the term to the leaders of the Church collectively. While the Kingdom is essentially identical with the pious and holy, it is also the episcopally organized Church. The contrast between the city of God and the city of the world (or, of the devil) is regarded as equivalent to that between Christianity and heathenism, between the good and the bad (including angels and devils), between the saints and the wicked even within the Church, between the spiritual and the carnal, between the elect and the non-elect. The evil world is never represented as *equivalent* to the State, but since the *civitas Dei* may be and is frequently conceived as the empirical Church, it is possible that – as is frequently said – he thought of the *civitas mundi* as finding its concrete embodiment in the State.

Augustine on the Kingdom of God

Augustine did not effect a true synthesis of his divergent views respecting the Church, and it may well be questioned whether such a synthesis is possible. Harnack calls attention to the fact that in Augustine 'the *externa societas sacramentorum,* which is *communio fidelium et sanctorum,* and finally also the *numerus praedestinatorum* are one and the same Church'. *Outlines of the History of Dogma,* p 362. Consequently a threefold answer may be given to the question, Who are in the Church? It may be said: (a) all the predestinated, including those who are still unconverted; or (b) all believers, including those who will relapse; or (c) all those who have part in the sacraments. But then the question arises, Which is the true Church, the external communion of the baptized, or the spiritual communion of the elect and the saints, or both, since there is no salvation outside of either? Moreover, how is the Church, as constituted of the number of the elect, related to the Church as the communion of the faithful? They are clearly not identical, for some may be of the faithful who are not of the elect and are finally lost. And when Augustine says that no one has God for a Father, who does not have the Church, that is the one visible catholic Church, for a mother, the question naturally arises, What about the elect who never join the Church? Again, if the one visible catholic Church is, as he maintains, the true body of Christ, does not this prove the contention of the Donatists that wicked persons and heretics cannot be tolerated in it? Once more, if the Church is founded on the predestinating grace of God, how is it possible that they who have once received the grace of regeneration and the forgiveness of sins in baptism, should lose this again and thus forfeit salvation? And, finally, if God is the only absolute source of all grace and dispenses it in a sovereign way, can it be considered proper to ascribe this power to the visible Church with its sacraments, and to make salvation dependent on membership in that organization? In connection with this point it may be said that Augustine's predestination views kept him from going as far as some of his contemporaries did in the direction of sacramentalism.

Want of synthesis in Augustine's view

2. IN THE MIDDLE AGES

It is a striking fact that, while the theologians of the Middle Ages have very little to say about the Church, and therefore contribute but few elements to the development of the doctrine of the Church, the Church itself actually developed into a close-knit, compactly organized, and absolute hierarchy. The seeds for this development were found in the writings of Cyprian and in the teachings of Augustine respecting the Church as an external organization. The other and more fundamental idea of the great Church Father, that of the Church as the *communio sanctorum*, was entirely disregarded and thus remained dormant. Two ideas became very prominent during the Middle Ages, namely, that of the primacy of Rome, and that of the identity of the Church and the Kingdom of God.

Development of the papal idea

The tradition gained currency in the fourth and fifth centuries that Christ had given Peter an official primacy over the other apostles, and that this apostle had been the first bishop of Rome. Furthermore, it was asserted that this primacy was passed on to his successors, the bishops of the imperial city. This idea was not only fostered by successive bishops, but also appealed to the popular imagination, because at the fall of the Western Empire it seemed to contain a promise of the renewal, in another form, of the ancient glories of Rome. In the year 533 the Byzantine Emperor Justinian recognized the primacy of the bishop of Rome over the occupants of the other patriarchal sees. Gregory the Great still refused the title 'Universal Bishop', but in 607 it was conferred on his successor, Boniface III, who had no scruples in accepting it. From this time on the spiritual primacy of the succeeding bishops of Rome was generally honoured in the West, though strenuously resisted in the East. It marks the beginning of Popery. The Church thus received an external and visible head, who soon developed into an absolute monarch.

Identification of the hierarchical Church with the Kingdom of God

Alongside of this the idea developed that the Catholic Church was the Kingdom of God on earth, and that therefore the Roman bishopric was an earthly kingdom. This notion was greatly encouraged by two notorious forgeries, the 'Donation of Con-

[232]

stantine' and the 'Forged Decretals', both of which were foisted upon the people in the ninth century to prove that the authority then claimed by the Popes had been conferred upon, and exercised by, their predecessors as early as the third century.

The identification of the visible and organized Church with the Kingdom of God had important and far-reaching consequences. If the Church alone is the Kingdom of God, then all Christian duties and activities must take the form of services rendered to the Church, for Christ speaks of the Kingdom as the highest good and as the goal of all Christian endeavour. Natural and social life thus assumed a one-sided churchly character. All that did not come under the control of the Church was considered as purely secular, and its renunciation became a work of special piety. The life of hermits and monks stood out as a grand ideal.

Another result was that an undue significance was ascribed to the outward ordinances of the Church. The Kingdom of God is represented in the New Testament, not only as the aim of the Christian life, but also as the sum-total of Christian blessedness. Consequently, all the blessings of salvation were thought of as coming to man through the ordinances of the Church. Without their use salvation was considered to be impossible.

And, finally, the identification of the Church and the Kingdom led to the practical secularization of the Church. As an external Kingdom the Church felt in duty bound to define and defend its relation to the kingdoms of the world, and gradually began to pay more attention to politics than to the salvation of souls. Worldliness took the place of other-worldliness. It was but natural that the Roman Pontiffs, in view of the superior character of the Kingdom of God and of its all-comprehensive destiny, should seek to realize the ideal of the Kingdom by demanding of the emperors subjection to the rule of the Church. This was the consuming ambition of such great Popes as Gregory VII (Hildebrand), Innocent III, and Boniface VIII.

It was not until after the Reformation that the Roman Catholic conception of the Church was officially formulated. Yet it is best to call attention to the form it finally assumed at this point, be-

Roman Catholic doctrine of the Church

[233]

cause the idea already found actual embodiment in the Church of Rome before the Reformation, and because the Protestant conception is best understood when seen against the background of the Roman Catholic idea of the Church. The Council of Trent did not venture upon a discussion of the proper definition of the Church. This was due to the fact that, while the highest officials of the Church desired recognition of the papal system, a great number of the bishops were thoroughly episcopal in their ideas. They were not ready to admit that all ecclesiastical authority belongs primarily to the Pope, and that the bishops derive their authority from him; but held that the bishops derive their authority directly from Christ. This clashing of views made it imprudent to attempt the formulation of a definition of the Church.

The Tridentine Catechism, however, defines the Church as 'the body of all the faithful who have lived up to this time on earth, with one invisible head, Christ, and one visible head, the successor of Peter, who occupies the Roman see'. Cardinal Bellarmine (1542–1621) surpasses all others of his day in giving a clear representation of the Roman Catholic conception of the Church. According to him the Church is 'the company of all who are bound together by the profession of the same Christian faith and by the use of the same sacraments and are under the rule of legitimate pastors and principally Christ's vicar on earth, the Roman Pontiff'. The first clause of this definition (profession of the same Christian faith) excludes all unbelievers; the second (use of the same sacraments), catechumens and those that are excommunicated; and the third (obedience to the Roman Pontiff) all schismatics, such as the Greek Christians.

The following particulars should be noted in connection with the Roman Catholic conception of the Church:

1. The visible nature of the Church is strongly emphasized. *Visible nature of the Church* The ultimate reason for the visibility of the Church is found in the *incarnation* of the divine Word. The Word did not descend into the souls of men, but appeared as a man among men, and in harmony with this appearance now carries on His work through a visible human medium. The Church can even be

[234]

regarded as a continuation of the incarnation. Christ Himself provided for the organization of the Church by appointing the apostles and by placing one of them (Peter) at the head of the apostles. The Popes are the successors of Peter, and the bishops, of the apostles in general. The former possess direct and absolute authority, while the latter have only a limited authority derived from the Popes.

2. A very important distinction is made between the teaching church (*ecclesia docens*) and the hearing, learning or believing church (*ecclesia audiens, discens,* or *credens*). The former consists of the whole clerus with the Pope at its head; the latter, of all the faithful who honour the authority of their lawful pastors. It is primarily to the *ecclesia docens* that the Roman Catholic ascribes the attributes which he applies to the Church. She is the one only, catholic, apostolic, infallible, and perpetual Church, which denies all others the right of existence, and therefore assumes an intolerant attitude over against them. The *ecclesia audiens* is altogether dependent on it, and has part in the glorious attributes of the Church only in a derivative manner.

Teaching and hearing Church

3. The Church is made up, like a human person, of body and soul. The soul of the Church consists at any particular time of 'the society of those who are called to the faith of Christ, and who are united to Christ by supernatural gifts and graces'. Not all the elect are in the soul of the Church; neither are all those who are in it elect, since there are always some that fall away; and some of those who are not in the body of the Church may be in the soul, such as catechumens possessing the necessary graces. The body of the Church is the society of those who profess the true faith, whether they be just or sinners. Only baptized persons belong to the Church; but some baptized persons, such as catechumens, do not yet belong to it.

Body and soul of the Church

4. In the Church Christ distributes the fullness of those graces and blessings which He merited for sinners. He does this exclusively through the agency of the clergy, that is, through the legitimate officers of the Church. Consequently, the institute of the Church logically precedes the organism, the visible Church precedes the invisible. The Church is a *mater fidelium* before she

The Church dispenser of grace

[235]

is a *coetus fidelium*. The *ecclesia docens* precedes the *ecclesia audiens*, and is far superior to it.

5. The Church is exclusively an institute of salvation, a saving ark. As such she has three functions: (1) to propagate the true faith by means of the ministry of the Word; (2) to effect sanctification by means of the sacraments; and (3) to govern believers according to ecclesiastical law. But it is only the *ecclesia docens* that can do all this. Strictly speaking, therefore, she constitutes the Church. She is (under Christ) the only Mediator of salvation, the depository and distributor of grace for all men, and the only ark of safety for the entire human race. The order in the work of salvation is, not that God by means of His Word leads men to the Church, but just the reverse, that the Church leads men to the Word and to Christ.

The Church institute of salvation

3. DURING AND AFTER THE REFORMATION

The conception of the Church that was born of the Reformation was quite different from that of the Roman Catholic Church. Luther was gradually weaned from the papal conception. The Leipsic disputation opened the way for new ideas on the Church and its authority.

[a] *The Lutheran view.* Luther rejected the idea of an infallible Church, of a special priesthood, and of sacraments that operate in a magical way; and restored to its rightful place the scriptural idea of the priesthood of all believers. He regarded the Church as the spiritual communion of those who believe in Christ, a communion established and sustained by Christ as its Head. He stressed the oneness of the Church, but distinguished between two aspects of it, the one visible and the other invisible. According to Seeberg Luther was the first to make this distinction. He was careful to point out, however, that these are not two churches, but simply two aspects of the same Church. His insistence on the invisibility of the Church served the purpose of *denying* that the Church is *essentially* an *external society with a visible head*, and of affirming that the essence of the Church is to be found in the sphere of the invisible: in faith, communion

Lutheran doctrine of the Church

with Christ, and in participation in the blessings of salvation through the Holy Spirit.

This same Church, however, becomes visible and can be known, not by the headship of the Pope, nor by the rule of cardinals and bishops, nor by all kinds of external paraphernalia, but by the pure administration of the Word and the sacraments. The really important thing for man is that he belongs to the spiritual or invisible Church; but this is closely connected with membership in the visible Church. Christ gathers the Church by His Spirit, but in doing this binds Himself to the chosen means, the Word and the sacraments. Hence the necessity of an outward ecclesiastical society, which Luther describes as 'the number or multitude of the baptized and believing who belong to a priest or bishop, whether in a city, or in a whole land, or in the whole world'. He admits that the Church, externally considered, will always harbour a number of hypocritical and wicked members, who do not share in the spiritual exercises of the Church. The Augsburg Confession defines the visible Church as 'the congregation of the saints in which the Gospel is rightly taught and the sacraments are rightly administered'.

[b] *The Anabaptist view.* The Anabaptists represent the most extreme reaction against the Roman Catholic externalization of the Church. While Rome based its Church organization largely on the Old Testament, they denied the identity of the Old Testament Church with that of the New, and insisted on a Church of believers only. Though children had a place in the Church of the Old Testament, they have no legitimate place in the Church of the New Testament, since they can neither exercise faith nor make a profession of it. In their insistence on the spirituality and holiness of the Church many of them even scorned the visible Church and the means of grace. In distinction from the Lutherans with their territorial system, the Anabaptists demanded the absolute separation of Church and State, some even going to the extreme of saying that a Christian cannot be a magistrate, may not swear an oath, nor take part in any war.

[c] *The Reformed view.* The Reformed conception of the Church is fundamentally the same as the Lutheran, though *Reformed doctrine of the Church*

[237]

differing from it in some relatively important points. Both agree that the real essence of the Church is found in the *communio sanctorum* as a spiritual entity, that is, in the invisible Church. But while the Lutherans seek the unity and holiness of the Church primarily in the objective ordinances, such as the offices, the Word, and the sacraments, the Reformed find these to a far greater extent in the subjective communion of believers. According to the former the blessings of salvation can be obtained only in and through the Church, since God in dispensing His grace binds Himself absolutely to the ordained means, the preaching of the Gospel and the administration of the sacraments. Some of the Reformed, however, were of the opinion that the possibility of salvation extends beyond the borders of the visible Church, and that the Spirit of God is not absolutely bound to the ordinary means of grace, but may work and save 'when, where, and how He pleases'. Then, too, the Reformed spoke of the invisibility of the Church in more than one sense: (1) as *ecclesia universalis*, because no one can ever see the Church of all places and all times; (2) as *coetus electorum*, which will not be completed and visible until the parousia; and (3) as *coetus electorum vocatorum*, because we are not able to distinguish absolutely the true believers from the false. Finally, the Reformed found the true marks of the Church, not only in the true administration of the Word and the sacraments, but also in the faithful administration of Church discipline. Besides all these there were also important differences as to the government of the Church.

[d] Divergent post-Reformation views

Socinian and Arminian views of the Church

(1) Socinian and Arminian. This altered conception of the Church had important practical consequences. Uniformity made way for multiformity, and this, in turn gave rise to various Confessions. The Reformers sought to maintain the proper connection between the visible and the invisible Church, but history proved this to be very difficult. And churches outside of the Lutheran and Reformed communions often sacrificed the invisible to the visible Church, or *vice versa*. The Socinians indeed spoke of the invisible Church, but in actual life forgot all

[238]

about it, since they conceived of the Christian religion simply as an acceptable doctrine. And the Arminians followed suit by denying explicitly that the Church is essentially the invisible communion of the saints and by making it primarily a visible society. Moreover, they robbed the Church of its independence by yielding the right of discipline to the State, retaining for the Church only the right to preach the Gospel and to admonish its members.

(2) Labadist and Methodist. The opposite tendency also manifested itself, namely, to disregard the visible Church. Jean de Labadie founded an 'evangelical congregation' at Middelburg in 1666, to which only true believers might belong. Pietism in general insisted strongly on a practical religion. It not only combated worldliness, but viewed the world itself as an organism of sin, which every 'awakened' Christian must shun, lest he put his soul in jeopardy. At the same time it made people indifferent towards the institutional Church with its functions and sacraments, and brought them together in conventicles. The real Church was considered ever-increasingly in such circles as the communion of those who shared in a special illumination of the Holy Spirit, and who, in virtue of the inner light, also agreed outwardly in their profession and life. This view is also found in some circles of Methodism, the consistent application of it being seen in the Salvation Army. The converts do not form a church, but a standing army of Jesus Christ, distinguished from the world by a distinctive uniform and a special mode of life.

De Labadie on the Church

(3) Roman Catholic. The Roman Catholic Church moved even further in the direction of an absolute hierarchy after the days of the Reformation, and became more pronounced in affirming the authority of the Pope. The Gallican Party, of which Bossuet was the original leader, maintained for two centuries, in opposition to the Jesuits and the Ultramontane Party, that the Pope may err in his decisions, and is always subordinate to an oecumenical council. This was also the common teaching of a large number of Roman Catholic textbooks. In 1791 fifteen hundred English Catholics signed a statement denying that papal infallibility was a dogma of the Roman Catholic Church. How-

ever, the opposition of the Gallicans was gradually overcome, and in 1870 the Vatican Council declared that 'the Roman *Papal* Pontiff when speaking *ex cathedra* – that is to say when fulfilling *infallibility* the office of pastor and teacher of all Christians – in virtue of his supreme apostolic authority defines a doctrine regarding faith or morals, *de fide vel moribus*, as a doctrine to be held by the universal Church, then through the divine assistance which has been promised him in the person of St Peter he enjoys fully that infallibility which the divine Redeemer wished his Church to have in defining doctrine touching faith and morals; and consequently such definitions of the Roman Pontiff are of themselves unchangeable and are not to be changed through approval of the Church'. The Germans were not willing to submit to this decision, and therefore constituted themselves the 'Old Catholic Church', with Dr Doellinger, the historian, as leader, and Dr Reinkens as its first bishop. Over against the Protestants the Roman Catholics continue to glory in their unity, though this is more apparent than real. The Church is not only divided on the question of papal infallibility, but also harbours an ever-increasing number of monastic orders, often leading to rivalries and bitter disputes, which show that they stand further apart than many of the Protestant denominations. Moreover, the Reform, the Los-von-Rom, and the Modernistic movements clearly show that the boasted unity of the Church of Rome is a mere corporate uniformity rather than a unity of spirit and purpose.

QUESTIONS FOR FURTHER STUDY

What special significance did Cyprian have for the development of the doctrine of the Church? Can Augustine's views on the Church be reduced to a consistent unity? How can we account for the duality in his representation? How did the priestly conception of the ministry arise? How do the Augustinian and the Roman Catholic conceptions of the Kingdom of God differ? What is the essential difference between the Roman Catholic view of the Church and that of the Reformers? How do the Roman Catholics, the Lutherans, and the Reformed respectively conceive of the relation between the Church and the State? How do present-day Modernists conceive of the Church?

LITERATURE

Bannerman, *The Church of Christ*, Vol I; A. Taylor Innes, *Church and State;* Schaff, *Church and State;* Hagenbach, *History of Doctrines*, I, pp 271–277; II, pp 62–67, 312–319; III, pp 122–140, 369–374; Neander, *History of Christian Dogmas*, I, pp 218–228; II, pp 394–398; Sheldon, *History of Christian Doctrine*, I, pp 133–136, 268–270, 384–391; II, pp 182–191, 378–382; Otten, *Manual of the History of Dogmas*, I, pp 171–179, 323–337; II, pp 214–233; Crippen, *History of Christian Doctrine*, pp 170–172, 182–189, 209–221; Seeberg, *History of Doctrines*, cf Index.

II: THE DOCTRINE OF THE SACRAMENTS

I. THE SACRAMENTS IN GENERAL

[a] Development of the doctrine before the Reformation

The term 'sacraments' is derived from the Latin *sacramentum* by which the Vulgate rendered the Greek *musterion*, which i used in the New Testament to designate something that wa not revealed in the Old Testament, but later on it acquired anothe connotation. It became the designation of all that was mysteriou and incomprehensible in the Christian religion and in othe religions, including mysterious actions or things. This meaning of the term was also transferred to the Latin word *sacramentum* which originally designated an oath required of a soldier, or a sum of money deposited as security in cases of litigation and forfeited to the State or to the gods, if the case was lost.

Sacraments in the early Church This accounts for the fact that the word 'sacrament' had a rather wide application in the early Christian centuries. It could be used of anything to which the idea of sanctity could be attached. Tertullian applies it to the works of the Creator, and to the work of the incarnate Son, particularly His death. The sign of the cross, the salt that was given to the catechumens, the ordination of the priests, marriage, exorcism, the celebration of the sabbath – they were all called sacraments. At the same time the term was applied predominantly to baptism and the Lord' Supper. The same loose usage of the term is found in the writings of Augustine, Hilary, Leo the Great, Gregory the Great and others.

The sacraments in the scholastic period On the whole it may be said that the Scholastics followed th Augustinian conception of the sacraments as visible signs and mediums of an invisible grace. There was no unanimity as to

[242]

their number which ranges all the way from five to thirty (Hugo of St Victor). Peter the Lombard was the first to name the well-known seven of the Roman Catholic Church. In virtue of the fact that his *Sententiae* became the general handbook of theology, his private opinion soon became a *communis opinio*, and finally the Council of Florence officially adopted these seven in 1439: baptism, confirmation, eucharist, penance, priestly consecration, marriage, and extreme unction.

This restriction of the number of sacraments naturally led to the delimitation of the concept. A doctrine of the sacraments was still a desideratum: the relation of the sensible to the spiritual element was not clearly defined; neither was there a clear representation of the manner in which the sacraments work. Augustine had occasionally made the operation of the sacraments so dependent on faith in the recipient, that the external sacrament became only an image of what God works in the soul. This notion was also clearly reflected in one of the views that was prevalent in the scholastic period and which, in fact, was dominant for some time, namely, that the sacraments do not contain but only symbolize grace, though God has covenanted to accompany the use of the sacraments with a direct operation of His grace in the souls of the recipients. This view is found in Bonaventura and Durandus, and became the prevailing one in the Middle Ages through the advocacy of Duns Scotus.

Alongside of this view, however, there was another, namely, that grace truly resides in the visible sacrament. This does not mean that it resides in the visible elements as a permanent power, but that 'the words of the institution effect a spiritual *virtus* (efficacy) in the external sign, which resides in the latter until this *virtus* has accomplished its end'. Hugo of St Victor and Thomas Aquinas advocated this view, which was finally adopted by the Church.

In connection with the question, whether the operation of the sacraments depends in any way on the worthy or unworthy reception or administration of them, Scholasticism gravitated to the opinion that they are effectual *ex opere operato*, that is, in virtue of their objective administration. This means, of course,

[243]

that the reception of sacramental grace is not dependent on the spiritual devotion of the recipient, nor on the character of the officiating priest, though a spiritual preparation for the reception of the sacrament will certainly bring its reward. The working of the sacraments *ex opere operato* was considered to mark the superiority of the New Testament sacraments over those of the Old Testament.

The Council of Trent on the sacraments   The Council of Trent passed several decisions respecting the sacraments, of which the following are the most important: (1) The sacraments are necessary unto salvation, that is, they must be received or at least desired by those who would be saved. It cannot be said, however, that they *are* all necessary *for every man*. (2) They contain the grace which they signify, and confer this *ex opere operato*, or through the act performed, upon one who does not present an obstacle to their operation, such as a mortal sin or some other obstacle. (3) The intention of the officiating priest to administer the sacrament in all sincerity, doing what the Church intends, is essential to its validity. He must intend to do what the Church does, but for the rest may be in mortal sin. (4) The sacraments of baptism, confirmation, and order (or, ordination) impress an indelible character on the soul of the recipient, and therefore are not repeated. (5) The priests, and the priests only are the legitimate administrators of the sacraments. However, confirmation and ordination can be administered by bishops only, and baptism may in cases of necessity be administered by laymen.

Besides baptism and the Lord's Supper the following sacraments are recognized: confirmation, penance, extreme unction, ordination (orders), and marriage. These may be briefly described as follows: (1) Confirmation is the sacrament in which, through the bishop's laying on of hands, unction, and prayer, those already baptized receive the sevenfold grace of the Holy Spirit, so that they may steadfastly profess their faith, and faithfully live up to it. (2) Penance is the sacrament by which forgiveness for post-baptismal *mortal* sins is obtained by those who are heartily sorry for their sins, sincerely confess them, and are willing to perform the penance imposed upon them. (3)

[244]

Extreme unction is the sacrament in which those who appear to be near death, by the anointing with holy oil, and by the prayer of the priest, receive special grace to confide in the mercy of God and to resist the final attacks and temptations of the devil. (4) Ordination or Holy Orders is the sacrament which communicates to those who receive it the full power of the priesthood, together with a special grace to discharge their duties well. (5) Marriage is the sacrament by which a man and a woman are joined in holy wedlock, and receive the necessary grace to discharge the duties of their state faithfully until death.

The following points deserve attention here: (1) Rome conceives of the grace communicated in the sacraments exclusively as an infused sanctifying grace that raises man to the supernatural order and makes him a partaker of the divine nature. It is regarded as a supernatural gift that comes to man from without. The forgiveness of sins, which is generally connected with baptism in Scripture, occupies a relatively unimportant place in the system of Rome. (2) The connection of the sacrament with the Word is practically ignored. The Word has some, but only a preparatory significance in that it works a purely historical faith, which cannot really save, except when it is informed by love, that is, by a *gratia infusa*. Since this love is communicated only by the sacrament, the latter acquires an independent significance alongside of the Word and really surpasses it in value. (3) Faith is not an absolute requirement for the reception of the sacrament. Sanctifying grace is present as a material element in the sacrament, is communicated by it *ex opere operato*, and presupposes at most that the recipient places no insuperable obstructions in the way.

[b] The doctrine of the Reformers and of later theology

In every one of the points just mentioned the Reformation subjected the doctrine of the sacraments to a scriptural revision. Luther, Calvin, and Zwingli were agreed in their opposition to Rome. They united in the position that the grace imparted in the sacrament is first of all the *forgiving* grace of God, which bears on the *guilt* of sin rather than on the lower nature of man de-

Points on which the Reformers agreed

[245]

prived of the *donum superadditum*. They also shared the conviction that the sacraments are signs and seals attached to the Word, which communicate no kind of grace that is not also imparted by the Word, and which have no value apart from the Word. And, finally, they also concurred in the opinion that, not the sacrament itself, but its operation and fruit is dependent on faith in the recipient, and therefore always presupposes saving grace.

Luther's view

But while they were at one on these particulars, it soon became manifest that they differed on important points. The sacraments became a bone of contention among them. In opposition to Rome, Luther at first stressed the fact that the operation of the sacraments is dependent on faith in the recipient, and later on gave greater prominence to their intimate and essential connection with the Word, of which they are signs and seals. They differ from the Word especially in this that they are not addressed to the Church in general, but to individuals. As a result of his struggle with the Anabaptists he, after 1524, emphasized the absolute necessity of the sacraments and their objective character, making their effectiveness dependent on the divine institution rather than on the subjective state of the recipient. Cf. Heppe, *Dogm.* III, p 380. The same controversy caused him to insist on the temporal, corporal, and local connection between the sign and the thing signified. In his opinion the divine power is present in the sacrament *as the visible Word*, and as such the vehicle of divine grace.

Zwingli's view

Since the sacraments are administered only to believers, Zwingli conceives of them as being first of all signs and proofs of faith, and only secondarily means for the strengthening of faith as reminders of the blessings appropriated by faith, and as directing our faith away from ourselves to the grace of God in Jesus Christ. For him the sacraments were memorials and badges of profession, though he also uses expressions which seem to point to a deeper significance.

Calvin's view

Calvin also regards the sacraments as acts of confession, but only secondarily. To him they are first of all signs and seals of the promises of God which direct attention to the riches of

[246]

His grace. He finds their essential element in the word of promise, in the covenant of grace, and in the person of Christ with all His blessings. But he did not conceive of these spiritual blessings as deposited in the visible elements, as inherent in these, making them more or less independent distributors of divine grace. For him God is and remains the only source of grace, and the sacraments are merely the instruments by which it is communicated. God communicates this grace only to believers by nourishing and strengthening their faith. Unbelievers may receive the external sign, but do not participate in the thing signified.

Outside of the Lutheran and Reformed Churches the Zwinglian conception of the sacraments enjoyed great popularity. The Anabaptists denied that the sacraments are seals and regarded them as signs and symbols only. They give a visible representation of the blessings conveyed to believers, but do this merely as acts of confession; they communicate no grace. *Zwinglian tendencies*

Socinians regarded the Lord's Supper as a memorial of Christ's death, and baptism merely as a primitive rite of profession for Jewish and pagan converts, without any permanent validity. The Arminians do speak of the sacraments as exhibiting and sealing the blessings of grace, but do not want to convey the idea that they are seals of the promise of God and communicate grace. They are rather simply signs of the covenant between God and man, in which the former exhibits His grace, and the latter pledges to lead a holy life.

Rationalists reduced the sacraments to mere memorials and badges of confession, aiming at the promotion of virtue. Schleiermacher made an attempt to maintain their objective character, and to unite all the different views in a higher synthesis, but did not succeed. In the nineteenth century many Neo-Lutherans and the Puseyites in England advocated a doctrine of the sacraments that reminds us very strongly of the Roman Catholic conception.

2. BAPTISM

[a] Development of the doctrine before the Reformation

Baptism was foremost among the sacraments as the rite of initiation into the Church. Even in the Apostolic Fathers we find *Baptism in the early Church* the idea that it was instrumental in effecting the forgiveness of sins and in communicating the new life of regeneration. In a certain sense it may be said, therefore, that some of the early Fathers taught baptismal regeneration. Yet this statement requires some limitations: (1) They held baptism to be efficacious in the case of adults only in connection with the right inner disposition and purpose, though Tertullian seemed to think that the very reception of the rite carried with it the remission of sins. (2) They did not regard baptism as absolutely essential to the initiation of spiritual life, or the life of regeneration; but viewed it rather as the completing element in a process of renewal.

Infant baptism was evidently quite current in the days of Origen and Tertullian, though the latter opposed it on the ground of the inexpediency of placing young children under the heavy responsibility of the baptismal covenant. The general opinion was that baptism ought in no case to be repeated; but there was no unanimous opinion as to the validity of baptism administered by heretics. The bishop of Rome asserted that it could be regarded as valid, but Cyprian denied this. The former finally gained the upper hand, and it became a fixed principle not to re-baptize those who had been baptized according to the trinitarian formula. The mode of baptism was not in dispute. While immersion was practised, it was not the only mode, and certainly was not considered to be of the essence of baptism.

Augustine on baptism

From the second century on, the conception of baptism gradually changed. The idea gained ground ever increasingly that the sacrament works more or less magically. Even Augustine promoted this view to some extent, though he considered faith and repentance as the necessary conditions of baptism in the case of adults. In the case of infants, however, he seems to have assumed that the sacrament was effective *ex opere operato*. He held that children which die unbaptized are lost, and that in the case of those who are baptized, the faith of the Church, represented by the sponsors, can be accepted as that of the child. Moreover, he maintained that baptism in every case impresses on the child a *character indelibilis*, in virtue of which it belongs by right to Christ and His Church. He defined the effect

[248]

of baptism more specifically than was customary by stating that, while it wholly removes original sin as a matter of guilt, it does not wholly remove it as a corruption of nature. In general, baptism was now considered as absolutely necessary, though martyrdom was regarded as a full equivalent for baptismal washing. In view of these facts, it stands to reason that infant baptism was generally practised.

The Scholastics at first shared the view of Augustine, that baptism in the case of adults presupposes faith, but gradually began to consider the sacrament as effective *ex opere operato*, and to minimize the importance of subjective conditions. Thus the way was paved for the Roman Catholic conception of baptism, according to which it is the sacrament of regeneration and of initiation into the Church. It contains the grace which it signifies and confers it *ex opere operato* on all those who do not put an obstacle in the way. The grace so conferred is of the utmost importance, since it includes: (1) The *character indelibilis*, which brings one under the jurisdiction of the Church. (2) Deliverance (a) from the guilt of original sin and from the guilt of sins committed up to the time of baptism; (b) from the pollution of sin, though concupiscence remains as the fomenting agent of sin; and (c) from eternal punishment and also from all temporal punishments, except in so far as these are the natural results of sin. (3) Spiritual renewal by the infusion of sanctifying grace and of the supernatural virtues of faith, hope, and love. (4) Incorporation into the communion of the saints, and into the visible Church of believers. Because of this importance of baptism, it was deemed quite essential that it should be administered as soon as possible, and in cases of necessity by laymen or even by non-Christians.

The Scholastic conception of baptism

[b] *The doctrine of the Reformers and of later theology*

The opposition of the Reformation to the Roman Catholic doctrine of the sacraments did not centre in baptism, but in the Lord's Supper. In fact, the German Reformers adopted much of the baptism of the Roman Catholic Church, even retaining many of the ceremonies connected with it, such as the sign of

Lutheran conception of baptism

[249]

the cross, exorcism, sponsorship, and so on. Luther taught that the Word of God with its intrinsic divine power makes the water of baptism a gracious water of life and a washing of regeneration. It is not simply common water, but 'the water comprehended in God's command and connected with God's Word'. *Smaller Catechism* IV. 1. At first he made the salutary effect of baptism dependent on faith, but in view of the fact that children can hardly exercise faith, he next held that God by His prevenient grace works faith in the unconscious child, and finally he turned the questions involved over to the doctors, saying 'We do not baptize upon that (faith in the infant), but solely upon the command of God'. Many of the Lutheran theologians, however, retained the doctrine of an infant-faith, either as a pre-condition for baptism, or as an immediately produced effect of its administration. In the latter case the implication is, of course, that the sacrament works *ex opere operato*. It works regeneration and takes away the guilt and power of sin, but does not entirely remove its pollution. The *radix aut fomes peccati* remains.

Anabaptist conception of baptism

In opposition to both Luther and Zwingli a new sect arose during the Reformation, in Germany, Switzerland, and the Netherlands, which denied the validity of infant baptism. Its adherents were called Anabaptists by their opponents, since they insisted on rebaptizing those who were baptized in infancy, when these desired to join their circle. They did not consider this a rebaptism, however, because they did not regard infant baptism as a true baptism. In their estimation there was no true baptism that was not preceded by a voluntary profession of faith in Jesus Christ. Children really have no standing in the Church. The spiritual successors of the Anabaptists prefer to speak of themselves as Anti-Pædo-Baptists.

Reformed conception of baptism

The Reformed proceeded on the assumption that baptism was instituted for believers and therefore does not work but strengthens faith. But by proceeding on this assumption they faced a twofold difficulty. They had to prove in opposition, especially to the Anabaptists, but also to the Roman Catholics and the Lutherans, that children can be regarded as believers before baptism, and as such ought to be baptized. And in addition to that they had to define the spiritual benefit which the child receives in baptism, seeing that it is not yet in a position to exercise active faith, and therefore cannot be strengthened in it. On the whole little attention was paid to the last point. It was generally said that baptism gives the parents the assurance that their child is incorporated in the covenant, is a rich source of consolation for the child as it grows up, and gives it, even in its unconscious state, a title to all the blessings of the covenant.

The answers to the question, how the children that receive baptism are to be considered varied from the start. There was general agreement in establishing the right of infant baptism by an appeal to Scripture and particularly to the scriptural doctrine of the covenant. Children of believers are covenant children, and are therefore entitled to the sacrament. Opinions differed, however, as to the implications of this covenant relationship. According to some it warrants the *assumption* that children of believing parents are regenerated until the contrary appears in doctrine or life. Others, deeply conscious of the fact that such children often grow up without revealing any signs of spiritual life, hesitated to accept that theory. They admitted that regeneration before baptism was quite possible, but preferred to leave it an open question, whether elect children are regenerated before, at (during), or perhaps long after baptism. It was felt that the cases varied and did not conform to a general rule. In harmony with this idea the spiritual effect of baptism as a means of grace was not limited to the time of the administration of the sacrament. Some even regarded baptism as nothing more than a sign of an external covenant. Under the influence of Socinians, Arminians, and Anabaptists it became quite customary in some circles to deny that baptism was a seal of divine grace, and to regard it as a mere act of profession on the part of man.

3. THE LORD'S SUPPER

[a] *Development of the doctrine before the Reformation.*

At first the Lord's Supper was accompanied with a common meal, for which the people brought the necessary ingredients.

The Lord's Supper in the early Church

These gifts were called oblations and sacrifices, and were blessed by the bishop with a prayer of thanksgiving. In course of time names derived from this practice, such as *prosphorai* (oblations), *thusiai* (sacrifices), and *eucharistia* (thanksgiving), were applied to the Lord's Supper itself. This was rather harmless in itself, but led to a dangerous development, when the clerical idea was strengthened and the bishop became a priest. Then the thanksgiving was regarded as a consecration of the elements in the Lord's Supper, and the Supper itself assumed the character of a sacrifice brought by the priest (bishop). This, in turn, affected the representation of the sacramental union. The symbolical or spiritual conception found in Origen, and essentially also in Eusebius, Basil, Gregory of Nazianzus, and others, was supplanted by the doctrine that the flesh and blood of Christ were in some way combined with the bread and wine in the sacrament (Cyril, Gregory of Nyssa, Chrysostom, John of Damascus), and this again passed into the doctrine of transubstantiation.

Augustine on the Lord's Supper

In the West the development of the doctrine of the Lord's Supper was slower, but led to the same result. Augustine admitted that the sacrament was in a sense the body of Christ, and in the language of Scripture often spoke of bread and wine as the body and blood of Christ. At the same time he clearly distinguished between the sign and the thing signified, and asserted that the substance of bread and wine remains unchanged. He stressed the commemorative aspect of the rite, and maintained that the wicked, though they may receive the elements, do not partake of the body. He even protested against the superstitious reverence that was paid to the ordinance by many in his day. In fact, the views of Augustine retarded the full development of the realistic theory for a long time.

Scholastic development of the doctrine of the Lord's Supper

During the Middle Ages the doctrine as taught by Augustine gradually gave way for the doctrine of the Roman Catholic Church. In AD 818 Paschasius Radbert formally propounded the doctrine that the material elements in the sacrament are by divine power *literally changed into* the very body that was born of Mary, the outward appearance of bread and wine being, after consecration, a mere veil that deceives the senses. This doctrine

[252]

was opposed by the foremost theologians of the day, and particularly by Rabanus Maurus and Ratramnus, who points out that the new teaching confounds the sign with the thing signified and replaces faith by a gross materialism. The new doctrine was defended, however by Gerbert (1003), and shortly after that became the subject of a furious controversy. About the year 1050 Berenger of Tours affirmed that the body of Christ is indeed present in the Eucharist, not in essence, but in power; that the elements are changed but not in substance; and that, in order to secure this change and power, not merely consecration, but faith on the part of the recipient as well is needed. His views were strenuously opposed by Lanfranc (1089) and Humbert (1059), who made the crass statement that 'the very body of Christ was truly held in the priest's hand, broken and chewed by the teeth of the faithful'. This view was finally defined by Hildebert of Tours (1133), and designated as the doctrine of *transubstantiation*. It became an article of faith, when it was formally adopted by the fourth Lateran Council in 1215. This doctrine suggested a good many problems to the Schoolmen, such as those respecting the duration of the change effected, the relation of substance and accidents, the manner of Christ's presence in both elements and in every part of them, the adoration of the host, and so on.

The Council of Trent dealt with the subject of the eucharist as recorded in Sessio XIII of its Decrees and Canons. The gist of what is contained in eight Chapters and eleven Canons may be stated as follows: Jesus Christ is truly, really, and substantially present in the holy sacrament. The fact that He is seated at the right hand of God according to the natural mode of existence does not exclude the possibility that He may be present in several other places at the same time according to a higher, spiritual and supernatural mode of existence. We may not be able to explain how, but we can conceive of the possibility of His substantial and sacramental presence in several places simultaneously. By the words of consecration the whole substance of bread and wine is changed into the body and blood of Christ. The entire Christ is present under each species and

The Council of Trent on the Lord's Supper

[253]

under each particle of either species, so that he who receives one particle of the host receives the whole Christ. He is present not only in the moment of the administration, but even before the reception of the elements by the communicant, since the Lord called the bread his body even before the disciples received it. In view of this presence of Christ in the eucharist the adoration of the host and the festival of the *Corpus Christi* are but natural. The chief effects of the sacrament are: 'increase of sanctifying grace, special actual graces, remission of venial sins, preservation from grievous (mortal) sin, and the confident hope of eternal salvation'.

[b] The doctrine of the Reformers and of later theology

Luther's conception of the Lord's Supper The Reformers one and all rejected the sacrificial theory of the Lord's Supper and the mediæval doctrine of transubstantiation. But that is about as far as their agreement in the matter went. When they addressed themselves to the positive task of constructing a scriptural doctrine of the Lord's Supper, their ways parted. Luther at first taught that bread and wine were signs and seals of the forgiveness of sins, but soon adopted another view, in which he opposed Zwingli's figurative interpretation of the words of the institution. He asserted the necessity of taking these words literally and assumed a real bodily presence of Christ in the Lord's Supper. At the same time he rejected the Catholic doctrine of transubstantiation, substituting for it the doctrine of consubstantiation, defended at length by Ockham in his *De Sacramento Altaris*. In his larger Catechism Luther expresses himself as follows: 'The very body and blood of our Lord Jesus Christ are, by the word of Christ, instituted and given to us Christians to be eaten and drunk in and under bread and wine.' According to him the body is also received by unbelievers who partake of the sacrament, but only to their condemnation.

Zwingli's view of the Lord's Supper Zwingli opposed especially the idolatry of the mass, and denied absolutely the bodily presence of Christ in the Lord's Supper. He interpreted the words of the institution figuratively, taking the word 'is' to mean 'signifies', as in Gen. 41:26; John

10:9; 15:1. In the bread and wine he saw mere symbols, and in the sacrament itself an act of commemoration. Yet he did not deny the spiritual presence of Christ. 'The true body of Christ', says he, 'is present to the contemplation of faith; but that his natural body is really and actually present in the Supper, or is eaten with our mouths . . . we constantly assert to be an error repugnant to the Word of God.' While he says, 'There is nothing in the eucharist but commemoration', he also uses expressions that would seem to point to a deeper significance. His position is not altogether clear.

Calvin held an intermediate position. He agreed with Zwingli *Calvin's* in rejecting absolutely the bodily, local, and substantial presence *view of the* of Christ in the Lord's Supper. But he had especially two objec- *Supper* tions to the view of the Swiss Reformer, namely that the latter, (1) stresses the activity of the believers rather than the gracious gift of God in the sacrament, and therefore conceives of the Lord's Supper one-sidedly as an act of profession; and (2) sees in the eating of the body of Christ nothing else and nothing more than an expression of belief in His name and confident trust in His death. While denying the bodily and local presence of Christ in the Lord's Supper, he yet agreed with Luther, that Christ is really and essentially present in his entire person, and is received as such by believers. His view is succinctly and correctly expressed by Sheldon when he says: 'His theory in brief was that the glorified humanity of Christ is a fountain of spiritual virtue or efficacy; that this efficacy is mediated by the Holy Spirit to the believing recipient of the eucharistic elements; that accordingly the body of Christ is present in the eucharist in virtue of efficacy; that the eating of Christ's body is entirely spiritual, by means of faith, the unbelieving having no part in it, and an oral manducation being out of the question.' *History of Christian Doctrine*, II, p 207. This view was incorporated in the Reformed Confessions, and became the common property of Reformed theology. The Thirty-Nine Articles of the Church of England are not very definite on the subject.

After the Reformation the Zwinglian conception of the Lord's Supper found favour in some circles. It was sometimes regarded

Later views of the Lord's Supper

as a sacrament of a purely external covenant, to which all who gave no offence were entitled. Thus the way was paved for Rationalism, which adopted the views of the Socinians, the Arminians, and the Mennonites, who saw in the Lord's Supper only a memorial, an act of profession, and a means for moral improvement. Under the influence of Schleiermacher the objective character of the sacrament as a means of grace was again stressed. Many of the mediating theologians (Vermittelungstheologen) rejected the Lutheran consubstantiation and *manducatio oralis*, and approached the doctrine of Calvin by teaching that Christ is spiritually present in the Lord's Supper, and in the sacrament imparts Himself and His spiritual blessings to believers. Others, such as Scheibel, Rudelbach, and Philippi reaffirmed the old Lutheran position. In England the Oxford Movement marks a return to the position of Rome. Many of the High Church party teach that the consecrated elements in the Lord's Supper are really, be it mystically, the body and blood of Christ.

QUESTIONS FOR FURTHER STUDY

What are the marks of a sacrament? Are the sacraments necessary to salvation? Do Roman Catholics defend the position that their sacraments were instituted by Jesus? What scriptural grounds do they adduce for their various sacraments? How did the idea of baptismal regeneration arise? How did the Anabaptist view of baptism differ from that of the Reformers? On what grounds do they deny infant baptism? How did the sacrificial idea of the Lord's Supper arise? Why do Roman Catholics withhold the cup from the laity? How did Calvin conceive of the presence of Christ in the Lord's Supper?

LITERATURE

Wall, *History of Infant Baptism;* Dimock, *The Doctrine of the Sacraments;* Hebert, *The Lord's Supper, History of Uninspired Teaching;* Ebrard, *Das Dogma vom heiligen Abendmahl;* Hagenbach, *History of Doctrines,* I, pp 277–299; II, pp 67–86, 319–377; III, pp 140–173, 219–226, 374–381; Neander, *History of Christian Dogmas,* I, pp 227–247; II, pp 398–413, 455–463, 527–537, 588–595, 613–619, 688–702; Sheldon, *History of Christian Doctrine,* I, pp 136–144, 270–281, 388–404; II, pp 191–212, 382–388; Otten, *Manual of the History of Dogmas,* I, pp 180–189, 338–356; II, pp 272–396; Crippen, *History of Christian Doctrine,* pp 189–207; Cunningham, *Historical Theology,* II, pp 121–154; Seeberg, *History of Doctrines,* cf Index.

THE DOCTRINE
OF THE
LAST THINGS

I: THE INTERMEDIATE STATE

The doctrine of the last things never stood in the centre of attention, is one of the least developed doctrines, and therefore calls for no elaborate discussion. Its main elements have been rather constant, and these constitute practically the whole dogma of the Church respecting future things. Occasionally deviating views occupied a rather important place in theological discussions, but these were never incorporated in the Confessions of the Church. It may be that, as Dr Orr surmises, we have now reached that point in the history of dogma in which the doctrine of the last things will receive greater attention and be brought to further development.

The Apostolic Fathers did not yet reflect on the intermediate state. According to the common opinion of their day the pious at death immediately inherit the heavenly glory prepared for them, and the wicked at once suffer the punishment of hell. It was only when it became apparent that Christ would not immediately return, that the Church Fathers began to reflect on the state between death and the resurrection. One of the first was Justin, who said: 'The souls of the pious are in a better place, those of the unjust and wicked in a worse, waiting for the time of judgment.' He denounced as heretical those who said that 'their souls, when they die, are taken to heaven'. *Development of the idea of an intermediate state*

The general opinion of the later Fathers, such as Irenæus, Tertullian, Hilary, Ambrose, Cyril, and even Augustine, was that the dead descend into hades, a place with various divisions, where they remain until the day of judgment or, according to Augustine, until they are sufficiently purified. In the measure in which it became apparent that the parousia of Christ was a far-distant event, it became increasingly difficult to maintain the

[259]

idea of hades as a merely temporal and provisional habitation of the dead. An exception was soon made for the martyrs who, according to Tertullian, were at once admitted into glory. The descent of Christ into hades was interpreted as having effected the deliverance of the Old Testament saints from the *limbus patrum*. And when the doctrine of the meritoriousness of good works became prominent, it was taught that those who were diligent in their performance were worthy of passing into heaven at once. Hades was gradually robbed of its *righteous* inhabitants. Finally, the wicked were about the only ones left, and it began to be regarded as a place of punishment, sometimes identified with gehenna. Origen taught explicitly that Christ transported all the righteous of former ages from hades to paradise, which from that time on became the destination of all departing saints.

In connection with the idea that many Christians are not sufficiently holy at death to enter the region of eternal bliss, the conviction gradually gained currency that these are subjected to a process of purification beyond the grave. The early Church Fathers already spoke of a purifying fire, which some of them located in paradise, and others associated with the final conflagration. They did not always have in mind a literal or material fire, but often thought merely of a spiritual test or discipline. Origen conceived of hades, including gehenna, and also of the final conflagration at the end of the world, as a purifying fire. Several of the later Greek and Latin Church Fathers, such as the three Cappadocians, Ambrose, Ephræm, Augustine, and others, entertained the idea of a purgatorial fire in the intermediate state.

Development of the idea of purgatory

It was especially in the West that the idea of a special purgatorial fire was developed. Gregory the Great already stressed it as a matter of unquestioned belief. Says he: '*It is to be believed* that there is, for some light faults, a purgatorial fire before the judgment.' Hence he is usually called 'the inventor of purgatory'. He was also the first one who clearly propounded the idea, vaguely entertained by others long before him, of deliverance from this fire by intercessory prayers and oblations. The mediæval Scholastics and Mystics were very explicit in their description of purgatory, and the majority of them conceived of it as a material fire. The Greek Church never cordially accepted the gross views current in the West.

The locality of purgatory was also discussed, and it was generally regarded as that division of hades that was nearest to hell. At a little remove from it was the *limbus infantum*, the place where, according to the Scholastics, children who died in an unbaptized state are confined, suffering no positive pain indeed, but yet kept for ever out of heaven. Still farther away from hell was the supposed *limbus patrum*, also called 'paradise' or 'Abraham's bosom', where, it was held, the Old Testament worthies were retained until the descent of Christ into hades. The doctrine of purgatory was solemnly affirmed by the Council of Trent in 1546. It was in connection with this doctrine that the vicious practice of selling indulgences grew up in the Church.

The doctrine of purgatory was opposed towards the end of the Middle Ages by such forerunners of the Reformation as Wyclif and Huss. Luther fulminated against the pernicious practices that grew up in the Church in connection with it, and the Reformers, one and all, rejected the whole doctrine of purgatory as contrary to Scripture. The Smalcald Articles speak of purgatory as belonging to 'the vermin brood of idolatry, begotten by the tail of the dragon'. And the Thirty-Nine Articles of the Church of England declare that 'the Romish doctrine concerning purgatory . . . is a fond thing vainly invented, and grounded upon no warranty of Scripture'.

Opposition to this idea

II: THE SECOND ADVENT AND THE
MILLENNIAL HOPE

Chiliasm in the early Church The early Christians were taught to look for the return of Jesus Christ, and it is evident even from the New Testament that some of them expected a speedy return. The literal interpretation of Rev 20:1–6 led some of the early Church Fathers to distinguish between a first and a second resurrection, and to believe in an intervening millennial kingdom. Some of them dwelt very fondly on these millennial hopes and pictured the enjoyments of the future age in a crassly materialistic manner. This is true especially of Papias and Irenæus. Others such as Barnabas, Hermas, Justin, and Tertullian, while teaching the doctrine, avoided its extravagances. The millennial doctrine also found favour with Cerinthus, the Ebionites, and the Montanists. But it is not correct to say, as Premillenarians do, that it was *generally* accepted in the first three centuries. The truth of the matter is that the adherents of this doctrine were a rather limited number. There is no trace of it in Clement of Rome, Ignatius, Polycarp, Tatian, Athenagoras, Theophilus, Clement of Alexandria, Origen, Dionysius, and other important Church Fathers.

The Millenarianism of the early Church was gradually overcome. When centuries rolled by without the return of Jesus Christ, when persecutions ceased, and when Christianity received a sure footing in the Roman Empire and even became the State religion, the passionate longing for the appearance of Jesus Christ very naturally gave way for an adaptation of the Church to its present task. The allegorical interpretation of Scripture, introduced by the Alexandrian school, and sponsored especially by Origen, also had a chilling effect on all millennial hopes. In the West the powerful influence of Augustine was instrumental in turning the thoughts of the Church from the future to the present by his identification of the Church and the Kingdom of God. He taught the people to look for the millennium in the present Christian dispensation.

During the Middle Ages Millenarianism was generally regarded as heretical. There were, it is true, here and there transient and sporadic buddings of the millennial hope in the sects, but these exercised no profound influence. In the tenth century there was a widespread expectation of the approaching end of the world, but this was not accompanied with chiliastic hopes, though it was associated with the idea of the speedy coming of Antichrist. Christian art often chose its themes from eschatology. The hymn *Dies Irae* sounded the terrors of the coming judgment, painters depicted the end of the world on the canvas, and Dante gave a vivid description of hell in his *Divina Commedia*. *Chiliasm during the Middle Ages*

At the time of the Reformation the doctrine of the millennium was rejected by the Protestant Churches, but revived in some of the sects, such as that of the more fanatical Anabaptists, and that of the Fifth Monarchy Men. Luther scornfully rejected 'the dream' that there would be an earthly kingdom of Christ preceding the day of judgment. The Augsburg Confession condemns those 'who now scatter Jewish opinions, that, before the resurrection of the dead, the godly shall occupy the kingdom of the world, the wicked being everywhere suppressed'. Art XVII. And the Second Helvetic Confession says: 'Moreover, we condemn the Jewish dreams, that before the day of judgment there shall be a golden age in the earth, and the godly shall possess the kingdoms of the world, their wicked enemies being trodden under foot.' Chapter XI. *Chiliasm during the Reformation period*

A certain form of Millenarianism made its appearance, however, in the seventeenth century. There were several Lutheran and Reformed theologians who, while rejecting the idea of a visible reign of Christ on earth for a thousand years, advocated a more spiritual conception of the millennium. Their view of the matter was that, before the end of the world and the return of Jesus Christ, there will be a period in which the spiritual presence of Christ in the Church will be experienced in an *Chiliasm in the seventeenth century; Post-millennialism* unusual measure and a universal religious awakening will ensue. The Kingdom of Jesus Christ will then stand out as a kingdom of peace and righteousness. This was the early form of Post- as distinguished from Pre-millennialism.

Chiliasm during the last centuries
During the eighteenth and nineteenth centuries the doctrine of the millennium again met with great favour in some circles. It was advocated by the school of Bengel and more recently by that of Erlangen, and numbered among its adherents such men as Hofmann, Delitzsch, Auberlen, Rothe, Elliott, Cumming, Bickersteth, the Bonars, Alford, Zahn, and others. There is great diversity of opinion among these Pre-millenarians as to the order of the final events and the actual condition of things during the millennium. Repeated attempts have been made to fix the time of Christ's return, which is with great assurance declared to be imminent, but up to the present all these calculations have failed. Though there is a widespread belief today, especially in our country, that the return of Christ will be followed by a temporary visible reign of Christ on earth, yet the weight of theological opinion is against it. In liberal circles a new form of Post-millennialism has made its appearance. The expected kingdom will consist of a new social order 'in which the law of Christ shall prevail, and in which its prevalence shall result in peace, justice and a glorious blossoming of present spiritual forces'. This is what Rauschenbusch has in mind when he says, 'We need a restoration of the millennial hope'. *A Theology for the Social Gospel*, p 224. Up to the present time, however, the doctrine of the millennium has never yet been embodied in a single Confession, and therefore cannot be regarded as a dogma of the Church.

III: THE RESURRECTION

Most of the early Church Fathers believed in the resurrection *The* *resurrection* *in the* *patristic* *period* of the body, that is, in the identity of the future body with that of the present. The views of Clement of Alexandria are somewhat uncertain, but it is clear that Origen, while defending the doctrine of the Church against Celsus, rejected the idea that the identical body would be raised up. He described the resurrection body as a refined and spiritualized body. Some of the Church Fathers shared his view, but the majority of them held that the resurrection body would be in every respect identical with the body formed in the present life. Augustine was in agreement with Origen at first, but finally accepted the prevalent view, though he did not consider it necessary to assume that the present differences of size and stature would continue in the life to come. In fact, he believed that at the resurrection all would have the stature of the full-grown man. Jerome, however, insisted on the identity of the very hairs and teeth. On the whole it may be said that the East manifested a tendency to adopt a more spiritual view of the resurrection than the West. The two Gregories, Chrysostom, and Synesius, were in general agreement with Origen. John of Damascus did affirm the restitution of the same body, but was satisfied with that view of identity which is suggested by the analogy of the seed and the plant. They who believed in a future millennium spoke of a double resurrection, that of the pious at the beginning, and that of the wicked at the terminatoin, of the millennial reign.

The Scholastics speculated in their usual way about the body *The* *resurrection* *in the* *Scholastics* of the resurrection. Their speculations were rather fanciful and had little permanent value. Thomas Aquinas seemed to have special information on the subject. He informs us that they who are alive at the coming of Christ will first die, and then be raised again with the rest of the dead. The resurrection will take place towards evening. That substance will arise which existed at the moment of death. All will be in the bloom of youth. The body will be tangible, but fine and light, and not subject to growth. In obedience to the impulse of the soul it will move swiftly and easily. The bodies of the wicked, on the other hand, will be ugly and deformed and capable of much suffering, though incorruptible.

The resurrection since the Reformation The theologians of the Reformation period were quite agreed that the resurrection body would be identical with the present body. This doctrine is also embodied in the confessional standards of the Churches of the Reformation. With the advance of the physical sciences some of the difficulties with which the doctrine of the resurrection is burdened were accentuated, and as a result modern religious liberalism either bluntly denies the resurrection, or explains the scriptural representations of it as a figurative representation of the idea that the full human personality with all its powers will continue to exist after death. This view is popular with many at the present time.

IV: THE LAST JUDGMENT AND
   THE FINAL AWARDS

The earliest Church Fathers have very little to say about the last judgment, but generally stress its certainty. Most of them are of the opinion that the saints in heaven will enjoy different degrees of blessedness, commensurate with the virtues which adorned them on earth. Some of their writings abound with sensuous representations of the pleasures of the future world. Those of Origen, however, reflect a more spiritual conception. The punishment of the wicked was generally thought of as eternal, Origen forming an exception. It is true that in his popular discourses he also speaks of eternal punishment, but in his *De Principiis* he tends to rule this out altogether. But even he does not conceive of the future punishment as purely spiritual. He really resolves it into chastisement by holding out hope even to the wicked, and expresses belief in the final restoration of all things. *The Fathers on the last judgment*

The later Fathers also stood firm in the conviction that there would be a final judgment at the end of the world. But they spoke of this mostly, just as of other eschatological events, in a highly rhetorical fashion, without conveying any definite information. Augustine proceeds on the assumption that the scriptural representations of it are figurative. He expresses the conviction that Christ is coming to judge the living and the dead, but maintains that Scripture leaves it uncertain how long this judgment will last.

There was no unanimous opinion as to what will constitute the blessedness of heaven. A more fully developed knowledge, intercourse with the saints, deliverance from the fetters of the body, and true liberty – these are some of the outstanding elements that were named. The sufferings of the damned were regarded as the very opposite of the joys of heaven. Some believed in degrees of bliss and torment, though both of these were generally regarded as eternal. Most of the Church Fathers also clung to the idea of a material fire, though some surmised that the punishment of the wicked would consist chiefly in separation from God and a consciousness of their own wickedness.

The Scholastics on heaven and hell The Scholastics paid particular attention to the location of heaven and hell. According to them heaven is divided into three parts, namely, (1) the visible heavens (the firmament); (2) the spiritual heaven, the dwelling-place of saints and angels; and (3) the intellectual heaven, where the blessed enjoy the immediate vision of God. They also conceived of the underworld as divided into different departments, namely, (1) hell, properly so called, the abode of devils and of the damned; and (2) regions that might be called intermediate between heaven and hell, of which there are three: (a) purgatory in close proximity to hell; (b) the *limbus infantum*, where unbaptized children remain; and (c) the *limbus patrum*, the abode of the Old Testament saints.

Post-Reformation period on the judgment The Reformers were content with the affirmation of the simple doctrine of Scripture that Christ will come again to judge the world. They were careful to distinguish between the general judgment at the end of the world and the secret and particular judgment which takes place at the death of each individual. The purpose of the former was understood to be the public vindication of divine justice in making final awards. They shared the common belief in the eternal bliss of heaven and the eternal torments of hell. Some Anabaptists taught restorationism, and some Socinians, the annihilation of the wicked. Some Protestant theologians held the opinion that material fire will play a part in the endless punishment of the wicked; others were non-committal on the subject; and still others interpreted all that the Bible says about fire in a figurative manner. The doctrine of future rewards and punishments, as taught by the Reformation, remains the official doctrine of the Churches up to the present day, though since the middle of the previous century the doctrine of conditional immortality has enjoyed great popularity in some circles.

[268]

Only thorough-going Universalists – and they are few – believe in universal salvation and in the restoration of all things in the absolute sense of the word.

QUESTIONS FOR FURTHER STUDY

Is it true that Chiliasm was the generally accepted doctrine of the Church in the second and third centuries? What accounts for it in the early Church? Was all Chiliasm even then of the same type? What was Augustine's view of the millennium? What can be said in favour of it? What accounts for the repeated re-occurrence of Chiliasm? Are the historical Confessions of the Churches favourable or unfavourable to it? Did the Reformers encourage chiliastic hopes? Is the Pre-millennialism of the present day the same as the Chiliasm of the early centuries? How did the Scholastics seek to prove the idea of purgatory from Scripture? Does Scripture favour the idea that the dead are in some intermediate place, neither heaven nor hell? Who taught the sleep of the soul and on what grounds? What are the doctrines of conditional immortality and of a second probation? What sects believe in the annihilation of the wicked? Does the doctrine of universal restoration find considerable favour?

LITERATURE

Mackintosh, *Immortality and the Future*, Chap V; Brown, *The Christian Hope*, Chap VIII; Alger, *Critical History of the Doctrine of a Future Life;* Hoekstra, *Het Chiliasme*, pp 9–59; Case, *The Millennial Hope;* Hagenbach, *History of Doctrines*, I, pp 301–322; II, pp 87–105, 378–405; III, pp 173–175, 226–229, 382–390; Neander, *History of Christian Dogmas*, I, pp 247–256; II, pp 413–417; Shedd, *History of Christian Doctrines*, II, pp 389–419; Sheldon, *History of Christian Doctrine*, I pp 145–155, 282–290; II, pp 213–217, 389–399; Crippen, *History of Christian Doctrine*, pp 231–253; Otten, *Manual of the History of Dogmas*, I, pp 105–107, 457–463; II, pp 418–437; Seeberg, *History of Doctrines*, cf Index; Addison, *Life Beyond Death in the Beliefs of Mankind*.

LITERATURE

LITERATURE

GENERAL

Allen, *The Continuity of Christian Thought*, Boston, 1885.
Boardman, *A History of New England Theology*, New York, 1899.
Cunningham, *Historical Theology*, Edinburgh, 1870.
Crippen, *History of Christian Doctrine*, Edinburgh, 1883.
Fisher, *History of Christian Doctrine*, New York, 1901.
Foster, *A History of New England Theology*, Chicago, 1907.
Hagenbach, *History of Doctrines*, Edinburgh, 1880.
Harnack, *History of Dogma*, Boston, 1897–1905.
Harnack, *Outlines of the History of Dogma*, New York, 1893.
Klotsche, *An Outline of the History of Doctrines*, Burlington, 1927.
Loofs, *Handboek der Dogmengeschiedenis*, Groningen, 1902.
McGiffert, *History of Christian Thought*, New York, 1932–33.
Neander, *History of Christian Dogmas*, London, 1858.
Orr, *The Progress of Dogma*, New York, 1902.
Otten, *Manual of the History of Dogmas*, St. Louis, 1922.
Seeberg, *Textbook of the History of Doctrines*, Philadelphia, 1905.
Shedd, *History of Christian Doctrine*, New York, 1889.
Sheldon, *History of Christian Doctrine*, New York, 1886.
Thomasius, *Dogmengeschichte*, Erlangen, 1874.

SPECIAL

Addison, *Life Beyond Death*, New York, 1932.
Bavinck, *Roeping en Wedergeboorte*, Kampen, 1913.
Berkhof, *The Assurance of Faith*, Grand Rapids, 1928.
Berkhof, *Vicarious Atonement Through Christ*, Grand Rapids, 1936.
Bruce, *The Humiliation of Christ*, New York, 1901.
Buchanan, *The Doctrine of Justification*, Edinburgh, 1867.
Candlish, *The Kingdom of God*, Edinburgh, 1884.
Case, *The Millennial Hope*, Chicago, 1918.
Dee, *Het Geloofsbegrip van Calvijn*, Kampen, 1918

LITERATURE

De Jong, *De Leer der Verzoening in de Amerikaansche Theologie*,
Grand Rapids, 1913.
Dimock, *The Doctrine of the Sacraments*, London, 1908.
Dorner, *History of Protestant Theology*, Edinburgh, 1871.
Ebrard, *Das Dogma vom heiligen Abendmahl*, Frankfort a. M., 1845.
Emmen, *De Christologie van Calvijn*, Amsterdam, 1935.
Emerton, *Unitarian Thought*, New York, 1916.
Flew, *The Idea of Perfection in Christian Theology*, Oxford, 1934.
Franks, *A History of the Doctrine of the Work of Christ*, New York.
Girardeau, *Calvinism and Evangelical Arminianism*, Columbia, 1890.
Hatch, *The Organization of the Early Christian Churches*,
Oxford and Cambridge, 1881.
Hebert, *The Lord's Supper, Uninspired Teaching*, London, 1897.
Henderson, *The Religious Controversies of Scotland*, Edinburgh,
1905.
Heppe, *Dogmatik des deutschen Protestantismus in sechzenten
Jahrhundert*, Gotha, 1857.
Heppe, *Geschichte des Pietismus*.
Hoekstra, *Het Chiliasme*, Kampen, 1903.
Hoffmann, *Die Lehre von der Fides Implicita*, Leipzig, 1903.
Illingworth, *The Doctrine of the Trinity*, London, 1907.
Innes, *Church and State, A Historical Handbook*, Edinburgh.
Impeta, *De Leer der Heiligmaking en Volharding bij Wesley en
Fletcher*, Leiden, 1913.
Kerr, *A God-Centred Faith*, New York, 1935.
Köstlin, *The Theology of Luther*, Philadelphia, 1897.
Kramer, *Het Verband van Doop en Wedergeboorte*, Breukelen, 1897.
Lindsay, *The Church and the Ministry in the Early Centuries*,
London, 1902.
Mackintosh, H. R., *The Doctrine of the Person of Jesus Christ*,
New York, 1912.
Mackintosh, H. R., *Immortality and the Future*, New York, 1917.
Mackintosh, R., *Christianity and Sin*, New York, 1914.
Mackintosh, R., *Historic Theories of the Atonement*, London, 1920.
Mathews, *The Growth of the Idea of God*, New York, 1931.
Mathews, *The Atonement and the Social Process*, New York, 1930.
McGiffert, *Protestant Thought Before Kant*, New York, 1911.
McGiffert, *The Rise of Modern Religious Ideas*, New York, 1915.
McPherson, *The Doctrine of the Church in Scottish Theology*,
Edinburgh, 1903.

Moore, *Protestant Thought Since Kant*, New York, 1922.

Morgan, *The Importance of Tertullian in the Development of Christian Dogma*, London, 1928.

Moxon, *The Doctrine of Sin*, New York, 1922.

Mozley, *The Doctrine of the Atonement*, New York, 1916.

Olthuis, *De Doopspraktijk der Gereformeerde Kerken in Nederland*, Utrecht, 1908.

Orchard, *Modern Theories of Sin*, London, 1909.

Ottley, *The Doctrine of the Incarnation*, London, 1896.

Peters, *The Theocratic Kingdom*, New York, 1884.

Ritschl, *History of the Christian Doctrine of Justification and Reconciliation*, Edinburgh, 1872.

Robertson, *Regnum Dei*, New York, 1901.

Robinson, *The Christian Doctrine of Man*, Edinburgh, 1920.

Rutgers, *Premillennialism in America*, Goes, 1930.

Sanday, *Christologies Ancient and Modern*, New York, 1910.

Schaff, *Creeds of Christendom*, New York, 1877.

Schweitzer, *Die Protestantischen Centraldogmen*, Zürich, 1854.

Stevens, *The Christian Doctrine of Salvation*, New York, 1905.

Storr, *The Development of English Theology in the Nineteenth Century*, London, 1913.

Swete, *The Forgiveness of Sins*, London, 1917.

Talma, *De Anthropologie van Calvijn*, Utrecht, 1882.

Tennant, *The Origin and Propagation of Sin*, Cambridge, 1906.

Van den Bergh, *Calvijn over het Genadeverbond*, 1879.

Walker, *The Theology and Theologians of Scotland*, Edinburgh, 1888.

Wall, *History of Infant Baptism*, Oxford, 1836.

Warfield, *Calvin and Calvinism*, London, 1931.

Warfield, *Studies in Perfectionism*, London, 1931.

Wiggers, *Augustinianism and Pelaganianism*, Andover, 1840.

Workman, *Christian Thought to the Reformation*, New York, 1911.

INDEX OF NAMES

INDEX OF SUBJECTS

Adoptionism, on relation of Christ to God, 111 f.

Alexandrian Fathers, on God and the Logos, 71 f; on man, 73; on person and work of Christ, 73 f; on salvation, 74 f; on the church, 75; on the last things, 75 f.

Anabaptists, on the church, 237; on the sacraments, 247; on baptism, 250.

Antignostic Fathers, on God, 63; on man 63 f; on the history of redemption, 64; on the Logos, 64 f; on redemption, 66 f; on salvation, 67 f; on the church, 68; on the last things, 68.

Antinomians, on the order of salvation, 222 f.

Apologists, on philosophy and revelation, 57; on God, 58; on the Logos, 58 f; on the new life, 59; their significance for the history of dogma, 59 f; Harnack's view of, 59 f.

Apostolic Fathers, formal characteristics of their teachings, 38 f; material contents of their teachings, 40 f.

Arminians, on sin and grace, 150 f; on the atonement, 188 f; on the order of salvation, 221 f; on the church 238 f; on the sacraments, 247; on baptism, 251; on the Lord's Supper, 256.

Assurance, Aquinas on, 214; the Reformers on 220; Wesleyan Arminians on, 222; Pietists on, 223.

Atonement, in Greek patristic theology, 165 f; recapitulation theory of, 165, ransom-to-Satan theory of, 166; Athanasius on, 166; Gregory of Nyssa on, 167; John of Damascus on, 167; in Latin patristic theology, 168 f; Tertullian on, 168; Augustine on, 169; Gregory the Great on, 169 f; satisfaction theory of, 171 f; moral influence theory of, 174 f; Bernard of Clairvaux on, 175 f; Peter the Lombard on, 176; Bonaventura on, 176 f; Aquinas on, 177 f; acceptilatian theory of, 179 f; Reformers on, 182 f; example theory of, 184 f; Governmental theory of, 186 f; Arminian view of, 188 f; Synod of Dort on, 189; school of Saumur on, 190; neonomian view of 192; Marrow-men on university of, 192 f; mystical theory of, 193 f; 198; Ritschl on,

194 f; in New England theology, 195 f; Bushnell on, 196 f; Maurice on, 197, Campbell on, 197 f.

Baptism in the patristic period, 247 f; Roman Catholic conception of, 249; Luther and Lutherans on, 249 f; Reformed on, 250 f; Anabaptists on, 250.

Baptismal regeneration, in the early church, 248; Augustine on, 248 f; Roman Catholics on, 249; Lutherans on, 249 f.

Chalcedon, Council of, on natures of Christ, 107.

Church, The, in the patristic period, 227 f; Cyprian on, 228 f; Augustine on, 229 f; in the Middle Ages, 232 f; Roman Catholic conceptions of, 232, 239 f; the Reformers on, 236 f; Socinian and Arminian view of; 238 f; Anabaptist and Labadist view of 237, 239.

Communicatio idiomatum, in John of Damascus, 110 f; in Lutheran theology, 115 f.

Concupiscence, scholastics on, 145 f.

Dogma, meaning of the word, 15 f; origin and character of, 16 f; Harnack's view of, 18 f; task of history of, 20 f; Newman's theory of development of, 22, 32.

Ebionites, 44.

Elkesaites, 44 f.

Eutichianism, on natures of Christ, 106 f.

Faith, in the early church, 203 f; Augustine on, 207; scholastic conception of, 212 f; in Roman Catholic order of salvation, 214 f; in the Lutheran order, 217 f; in Arminianism, 221 f.

Generation, eternal, Origen on, 83 f; Arius on, 84 f; Athanasius on 86; Marcellus on, 88 f; Calvin on, 95 f; Emmons and Stuart on, 97.

Gnosticism, its origin, 45 f; its essential character, 46 f; its main teachings, 47 f; its historical significance, 49 f.

Grace, Greek fathers on, 203 f; Pelagius on, 205 f; Augustine on, 206 f; Semi-Pelagianism on, 207 f; Roman Catholics on, 211 f; Reformers on, 217 f; Arminians on, 221; Wesleyan Arminians on, 222.